N

○ Bakewell

21 26

22 27 28 Matlock ○

15,16

3,4

25

5,6 17,18 23

8

29 30
○

24 Wirksworth

10,11 19

PEAK DISTRICT
NATIONAL PARK BOUNDARY

00 400 188 055

20 Ashbourne
○

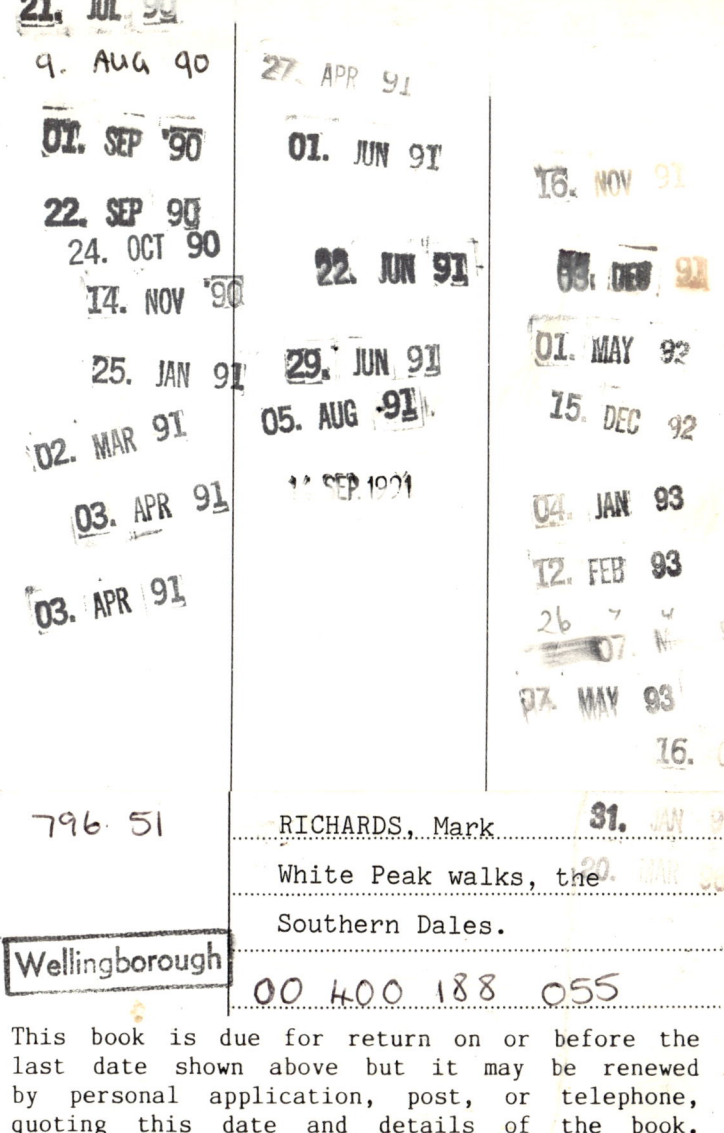

Parkhouse Hill, Dowel Dale

WHITE PEAK WALKS
THE SOUTHERN DALES

by

MARK RICHARDS

CICERONE PRESS
MILNTHORPE, CUMBRIA

© Mark Richards 1988
ISBN 0902 363 88 3
First published 1988
Reprinted 1989

Northamptonshire Libraries

796.51

TO
ROLAND SMITH
For his good humour and genuine concern for
for the well-being of Peakland

Acknowledgements

I would like to take this opportunity to thank Harry Jones and his colleagues at Aldern House for their valuable assistance during the making of this guide. I pay tribute to all their good works.

To Iain Liddell for his keen-eyed proof-reading and command of the English language, and the good company of friends (Martin Barnsley, Ron Bridger, Rodney Busby, Mike Devas, John McGrillis and Mike Walker) who shared my pleasurable forays through fair weather and foul during the extended period of this guide's production.

Lastly, and by no means least to my dear family for their support and Dorothy Unsworth for her forbearance!

Mark Richards

00 400 188 055

CONTENTS

			Page No's
Map locating the start of the walks			inside front cover
Introduction			I
Symbols on the route maps			1
WALK 1	Morridge from the Rey Monument	5 miles 2¾ hours	2-9
WALK 2	Butterton Moor from Onecote	5½ miles 3 hours	10-17
WALK 3	Revidge from Hulme End	6 miles 3½ hours	18-28
WALK 4	Ecton Hill from Hulme End	5¼ miles 2¾ hours	29-36
WALK 5	Thor's Cave from Wetton	5¼ miles 3 hours	37-48
WALK 6	Bincliff from Wetton	5½ miles 3 hours	49-58
WALK 7	Hamps Valley from Grindon	6 miles 3¼ hours	59-64
WALK 8	Throwley Moor from Weag's Bridge	5¼ miles 2½ hours	65-70
WALK 9	The Weaver Hills from Waterhouses	6¾ miles 3¾ hours	71-80
WALK 10	Musden from Ilam	5 miles 2½ hours	81-87
WALK 11	Ilam from Blore pastures	4 miles 2¼ hours	88-95
WALK 12	Flash from Cistern's Clough	7½ miles 4¼ hours	96-105
WALK 13	Dove and Dowell from Hollinsclough	4¼ miles 2½ hours	106-113
WALK 14	High Wheeldon from Longnor	5½ miles 3 hours	114-125
WALK 15	Pilsbury Castle from Hartington	5½ miles 3 hours	126-131
WALK 16	Wolfscote Dale from Hartington	5¼ miles 2¾ hours	132-139
WALK 17	Wolfscote Dale from Alstonefield	7 miles 4 hours	140-147

CONTENTS (continued)   **Page No's**

WALK 18	Milldale	4¾ miles	
	from Alstonefield	2½ hours	148-153
WALK 19	Dove Dale from Dove Dale car park		
	Valley path to Milldale	2¾ miles	154-165
	Thorpe Cloud	½ mile	166-167
	Eastern Skyline	1¾ miles	167
	Return from Milldale via Ilam Moor	3 miles	168-169
	Return via Hall Dale	1¼ miles	170
	Return via Air Cottage	1½ miles	170-171
WALK 20	Dove Dale Approach	8 miles	
	from Ashbourne	4 hours	172-179
WALK 21	Trail Walking	3½ miles	
	from Parsley Hay	2 hours	180-185
WALK 22	Trail Walking	5¾ miles	
	from Hartington Old Station	2¾ hours	186-189
WALK 23	Biggin Dale	6¼ miles	
	from Alsop Moor	3 hours	190-197
WALK 24	Tissington's Trail	8½ miles	
	from Tissington Old Station	4½ hours	198-207
WALK 25	Minninglow	5½ miles	
	from Minninglow Picnic Site	2¾ hours	208-215
WALK 26	Harthill Moor	3½ miles	
	from Elton	2 hours	216-223
WALK 27	Gratton Dale	8 miles	
	from Youlgreave	4 hours	224-237
WALK 28	Stanton Moor	6½ miles	
	from Winster	3½ hours	238-249
WALK 29	Rainster and Harborough Rocks	9 miles	
	from Middleton Top Picnic Site	5 hours	250-259
WALK 30	Cromford Heights	9¼ miles	
	from Middleton Top Picnic Site	5½ hours	260-275
Postscript			276

Thorpe Cloud from Air Cottage

INTRODUCTION

It is perhaps inevitable to find 'travel writers', once they have been drawn to explore the southern uplands of the White Peak, sitting in judgement over the qualities of the various dales: equally inevitable is the tendency to bestow the laurel wreath of 'Dale of Dales' on that valley which so distils the essence of the area, Dove Dale. And yet, having spent the best part of four years regularly visiting the area I cannot help but feel that the bias of promotional comment is tilted too heavily upon that one valley. There is no denying its particular claims for adulation, but, having ranged to the wider bounds of these southernmost Pennine hills, I would like to think that I would be failing in my mission if, through the medium of these thirty walks, I could not persuade walkers to a broader appreciation.

Nevertheless, the whole of the Dove valley within the National Park fully merits respect, and not just the short passage between Milldale and Thorpe. That hard-pressed section, which receives the brunt of visitor attention throughout the year, underwent major path restoration in 1984, a process which is to be sensitively extended. Clearly, there are stretches of path ill-suited (by the nature of the underlying soil) to the legions of pedestrian visitors who lay siege. Beresford Dale is a case in point, where the laying of a graded limestone rubble path is relieving the unsightly mudbath. However, such 'improvements' can, and certainly in the short term do, impinge on the aesthetic integrity of the place, but critics should never doubt the amazing healing capacity of Nature, for all man's unremitting assaults.

INTRODUCTION

Even though increased mobility has extended the diversity (in terms of sights and sites) of beautiful countryside within range of the millions who inhabit middle England, the White Peak remains tremendously popular among casual walking visitors. The area offers an amiable landscape despite the vagaries of its climate, dissected by countless walls, abundant in pastures and woodland, its limestone outcrops completing the interplay of green and white. It also offers a well maintained footpath network. The 'net' effect ensures that walkers feel at ease and relaxed in their wanderings as in few other places in England, and it is here that the efforts of the Park Authority deserve a special mention.

Since its establishment in 1951 as the first National Park in Britain, the Peak Park has gained an honourable reputation in defence of the intrinsic character of these uplands, frequently having to strike a delicate balance between serving the vital recreational needs of a vast 'on the doorstep' urban populus and compliance with purely local aspirations. No planning authority can ever claim a blemish-free existence, and whilst it is seen by a tiny proportion of the 40,000 people who live within the Park's bounds in a negative light, it is clear to me that the long-term well-being of the resident population is the prime concern of the Board. True, it imposes a tighter scrutiny than is considered necessary outside the Park's bounds, but it will only be through the continued fostering of a closer harmony of interest that the future well-being of the area can be secured. The Park Board has a strong local composition, thus ensuring a genuine care for the land and its economic viability.

A journey across the girth of the White Peak from east to west reveals a dichotomy. Communities surrounding the Derwent valley have flourished because they lie within dormitory range of Sheffield and Chesterfield. Commuters can afford to lay extra stress on preservation of the National Park characteristics since they do not rely on the productivity of the land to determine their lifestyles. The short journey west across the high limestone plateau brings a progressively different state of affairs to light. Rural decline, accelerated in recent years by milk quotas and the general levelling-off in livestock prices, coupled with the loss of local employment opportunities through increased mechanisation of quarrying and similar industries, has brought about despondency among these hardy folk. This has often directed unwarranted calumny at the National Park Authority in its perceived insistence on the preservation of the natural landscape.

All is not black, as the 'Integrated Rural Development Scheme' pioneered at Longnor and Monyash can testify. At Longnor, for instance, the parish has witnessed a quite remarkable turnaround through the establishment (aided by cash injection) of a special Project Officer, and 35 jobs have been created among a population of just 400. Visitors arriving in the cobbled Square will be immediately attracted to the old Market Hall. The sign over the door advertising 'SCVLPTVRE' should encourage entry to admire the imaginative ceramic works created on-site. The enterprise's name 'Woodstringthistlefoss' derives from old Staffordshire dialect and means 'make do and mend'. However, much more than that has already been achieved, but the message is sound enough, and the potential for the extension of such schemes within

The Manifold Track

INTRODUCTION

many other upland village communities is equally valid.

The geographical position of The Peak has long made it a target for people earnest for informal country pursuits, of which walking is undoubtedly pre-eminent. Perhaps the single most influential contributory factor in the early great surge of interest (during the inter-war years) was made possible by the railways. Whilst today it is clear that the overwhelming majority of walking visitors arrive in private cars, public transport still figures large. The extensive network of bus and train services provides splendid opportunities to enjoy a surprisingly varied cross-section of the district. With the survival of the rural public transport network a very real concern, the Peak Park has co-ordinated two important initiatives with British Rail and bus operators - the 'Peak Wayfarer' and 'Day Discoverer' travelcards. The Peak Wayfarer, originating in Greater Manchester, serves the Peak Park (and overspills into Lancashire and Cheshire too), whilst the Day Discoverer covers Derbyshire, the latter being the spearhead of the County Council's drive to retain rural public transport, particularly on Sundays. Both schemes operate with scratch-cards, giving walkers (and others) the freedom to buy in advance and choose the day of use, and have the liberty to roam the network, exploring widely by bus and train. Individual and 'family' cards are available.

THE AREA COVERED BY THIS GUIDE

The boundaries of this guide are defined on the east by the long spine of Axe Edge and Morridge, to the south by the Weaver Hills and Ashbourne, continuing north-eastward with the B5035 to Cromford and Matlock, cutting west via Youlgreave to Parsley Hay and Earl Sterndale back to the source of the Dove.

This is predominantly limestone country, with only the shale uplands west of the upper Dove and lower Manifold and the gritstone of Harthill and Stanton Moors to lend contrast. To strong walkers, the selection of outings may seem of modest ambition, but for the majority of casual visitors they will be found to be of perfect length for refreshing exercise and a gentle introduction to this truly beautiful walking region.

Note: Companion volumes to the Peak District by Mark Richards are:
White Peak Walks: The Northern Dales
High Peak Walks

SYMBOLS
ON THE ROUTE MAPS

Described walk — match arrows for continuity

Walk on motor road

Other paths or tracks

Starting point of route description **S**

Distance from starting point cross-referenced to route description **4**

Map scale 2" to 1 mile   Direction of North

Stream or River arrow indicates direction of flow   lake

Cliffs   Marshy ground

Buildings   Church +   Youth Hostel ▲

Trees   Tumulus ⁂   Trig. column △

Hedge or fence

Wall   Broken wall

Major road

Minor road

Other road

Railway

Abbreviations ——————— ON MAPS

fb : footbridge   k : kissing gate
G : field gate   PH : Public House
Gy : gateway   S : Stile
g : narrow gate   tel : telephone kiosk

——————— IN ROUTE DESCRIPTION

L/R : turn left or right
N/S/E/W : being the compass points
    North, South, East and West
All distances/heights in miles/feet

1

Hen Cloud, The Roaches and Ramshaw Rocks from Blake Mere

WALK 1   MORRIDGE

from the Rey Viewpoint   5 miles

Simply told, the central limestone plateau of the White Peak is flanked to east and west by gritstone moors. But they are not mirror images. The scarp/dip formation of the eastern edges fails to materialise on the west, where the Millstone Grit was subjected to pressure which created a folded structure. The outcrops that do occur do not face east despite the north-south axis of the folding. In the main, this is moorland country-the domain of grouse, curlew and sheep, making it a splendid place to wander. Far-ranging views, obtained particulary from the Rey Memorial Viewpoint, Merryton Low and Royledge complement the serene moments delving into the attractive headwaters of the Hamps and Warslow Brook valleys.

Morridge (moor ridge), that long arm of high ground extending south from Axe Edge; discreetly defines the south-western limits of Peakland, an horizon between the populated plain and the lonely heartland.

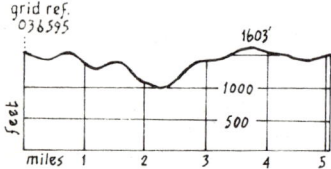

grid ref. 036595

S   Park upon the generous verges at the road junction near the Rey Viewpoint lay-by (grid ref. 028596). Follow the unenclosed farm track leading SE which passes the Newcastle-under-Lyme motocross course to the R of the depression.

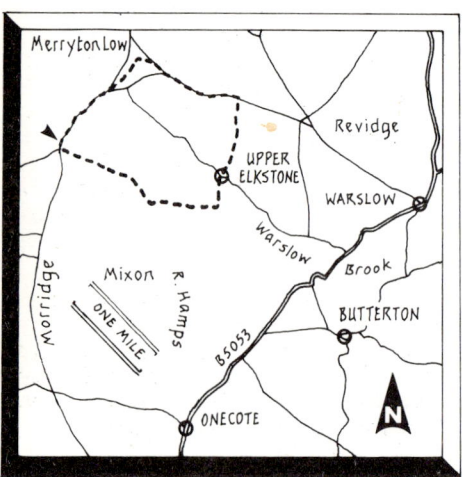

The track rises to a cattle grid/gate then descends through a gateway onto a rough pasture, a legacy of old lead mining ventures. Where the track forks, go through the gate R, descending into the farmyard of Upper Green.

Turn R entering the the field via a gate opposite the farmhouse, follow the wall **1** to a stile in the corner. Slant L to enter Lower Green Farm by a stile/gate. From the farmhouse go R, not along

——— continued on facing page

continued from facing page

the access road, but close by the Atcost building to a field gate. Then turn immediately L to a fence stile and cross the footbridge over the stripling Hamps. The path mounts the slope in a hollow way beside the wall, keeping parallel to the metalled farm road. The angle of the R hand fence indicates the line of the path to the stile, not the gateway. Thereafter it rises beside the fence, not on the road, aiming directly uphill to a stile/gateway and therefrom to the ridge road. Cross to the stile and proceed to the O.S. trig pillar (S4170) at 1394' (see drawing above), unfortunately situated on a burial mound. Hillocks in the vicinity of the summit are suggestive of mine shafts.

Sandwiched between the upper Hamps and Warslow Brook valley this S running ridge off Morridge has a prominence recognised by the Bronze Age folk who dwelt in its shadow: witness the tumulus.

Discriminating walkers (readers of this book amongst their number!) can discover the merit of this location as a viewpoint with an E bias, down the Warslow Brook valley to Ecton Hill and the Dove Dale hills about Wetton and Alstonefield. The distinctive bedraggled clump of trees on Minninglow, ten miles distant as the crow flies, is visible on a line directly above the Ecton copper mine spoil (Dutchman Level), slightly L of Johnson's Knoll clump. To the SE, Hazelton Clump, seven miles off, also claims attention above Ilam.

The footpath plummets down the hill, no carefully graded zig zags
— *continued on page 6*

continued from page 5

here to save creaking knees! The fence stile indicates the way to a wall stile; thereafter the route turns L along the Under the Hill Farm road to enter Upper Elkstone. It is with regret that I have to report that O.S. map information is out of date, for no longer can the walker find welcome refreshment in the village inn (the thirst will have to wait till The Mermaid - appropriately elusive to lunchtime opening during winter months). However, do take time off to admire the charming little parish church which obviously plays an important role in the community, being beautifully tended and decorated within. A plaque on the interior wall states ' This Chapel was built under the care and inspection of William Grindon of Stonfold. Who with the sum of two hundred pounds (£140 of which was collected by a brief and the remainder by a levy throughout the Township) completed the whole in the year of our Lord 1788'. There are other plaques with prayers and a superb Royal Heraldic Shield (G.R.) which forms the central focus about the altar decorated with gorgeous drapes; there is also a fine gallery - in all, quite the perfect meeting house.

continued on page 8

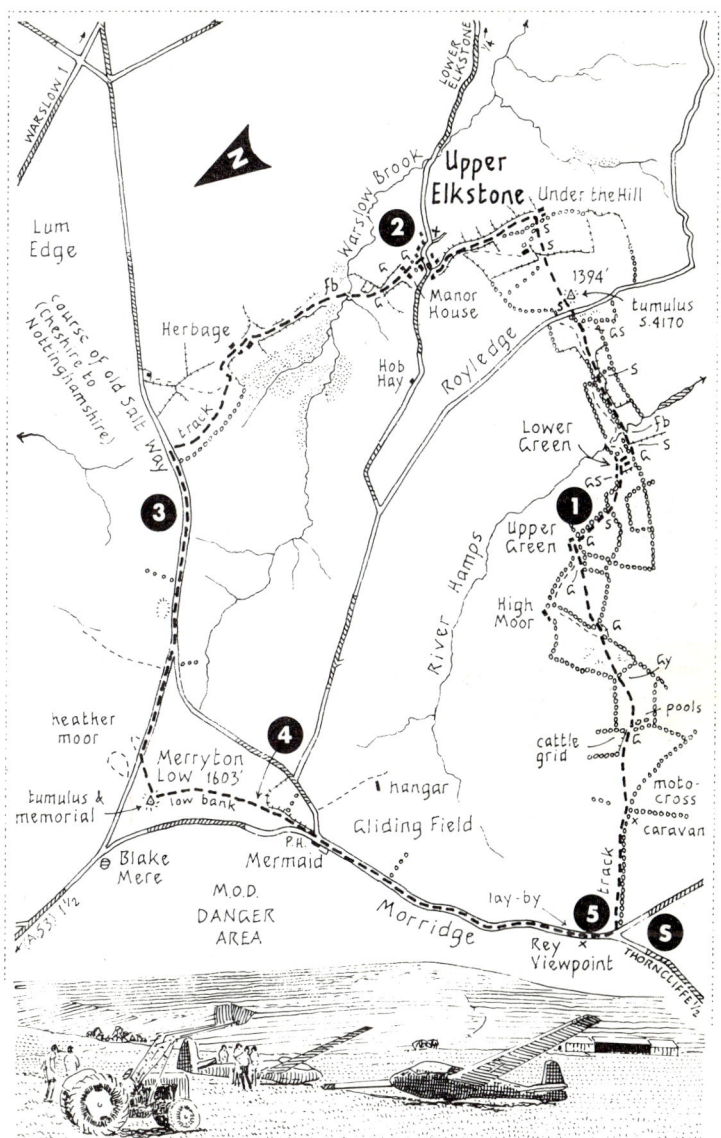

continued from page 6 ————

Go R, then first L (road sign 'No Through Road'), leading to Manor House farm (and bus depot); the house itself has 17th century origins. ❷ Pass directly through between the buildings, via gates, down a track to a fence gate thence continue to a footbridge with fine views of the steep clough banks.

The path ascends the shallow valley keeping near to the L hedgeline, at the valley head it drifts R, across boggy ground, to join the farm track that runs between the buildings and Herbage Farmhouse. Keep on the access track to the public highway (strictly this track is not a right of way, the footpath diverging to Herbage Barn). The farm notice imploring 'No Military Vehicles' is an indication of the hassle the proximity of military training grounds can inflict upon local life, so leave no cause for the farmer to rue your passing either! Turn L along the ridgetop road with heather moor to the R ❸. Follow the minor road R at the junction, branching L to the summit of Merryton Low at the second entrance of the vehicle turning loop.

The triangulation pillar, the second en route and again surmounting a tumulus, carries the memorial "to the 5th Staffordshire Leek Battalion Home Guard 'C' Company, Roll of Honour, World War 1939-1945." (see drawing)

———— *continued on facing page*

8

Mermaid Inn

continued from facing page ———

If blessed with clear visibility, the visitor can marvel at a remarkably extensive panorama from this, the highest point on the long Morridge (moor ridge) ridge at 1604'. The name Merryton deriving from the Old English myrige, meaning 'enclosed marsh'. Spent rifle cartridges abound among the tussock grass and heather underfoot. Walk SSW from the summit, dryshod on the ridgetop turf bank. **(4)** Descend with the fence to the road junction beside the Mermaid Inn, its name derives from the legendary 'Lady of Blake Mere.' The steep W flank of Morridge is harnessed by members of the Staffordshire Gliding Club, taking advantage of the strong updraughts and thermal currents to soar and wheel.

The walk concludes along the road rising to the Paul Rey (1925-1977) Memorial. **(5)** The happy inscription to this man of Hanley reads: 'A rambler and world traveller who inspired so many with his love of the countryside' - a splendid epitaph for any true lover of the great outdoors.

Looking NW from the Rey Memorial

River Hamps downstream from the Jervis Arms, Onecote

WALK 2   BUTTERTON MOOR
from Onecote   5½ miles

Alongside the rigours of walking around the Hamps and Manifold valleys east of Grindon, it must come as a relief to less energetic walkers to be able to stride forth to enjoy this easy-going excursion on the Staffordshire Moorlands. The broad rolling gritstone hill country forming the headwaters of the River Hamps, which drains Morridge from The Mermaid, provides a no less pleasurable landscape contrast to the limestone heartland of the White Peak. The scenery may seem subdued in the initial stages of the walk to Mixon and Black Brook, but on breasting Butterton Moor, the walker is rewarded with a great panorama to admire. The Butterton locality, together with the crossing of Grindon Moor back to Onecote (pronounced 'on cot'), are notable elements which lend that vital ingredient of historic and topographic diversity in a farmed countryside won from wild uplands.

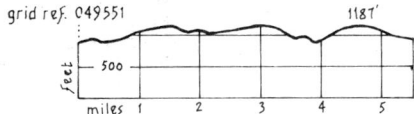

grid ref. 049551   1187'

S The walk starts from the broad verge in front of the old primary school, closed in 1984, and proceeds W along the minor road to the parish church. Usually, a church will hold something to mark it out as different

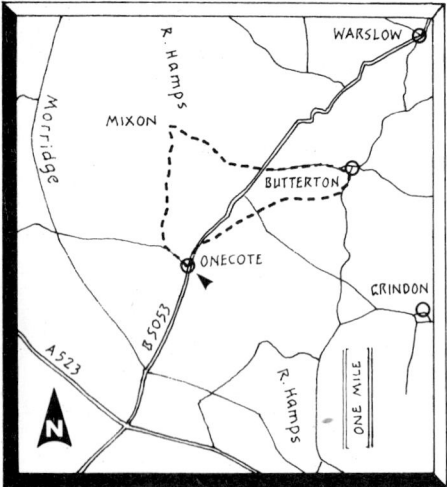

in some way, this little church is no exception as it boasts a superb old oil painting depicting Moses receiving the ten commandments on Mount Sinai. Across the road from the church is a steeply gabled Victorian farmhouse associated with the Robinson family; their bravery is recounted by Dougal Robinson in 'Survive the Savage Sea'. Their voyage around the world ended abruptly off the Galapagos Islands when their yacht sank within two minutes of an attack by killer whales.

—— continued on page 14

The Black Lion, Butterton

Jervis Arms, Onecote

continued from page 12

The Robinson family resorted to an inflatable dinghy and managed to survive for 53 days on a pitiful diet until their rescue by Japanese tuna fishermen.

Branch from the road down the lane R to Onecote Grange (Pedigree Ayrshires) signposted 'Mermaid 3¼, Mixon Mines 1¼'. Go R by the cattle grid between the farm buildings and the farmhouse, then through two yard gates and along the trackway to the former Mixon Mine ❶. Mixon derives from 'mixen', a dungheap or midden.

continued on facing page

Onecote Church

Onecote Grange

continued from facing page

Beyond the third cattle grid go R, through the gate (before the cottage), passing the workshop. Descend the spoil bank (galena ore) to reach the path through a young plantation to a fence stile. Continue via a wall stile to a footbridge over the infant River Hamps. The path rises to a gate, follows the fenced bank to a further gate, slants R
② to a fence stile (off the strict line of the footpath) and onto a rough track in a lane. A gate gives access to Black Brook farmyard (below).

The track leads uphill to a gate on course for the lane to the B5053, Warslow/Onecote road. There is an evident change detectable in crossing Butterton Moor, not only in the more extensive views, but in agricultural terms too. Black Brook you will remember for its rustic charm, whilst the Butterton locality exudes a far more prosperous air. Indeed the place-name derives from 'butter don' meaning 'the hill with rich pastures for the production of milk and butter,' obviously noted for such since Saxon times. The walk advances from the B5053 'T' junction with the road to Butterton. ③
—— *continued on page 16*

continued from page 15

Beyond the village shop fork R, then L with the village road to the Black Lion (P.H.) opposite the parish church (locked) whose spire vies with the neighbouring Grindon for the travellers' admiration. Both are startling examples of the Victorian eagerness to recapture former glories in church architecture.

Go R, quite steeply downhill, to the long road ford with its dry pedestrian passage.

The footpath from Coxon Green is not signposted, but is easily located - diverting R midway along the ford up steps to reach a stile leading to pastureland. Follow the wall L, with a well defined path ❹ proceeding by thirteen stiles across a series of strip enclosures. Pass the remote cottage (Little Twist) and onto the track ascending to a gate by Twistgreen Farm continuing to the Grindon Moor road (stile). A memorial plaque in Grindon church records a tragedy on this moor during the severe winter of 1947 when an RAF mercy misson carrying provisions for the beleaguered people of Grindon crashed in a blizzard. The flight was considered locally as little more than a misinformed publicity exercise, for among the seven who died were two journalists. The village was not in dire straits at the time.

Cross directly through the heather to a fence stile. Ahead the path is poorly defined, keep L of the ruined farm, stranded like 'Wuthering Heights' amid rough pasture. Follow the stream with a less illusory path ❺ to a stile onto Titterton Lane, continuing downhill past Home Farm to join the B5053. Proceed with caution, crossing the Hamps once more at the Jervis Arms to conclude the walk R at the next road junction.

16

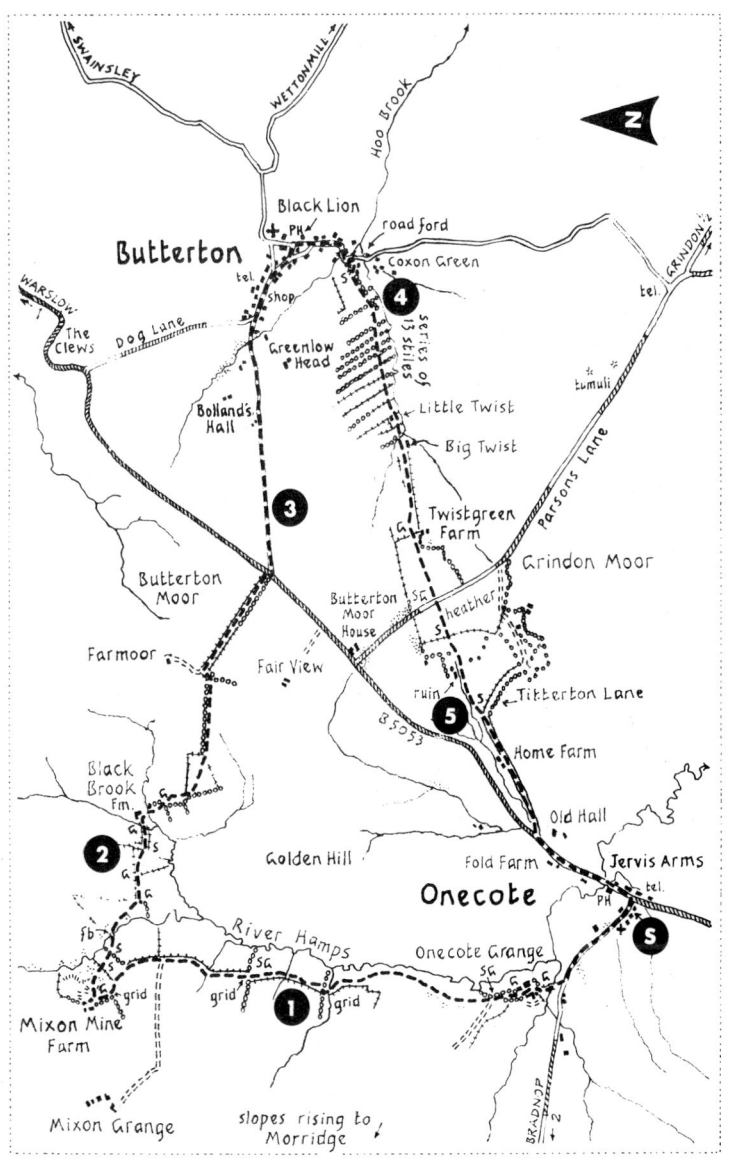

Manifold valley at Ecton

WALK 3
from Hulme End

REVIDGE
6½ miles

Revidge (edge frequented by foxes) is a retiring, unsung hero, a viewpoint with the right sort of credentials. True, it is not an all round panorama, but there is no finer stance or promenade from which to consider the upper Manifold valley. Filling the eastern gaze, a tantalising hillscape includes Axe Edge, the Dowel Dale hills, Sheen Hill and the rich tangle of hills south of Hartington and Hulme End. As a backdrop, the White Peak plateau reaches the far horizon with stretches of the Tissington Trail apparent due east. As like as not your happy deliberations will be solitary, for few walkers pass this way to idle a merry afternoon away, repelled, no doubt, by the thought of disturbance by khaki manoeuvres. It may be a coincidence but the place-name Warslow means 'watch tower' or perhaps 'lookout hill' and though it is unlikely to be alluding directly to Revidge, here is an ancient recognition of the merits of this locality as a station of vantage.

The walk does not round exclusively on this high edge; there are also choice encounters with the Manifold, as a serpentine glen backed by Ecton Hill and in pastoral mood about Brund.

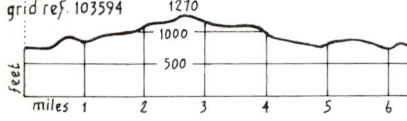

grid ref. 103594

Brund, which means 'the broom covered bank', will be remembered for its delightfully renovated mill buildings — rejuvenating a lovely scene.

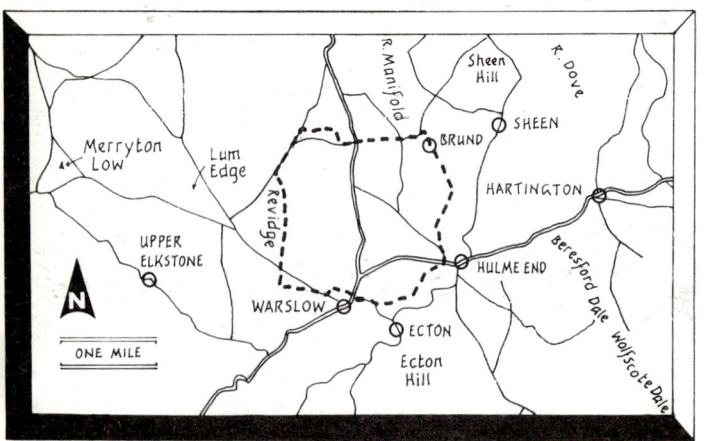

from Ecton Hill

Two views of Revidge

from Brund Mill

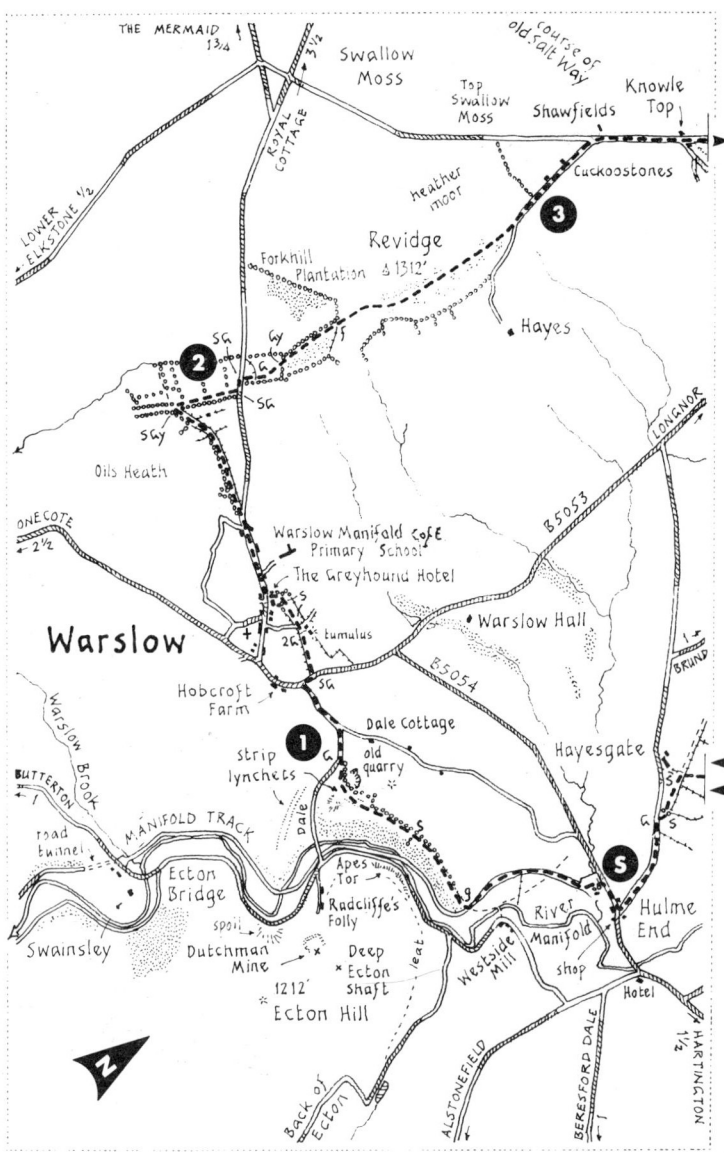

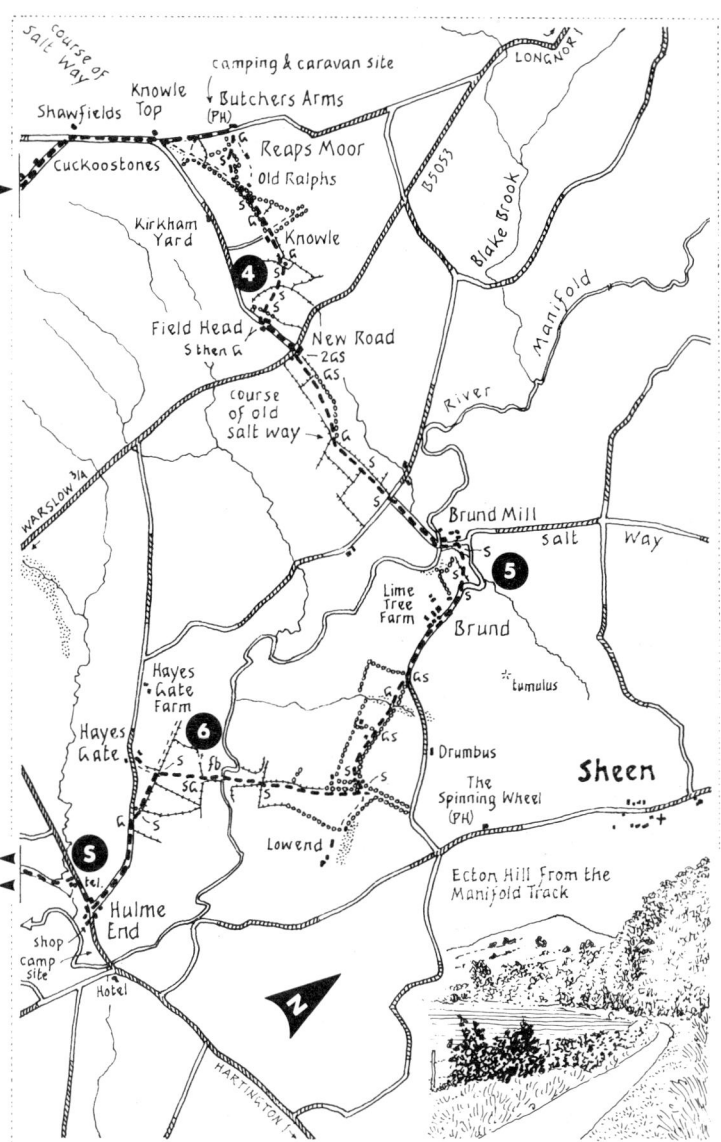

S From the National Park car park at the northern terminus of the Manifold Track walk S along the Track (a surfaced path replaced the rails in 1935), leaving it R just short of the first tight righthand bend where a footpath from Westside Mill crosses the Track (field gate L, kissing gate R). This point also coincides with a major change in the career of the River Manifold. Hitherto the product of the shaley grit hills, it now embarks upon a deeply entrenched incision into the carboniferous limestone land block.

There is no path on the ground during the steady ascent along the scarp edge. The scenery certainly justifies this early decision to enshew the popular Track to gain a mid-height perspective of Ecton Hill. Down in the valley, across the narrow strath the tightly contorted strata of Apes Tor are clearly seen just above the road. Copper, deposited in vertical pipe veins some 200 million years ago when mineralised fluids surged up fractures in the upfolded limestone, brought considerable wealth, particularly to two landowning families who controlled Ecton's mining operations at the zenith of their production during the latter half of the 18th century. The Dukes of Devonshire (Chatsworth Park, Derbyshire) and Burgoynes (Sutton Park, Bedfordshire) were the principal beneficiaries. The ore was laundered in the Manifold and dispatched on pack mules from Wettonmill Bridge, via Waterslack and Winkhill, to Whiston, beyond Cauldon Low, where a smelt works was established powered by Cheadle coal. The last hundred years since the final demise of the mines has seen a considerable softening of the harsh legacy of spoil and dereliction, the valley stepping back from the limelight of industrial exploitation for good (let's hope).

Subsequent to crossing a stile the view of the winding Manifold valley opens still further, beneath your feet tell-tale ledges betray ancient strip lynchet cultivation terraces. The path slants round R with the slope, keeping above old mine shafts and below an old quarry, to reach a stile/gate onto the minor road rising up the re-entrant valley known as The Dale.

Follow the road uphill, **1** keeping L at the first junction then R at the junction with the B5053. After 40 yards cross over to a gate/stile and follow the hedge to the farm buildings passing directly through by stiles/gates. The light green portal barn to the R of this group of buildings has been constructed upon a tumulus. Such happenings are not uncommon but there may be more cause to rue the insensitive building in this instance because of the village name. Warslow means 'tumulus with a watch tower or lookout', its location close to the village nucleus raises the question, could this be the precise mound from which the place-name derives?

Cross the facing fence stile (or follow the lane L onto the village street). Proceed by the hedge to a stile in the succeeding length of wall L. The route enters the street via a short lane above the Greyhound Hotel. Across the way the sad sight of a chapel of 1848 once transformed into a garage workshop and now lying derelict. Go R, uphill with the road forking L along a lane 40 yards after a minor road also on the L. Notice the curious shallow

—— continued on facing page

24

continued from facing page

roadside well with white metal railings. The green lane passes a cottage backing onto the lane and therefore sensibly facing 'the view' across the Warslow Brook valley. Notice the unusually large dock leaves near the cottage; can anyone explain this freak strain? Keep within the lane until the L bend. Where the lane descends, cross the facing stile beside the wired off gateway; turning R, follow the wall uphill ❷ A stile/gate gives access onto the minor road: go L 50 yards, to a footpath sign and stile/gate. The track leads, via a fence gate, diagonally across the pasture. Go through a gateway to follow a wall beside an open deciduous plantation: this light woodland contains an interesting mixture of trees, though sessile oak predominate. Crossing an awkward barrier (in best commando style!) follow the track over open moorland, gently rising to a fringe of conifers. Here, just below the summit of Revidge, the high prow of Merryton Low's eastern ridge, we can admire a view of exceptional merit affording a comprehensive picture of the hill country surrounding the Manifold and Dove valleys. Can you spot High Wheeldon, Sheen Hill, Frank i'th' Rocks in Wolfscote Dale and Thor's Cave?

N from Revidge

Panorama labels (left to right): HOLLINSCLOUGH, AXE EDGE MOOR, LEAP EDGE, HIGH EDGE, HOLLINS HILL, UPPER EDGE, BLACK EDGE, CHROME HILL, BRIER LOW, HITTER HILL, CHELMORTON LOW, SOUGH TOP, HIGH WHEELDON

Foreground labels: BARROW MOOR, FAWFIELDHEAD, PARKHOUSE HILL, ALDERY HILL

The track, etched to bedrock by military vehicles, descends to join Hayes Lane ❸ passing the intriguingly named farmstead Cuckoostones, before joining a minor road at Shawfields going R. Proceed beyond the next junction at Knowle Top to reach the Butchers Arms (public house).

―― *continued on page 26*

Old Ralphs

continued from page 25 ———

Finding a pub on Reaps Moor is quite a convenient surprise, this lonely station lending it a special appeal hard to ignore, as to boot it offers a useful base for caravan/campers. Opposite the Butchers Arms leave the road R through a gate, rising off the track to an obvious stile R, the ensuing paddock funnelling into a short passage above Old Ralphs. A stile is crossed into the next enclosure: continue with the R hand wall as the field broadens out, down via a gate to Knowle Farm, passing straight through to a gate and the derelict Knowle Cottage, a dwelling of humble proportions in a delightful setting.

Cross the fence stile to the R descending the bank to a slightly boggy hedge stile: **4** heading across the pasture R tread cautiously through a second marshy patch to reach a stile in a wall. Go beyond the water trough to a fence stile in the paddock corner, then join the road via the gate at Field Head Farm. Go L, down to the road junction, cross over to the gate to the R of New Road Farm. Passing through the farmyard by a second gate/stile and down the field to another gate/stile, the path angles R with a discernible track to a gate where the field bottlenecks. Hold to the L hedgeline, subsequent to the stile boggy ground hampers progress again but not for long. The stile onto the road might prove more of an obstacle, being a case for geriatric repair.

Advance straight on from the junction to cross the Manifold bridge at Brund Mill. It would be a surly wretch who thought the transformation of the Mill and attendant buildings into private homes not worthy of praise: better this than ruinous neglect so apparent elsewhere. Seek a stile R, short of the road junction, cross the stream before climbing the bank to a fence stile **5** and continuing to a partially obscured wall stile onto the minor road.

Go R, past the attractive and tidily managed farming community of Brund. Ignore the first inviting stile off the road R, this being for private use:

Greyhound Hotel, Warslow ——— *continued on facing page*

continued from facing page ———

instead divert R at the road corner through the gate/stile. Follow the wall with a track underfoot down to a bridge rising to a gate, maintaining course via a gate/stile keeping above the barn. Slip through a small deciduous plantation via stiles, turning down R beside the hedgeline to the sturdy footbridge across the meandering River Manifold (clearly living up to its name).

River Manifold

Advancing to a stile/gate **6** notice the long abandoned course of the river beneath the steepening meadow bank. Ascend the pasture to a stile/gate, turning L along the hedgeline to a wall stile, slant R to a gate onto the minor road. Follow this road L into the hamlet of Hulme End (shop/camping site), concluding the walk R along the B5054.

27

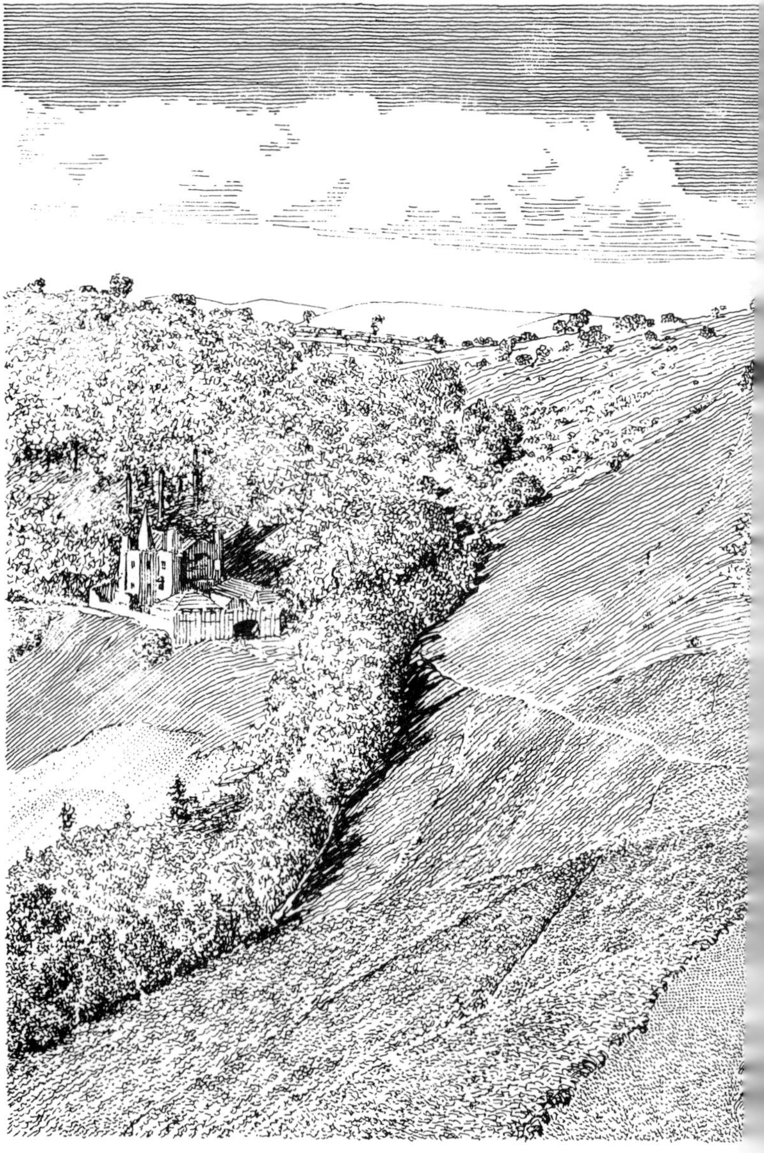

Radcliffe's Folly and the Dutchman Mine

WALK 4   ECTON HILL

from Hulme End   5¼ miles

Although created as long ago as 1937 the Manifold Track is still one of the prime visitor facilities of the White Peak, finding steady appreciative use and is particularly welcomed by those less fortunate who are confined to wheel-chairs or shackled by age (young and old alike). The recently enlarged Hulme End car park provides the perfect springboard, not merely to sample the Track, but also to explore Ecton Hill

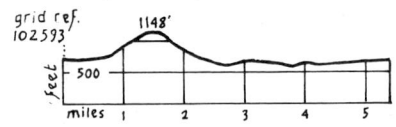

grid ref. 102593   1148'

S   From Hulme End car park (former terminal of the Leek and Manifold Light Railway) follow the track S to Dale Bridge. Leave the Track rising L with the minor road. Cross the road junction and ascend the metalled lane to Radcliffe's Castle. Pass through the archway to a stile L. Proceed along the path mounting the scarp obliquely beneath the mine spoil plantation **1** and above the scree quarry. The views throughout this section are quite delightful and frequent halts to survey the scene are in order, the severity of the slope dictating that walkers keep their eyes resolutely on the narrow trod whilst actually moving! At the crest, contour to a short hedge rising to a stile. Follow the wall to a passage, cross the pasture to a further short passage - entering the field, glance at the old limekiln and quarry R.

Whilst the underlying rock may be calcium rich the surface soil is leached, so to counteract this acid state farmers have long resorted to applications of burnt-lime to 'sweeten' the ground.

Cross to a gate going L with the wall to the Broad Ecton Farm access road, then R following the wall into the dale via stile/gate. **2** Note that the tension on the accompanying wire fence affords scope for the more musical of walkers to pluck out quite tuneful bass notes!

—— continued on page 32

Swainsley and Morridge up the Warslow Brook valley

Dale Farm

continued from page 30 ———

Approaching the Sugar Loaf bluff, cross two stiles and pass down to the R of the resilient reef outcrop into the dale bottom. Track down The Dale meadow, in all probability slipping discreetly past a contented herd of Friesian cows to Dale Farm, watching your head on the overhead vacuum line as you enter the farmyard gate. The cafe at Wetton Mill may conveniently be visited, with the detour including a brief digression up to Nan Tor Cave from the road corner descending directly to the Mill (via stiles).

The walk continues along the old gated road from Dale Farm ❸ undulating to Swainsley, the intimate views of the winding Manifold (the characteristic from which its name derives), its meadows and wooded banks sustaining the quality of the walk. After the second gate go L with the minor road over the river bridge then immediately turn R at the stile. The meadow path crosses Warslow Brook footbridge, rising to a kissing gate ❹ where the Manifold Track is rejoined. Go R retracing the approach via Ecton, the lost mining centre reclaimed by Nature. ❺

Swainsley Dovecote

32

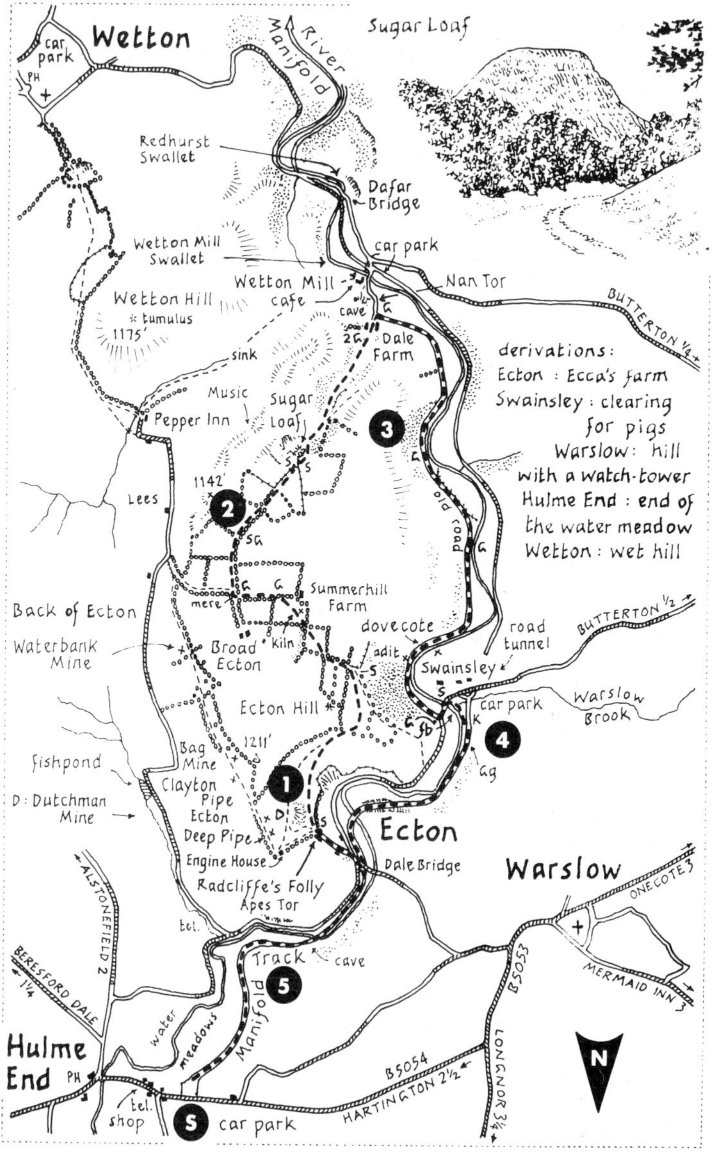
Wetton
car park
PH
Sugar Loaf
River Manifold
Redhurst Swallet
Dafar Bridge
Wetton Mill Swallet
car park
Wetton Mill cafe
Nan Tor
Wetton Hill
tumulus
1175'
cave
Dale Farm
BUTTERTON 1/4
derivations:
Ecton : Ecca's farm
Swainsley : clearing for pigs
Warslow: hill with a watch-tower
Hulme End : end of the water meadow
Wetton : wet hill
sink
Music
Sugar Loaf
Pepper Inn
3
1142'
2
Lees
old road
Back of Ecton
Summerhill Farm
mere
dovecote
road tunnel
BUTTERTON 1/2
Waterbank Mine
Broad Ecton
kiln
adit
Swainsley
car park
Warslow Brook
Ecton Hill
4
Bag Mine
1211'
Fishpond
Clayton Pipe
Ecton Deep Pipe
1
D : Dutchman Mine
Ecton
Engine House
Dale Bridge
Warslow
Radcliffe's Folly
Apes Tor
ONECOTE 3
ALSTONEFIELD 2
tel.
Track
cave
B5053
BERESFORD DALE 1 1/4
5
Manifold
water meadows
MERMAID INN 3
Hulme End
PH
B5054
LONGNOR 3 1/4
N
HARTINGTON 2 1/2
tel.
shop
S
car park

Leek and Manifold Light Railway —

Completed in 1904, the Leek and Manifold Railway was described prophetically by a local thus "it's a grand bit of line but they wunna mak a go on it for it starts from nowhere and finishes up at the same place".

Conceived to regenerate the Ecton copper mines and serve the farming communities W of Hartington, the enterprise limped from the outset, never establishing a realistic passenger or goods trade it met its inevitable demise in 1934. Shortly afterwards Staffordshire County Council adopted it as a bridleway, applying a tarmac surface thereby creating a revolutionary amenity along the 8 mile section from Waterhouses to Hulme End. The scenery is of exceptional quality throughout, richly wooded and punctuated by limestone bluffs and buttresses with green pastures and two rivers each adept at playing the disappearing act. Between Swainsley Tunnel and Wetton Mill the main thoroughfare was switched to the former railway trackbed giving walkers the undoubted pleasure of following the undulating old road.

Swainsley Tunnel

Ecton Hill

Today Ecton is a quiet place which, during the C17th and C18th throbbed with the frenzied life of copper fever. Evidence of those years remains in spoil (though a great deal was removed and used as ballast for the railway) ruin and shaft (some, like the top of Deep Ecton, poorly protected, so risk not a peer in!). The walk passes two buildings surviving from those days on the rise to Radcliffe's Folly, the former sales office and the mine agents (captain) house. Radcliffe's Folly is a classic example of pre-planning regulation eccentricity. Despite its copper hood this oddity has no links with Ecton's mining days, having been shoddily built in the 1930s by Arthur Radcliffe.

Visitors who have been delighted by the grandeur and pomp of Chatsworth House and Buxton Spa would do well to consider from whence much of the wealth derived for their creation. The productivity of the exploitation of Ecton Hill's copper, lead and zinc deposits (though prone, like all mining ventures, to great variation) tended to reach its zenith whenever the Dukes of Devonshire desired the top returns to satisfy their various building enterprises, the mounting rich pickings probably prompting equally big ideas! During the heyday years in the latter half of the C18th, the principal beneficiates were the Devonshire's from Ecton Pipe Vein and the Burgoyne's from Clayton Pipe Vein. The C19th saw an appreciable decline in the ventures due to flooding and the likely exhaustion of easily obtained ore. The horse-shoe of conifers seen on the ascent from the Folly surrounds the spoil from the Dutchman Mine (the level is blocked, though easily located by the spring of water). The ruins here are of an engine house, smithy and carpenters' shop used chiefly during the construction of the Goodhope Level in the 1850s. Above this is a barn adapted for farm use but which was erected in 1788 to house a Boulton & Watt steam engine which raised ore and pumped water from the Deep Ecton Mine. When sunk in the years to 1795 the shaft was the deepest in Britain some 924' below adit level (by 1840 the shaft from the surface was 1312' deep, hence my warning about the open top).

Speleological access is strictly controlled.

The gaping shaft of Deep Ecton

The Manifold valley, N from Thor's Cave

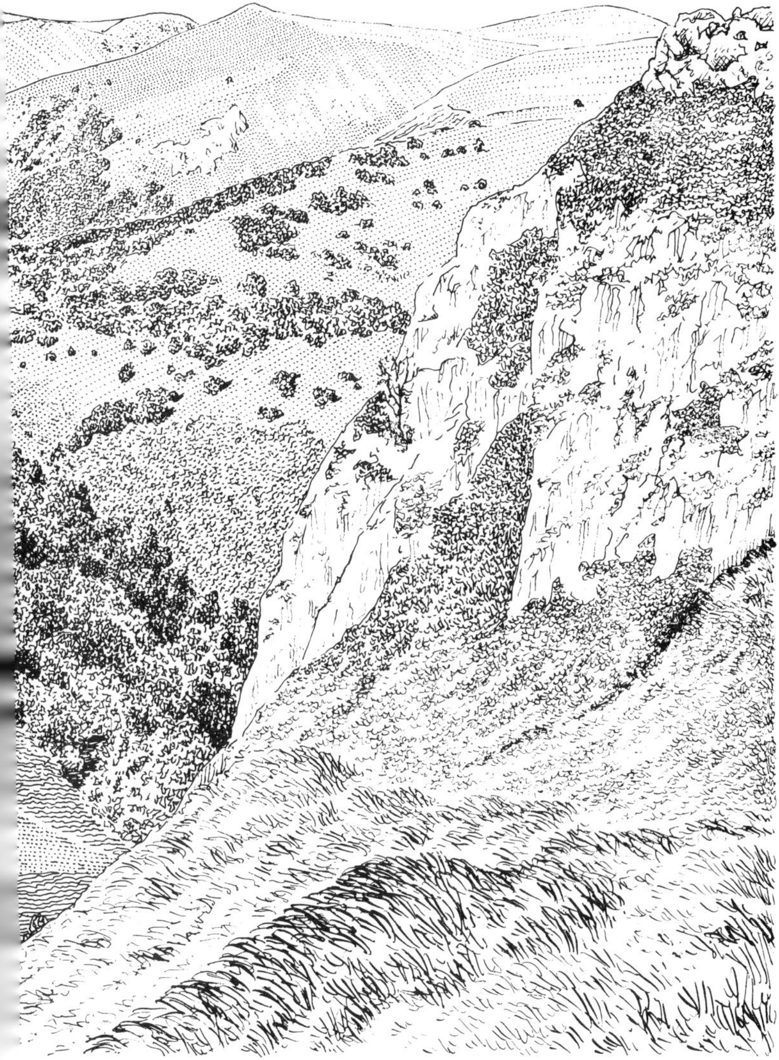

WALK 5
from Wetton

THOR'S CAVE
5¼ miles

Thor's Cave, some 60' high at its entrance, is set 250' above the Manifold valley. Though caving enthusiasts may deem it something of a sham cavern, no visitor will be disappointed by its visual impact. It is one of the thrills bestowed on walkers to the White Peak to inspect at close hand this gaping cavity and perch upon its topmost knot to survey the Manifold hillscape betwixt Wetton and Grindon.   Walkers may limit their steps to simply embracing this one special objective, yet a route sweeping across this beautiful valley to and fro reveals a fuller compositon with the discovery of secret dales - in all a walker's preserve par excellence.

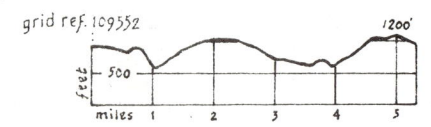

grid ref. 109552   1200'

S From the Wetton village car park follow the road R.   At the junction where the Wetton Mill road enters Wetton street go L, forking L along the lane signposted 'concessionary path to Thor's Cave.' An alternative footpath descends the fields into the wooded re-entrant valley below Thor's Cave, and whilst there is a branch path in the woodland giving good access to the Cave from below, there is little doubt that the higher route is superior.   Following a stile/gate in the lane, a signpost directs R at a stile into a field ; keep close to the upper wall descending, rising and contouring to a fence stile. Thor's Cave is located round to the R, but would encourage walkers to complete the ascent to the crag summit L before visiting the Cave.

Be sure to return precisely by the (only) ascent path as the N and W faces fall away precipitously. N.B.- avoid the apparent impromptu slither path just S of the summit near Seven Ways Cave.

— continued on page 41

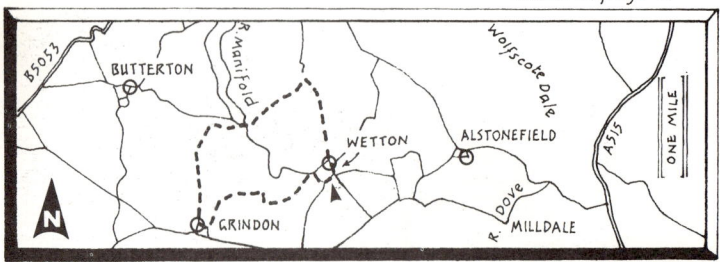

Thor's Cave dominating the Leek & Manifold Light Railway — taken from a photograph of c. 1907 in the possession of the PPJPB.

Thor's Cave

continued from page 38 ———

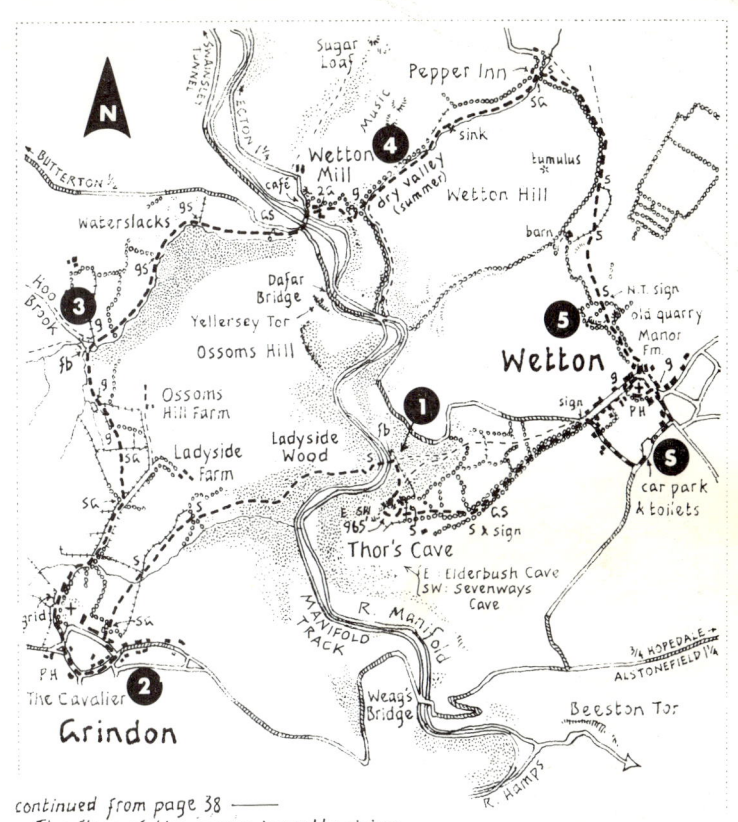

   The floor of the cavern is gently rising
bedrock, which can be very slippery when wet. Upon entry the muffled
cooing of resident pigeons can frequently be detected emanating from
the dark recesses of the roof.   The great domed cave within the reef
limestone, eroded away during the formation of the Manifold valley
during the many phases of the Ice Age, is the remnant of an ancient
subterranean cave system of potentially vast proportions. The earliest
reference to this cave was as 'Thyrsis Cavern', clearly pointing to the
traditional Scandinavian superstition associating such natural
phenomena with their thunder-god Thōrr. A giant fissure known as
the West Window marks a change of rock level within, and whilst the
scrambler (with a torch) may venture a little farther in, this is sufficient
for the majority of visitors. The prospect out through the main entrance
is one of the high points of this walk.   ——— *continued on page 42*

continued from page 41 ——— Refrain from descending the West Window gully, above and to the L of which is Thor's Fissure Cave, a large joint passage which, along with Seven Ways and Elderbush Caves, found higher up the reef limestone knoll, have been excavated archaeologically revealing a climatic and occupational record from Late Pleistocene to Romano-British times. Thor's Cave itself was excavated along the enlarged joints on three occasions in the latter part of the C19th (which helps to explain the total lack of cave floor deposits today).

From the cave entrance, descend the steps (lower, a potentially slippery path) to the Manifold footbridge ❶. In summer, in its normally dry state, it is an eerie sight, with only the broad boulder-strewn dry river-bed on view. The river disappears at Wettonmill Swallet to reappear near Ilam Hall; only in times of high flood does the subterranean system fill to capacity and the river flow the whole way. The Manifold running from Axe Edge drains the Millstone Grit uplands W of the Dove, encountering limestone country at Hulme End. Because the Ecton Limestones are tightly folded and virtually impervious, the river flows over thin shaly limestones until the reef limestone is met at Wetton Mill.

Walkers may care to return directly back up to Wetton or follow the Manifold Track R on course for the Wetton Mill café. If you take this option, choose for preference the old road via Dafar Bridge from where Ossom's Eyrie can be detected 80' up the face of Yellersey Tor. It has been entered for archaeological investigation via a rope ladder off the top of the cliff. At its foot is Yellersey Tor Cave, a rock shelter with an upward fissure which was found to contain Late Palaeolithic remains including the bones of reindeer and bison - presumably part of the diet of those early men of some eight thousand years ago. Remarkably, Ossom's Eyrie had been occupied by man from Early Stone Age!

——— *continued on facing page*

Wettonmill Bridge

continued from facing page ──── The main route crosses the Manifold Track to a fence stile with attendant National Trust sign 'Ossoms Hill'. A footpath, with waymark posts, zig-zags up Ladyside Wood. At the outset, the principal attraction is the Thor's Cave buttress with the West Window fissure prominent, but as height is gained there is one delightful glimpse down the winding Manifold valley before the side valley closes in. The path comes to a stile beside a stone trough here entering a field. Slant L up to a stile then cross the stream by a simple stone slab, aiming up the pasture to the L of the prominent trees, entering Grindon by way of a stile and gate. **2**

This charming village has retained its strong upland identity without forfeiting its soul to holiday lets. There is a friendly public house, The Cavalier, and several homes provide B & B (of which the author can recommend Porch Farm). But the principal focus for the visitor is the parish church, often referred to as 'the Cathedral of the Staffordshire Moorlands'.

──── *continued on page 44*

43

continued from page 43

The church, as we look at it today, is totally Victorian. It stands, however, on an ancient church site: indeed, the tower vestry now plays host to two Saxon stone coffins and a font embraced with a serpent motif - these artifacts were presumably discovered during the rebuilding in the last century. Within the church, notice the wall board above the door referring to Robert Port of Ilam Hall, a former Grindon landowner whose name survives corrupted in Porch Farm. Also the plaque to the air disaster during the Arctic winter of 1947 when, on a mercy mission for the beleaguered village, a plane from R.A.F. Fairford in Gloucestershire crashed on Grindon Moor. Sad to report falling attendances threaten this proud church's future. On the tiny Green beside the church gate stands the Rindle Stone, an inscription all but indecipherable apart from the date 1807, it is locally associated with the now crudely culverted occasional stream that passes here from the new pond, and ran down to the now filled in village mere below. Incidentally, the village name means 'green hill' evidence of sweet grazing certainly recognised in Saxon times.

From the car park at the church, follow the road (which leads to Ladyside Farm) N, leaving it to the L at a stile beside a field gate just short of the fork for Ossoms Hill. A discernible footpath leads diagonally across the field to another stile by a gate. En route, notice Butterton church spire ahead set high upon the ridge of rank hedges whose spur of land furnished Hoo Brook with its name. The path heads on downhill by two wicket gates into the deep Hoo Brook valley. Cross the footbridge, go R to a wicket gate, ❸ advancing with the stream to a wall gateway with the dense ashwood of Ossoms Hill and steep pasture flanking the valley. Proceed beneath the scrubby bank of Waterslacks (the name means 'wet hollow') crossing two stiles. The valley curves to reach the Wetton Mill

——— *continued on facing page*

The Cavalier

continued from facing page ─────

camping site. The sign on the gate holds little comfort for owners of unruly dogs that love to roam!

Reaching the road, go L to Wettonmill Bridge. The adjacent signboard informs the visitor of the history and uses of the Manifold Track (at this point, between Swainsley and the Wetton road beyond Yellersey Tor, a motor road) and the erratic course of the river in the vicinity. The bridge was rebuilt in 1801 (where have you seen that date before?) by the Duke of Devonshire to service his copper mining enterprises on Ecton Hill. Wetton Mill ceased to function as a grist mill in 1857. This attractive group of buildings is part of the National Trust's Manifold estate holdings and, in response to an obvious need, provide café and toilet facilities for the car park across the bridge. The river here is normally shallow enough for children to enjoy paddling among the boulders, and families will have fun watching the river sink, according to the season of the year either here, at Redhurst Swallet by Dafar Bridge, or a little farther on at Snow Hole — though sometimes it persists to Beeston Tor and beyond. Just above the café is Nan Tor: like a giant Gruyère cheese, it contains one large cave or rock shelter which contained evidence of use by Mesolithic man in early post-glacial times some 8½ thousand years ago. — *continued below*

Nan Tor

continued from above ───── The walk passes in front of the millhouse via two gates to a clear ascending track, from where there is an uninterupted and beautiful view up of the winding Manifold at its scenic best. Rising by a rock cutting, the track is lost on the ridge pasture. However,

───── *continue on page 46*

Waterslacks in the Hoo Brook valley

Dry valley below Pepper Inn

continued from facing page

slant L seeking a somewhat well-concealed wicket gate in the light scrub. The path proceeds up the (summer) dry valley in marked contrast to the opposing Hoo Brook valley. For such a striking valley with its steep open hillsides, it seems strange that mapmakers apply no name to it. Can any reader supply a 'lost' local name? **4** Quite by surprise, a sink is passed and as the valley narrows, a tiny stream accompanies the path in cressbeds to a stile by a gate at Pepper (derived from pauper) Inn.

Briefly entering a lane, turn R at a stile and cross the slab footbridge, rising with the wall on the flanks of Wetton Hill. Cross the stile into a fenced enclosure, which is traversed diagonally to a second fence stile. Follow the clear footpath over the shoulder to a wall stile by a National Trust sign. **5** The walk concludes through an old quarried enclosure to enter a lane into Wetton. The walk takes advantage of a stroll through the churchyard by turning R upon entering the street, then L to rejoin the street by the pub. Go R to the road junction and R again.

Wetton has a slightly busier air than Grindon and amid the grey-toned buildings there exist some noteworthy vernacular C18th farmhouses, an interesting church and the Ye Olde Royal Oak public house - but alas no shop.

Pepper Inn, built c.1740 by the mine owners of Ecton (the Burgoynes). Originally an alehouse for miners, over the years it has served as a smallpox isolation hospital and a button factory.

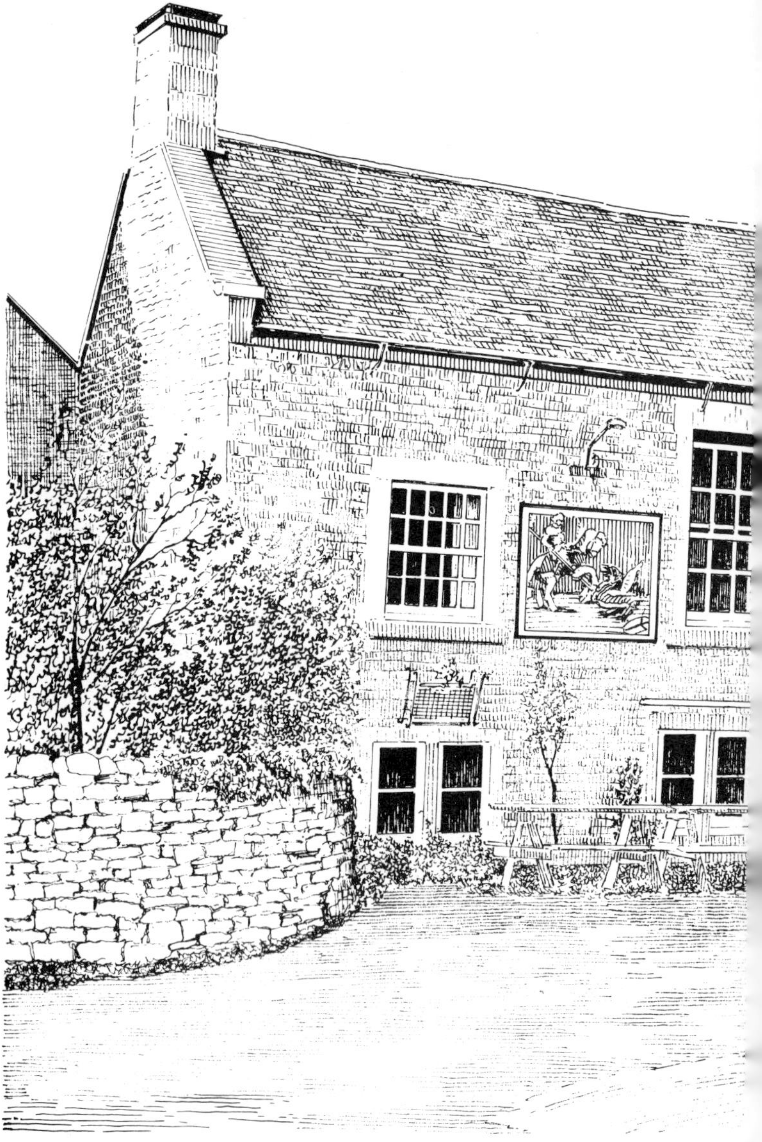

The George, Alstonefield

WALK 6   BINCLIFF
from Wetton   5½ miles

The gorgeous contortions of the Manifold valley from Beeston Tor to Rushley Bridge can only be admired from on high, there being no valley bottom path. However, the path along Bincliff is more than ample compensation. The walk turns on Castern Hall, one of the grander houses of the district, commanding a fine prospect of the Musden banks of the Manifold. Crossing Ilam Moor, a name that harks back to pre-enclosure times, the walk passes through Stanshope, a hamlet of dairy farms, into the depths of Hopedale via Brunister Lane. Attaining Alstonefield (the second opportunity for refreshment en route, or only, if Barn Close is not open!), the last westward stretch of the triangular route begins. Upon the crossing of Hope Marsh, the walker encounters the only surface stream as it drains Windledale Hollow on course for shack holes and a subterranean career down Hopedale. The Marsh is drained and boggy going need not be anticipated. The whole walk is, in fact, on firm footing, though after prolonged rain the crossing of Hopedale can be slippery.

grid ref. 109552

S From the Wetton village car park head S along the road signposted to Grindon (Carr Lane), at the ruined barns diverging L through to a stile. Follow the wall uphill, gradually slanting R via a waymark post to reach a stile L of the barn on the brow.

The summit of Wetton Low is visible L, but the trig. pillar, built upon a tumulus mound is out of bounds. The path descends beside the wall (notice a wall has been removed half way down) to reach Larkstone Lane at a stile (with a sign affixed encouraging a visit to Barn Close).

The next phase of the walk may quite fairly be described as the highlight of this outing, and an ambling pace should be cultivated not least out of

—— continued on facing page

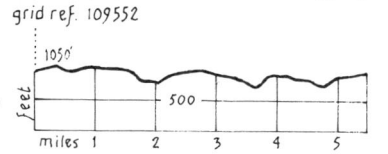

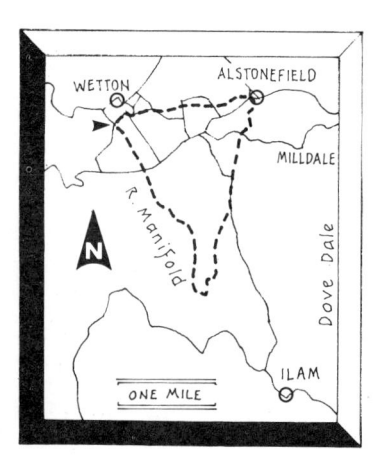

continued from facing page

cautious respect for the steep Bincliff slope. Going directly across the lane, descend to a stile into a funnelling enclosure, presumably so designed to assist in the sheep gathering process (notice the curious bulbous wall junction opposite?). Contour R to a stile, hereafter keeping with the scarptop path. Glancing R the concrete dish of a mere can be seen below the path, proof of the scarcity of drinking water for grazing animals, especially during summer months when even the River Manifold fails (running underground).

Waterfall Low

The Manifold valley from Bincliff

The proximity of the old Bincliff mines are soon apparent with large heaps of spoil adjacent to shafts seen littering the plateau. This is not an area for the wandering spirit: indeed the steep slope down to the Manifold valley floor is honeycombed with galleries definitely not for casual visitation! The path passes a collapsed adit entrance, the adopted home of badgers. Notice the freshly excavated sett soil down the bank. Foxes too have found safe haven in this vicinity. Beeston Tor is visible R, but its the beautiful curvature of the valley that holds attention.

continued on page 52

strolling along Bincliff

continued from page 51

1 A few yards subsequent to crossing a stile, rise to a second stile L, near a caravan. Pass by the Highfield Mine (lead) spoil to a gateway, crossing the recently enlarged pasture to a stile/gate. Go forward with the sweep of the strip lynchets, confirmation of the former intensive tilling in this neighbourhood (one might say 'prior to the Prior'). When Burton Abbey held these lands, the monks would have adopted a pastoral system of sheep rearing, so it can be assumed the many instances of terracing about these Manifold banks came into existence in the Dark Age period and reflect little medieval activity. Arriving at a gate/stile, follow the track (an optional short-cutting track slants uphill L, above Castern Farm) via further gates to Castern Hall. A brief detour along the access road round to the front of the Hall is recommended. Notice the Hurt family rebus, a wounded hart, on the entrance gates. Nicholas Hurt came to Castern in 1560 and

continued on facing page

Castern Hall

52

continued from facing page

whilst nothing of his time is evident in the present building (though he was party to the rebuilding of St Bertram's Chapel at Ilam and that remains intact) his family influenced the Hall's development in succeeding centuries.

2 The walk now sets its face to the N: before we leave the topic, however, it is interesting as an aside to note that the original Hurt estate extended over Ilam Tops to define its N limits below Hurt's Wood in (Castern) Hall Dale. Follow the farm road as to Castern Farm, heeding the advice to cross the fence stile L short of the farmyard, and climb the bank directly to a stile. Go R to squeeze behind the circular cattle drinking trough, descending with the farm track (cattle corridor!) to the rear of the farm buildings there locating a stile/gate (with the footpath's destination welded to the metal post - quite a novel idea!). The fields around Castern, Ilam and Throwley are distinctly larger than elsewhere on the limestone plateau, indicating old untouched Grange pastures, where walls wind without a hint of grid-like regimentation. The mere drinking place (above) shows an interesting device by which sheep from an otherwise dry enclosure were enabled to access a spring without mixing with neighbouring flocks, the enclosure on the L having its own spring supply somewhat higher up the valley. The walk crosses a stile R above the illustrated mere, following the wall up the valley to a stile just beyond the upper spring. Crossing the saddle of the ridge via two further stiles and a gateway, an optional return route beckons, where a wicket gate L gives access to the old

continued on page 54

continued from page 53 ───────

ridge way via Stable and Ashbourne Lanes back into Wetton (Stable Lane could also have been entered off Bincliff).

Continuing in the author's footsteps, cross the facing stile (noticing the interesting toppled willow L in a spring) maintaining course via two further stiles onto Ilam-moor Lane below Damgate (this place-name means 'the pond on the old road'). (3) Go L into Stanshope, following the farm road forking R to Grove Farm (Ravenstorr Herd of pedigree Friesians). Beyond the farmyard entrance, Brunister Lane continues downhill, delightfully lined with a host of golden daffodils in late Spring. One fascinating and unusual feature of this evidently old drove way between the valley and hill pastures is the lay-by fold. In times when sheep were in frequent passage, perhaps to have their fleeces washed prior to the annual clip, small flocks would be travelling to and from the Milldale sheepwash. To avoid confusion when two flocks met, the rising flock were deftly slipped temporarily into this fold, thereby giving priority to the dirty sheep in descent.

continued on page 56 ───────

lay-by fold, Brunister Lane

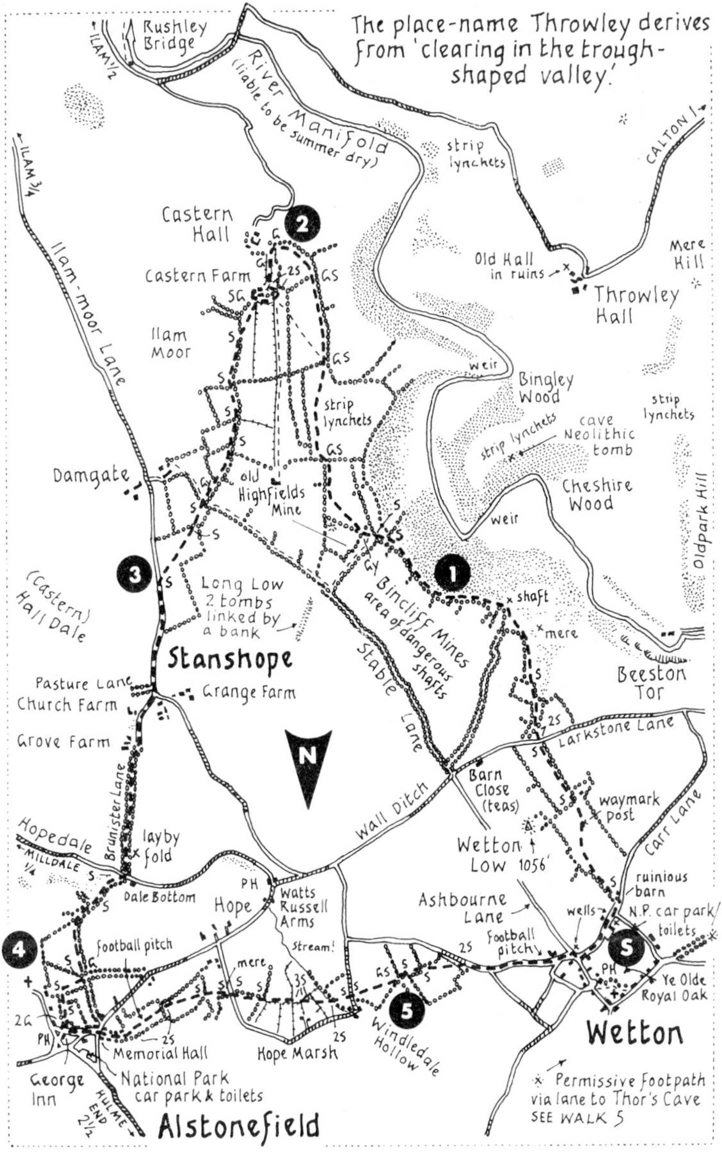

The place-name Throwley derives from 'clearing in the trough-shaped valley.'
Rushley Bridge
ILAM ½
River Manifold (liable to be summer dry)
strip lynchets
CALTON 1
ILAM ¾
Castern Hall
Castern Farm
Old Hall in ruins
Throwley Hall
Mere Hill
Ilam-moor Lane
Ilam Moor
weir
Bingley Wood
strip lynchets
cave
Neolithic tomb
Damgate
old Highfields Mine
Cheshire Wood
Oldpark Hill
(Castern) Hall Dale
Long Low 2 tombs linked by a bank
Bincliff Mines area of dangerous shafts
shaft
mere
Stanshope
Pasture Lane
Church Farm
Grange Farm
Beeston Tor
Grove Farm
Stable Lane
Larkstone Lane
Barn Close (teas)
waymark post
Brunister Lane
Wall Ditch
Carr Lane
Hopedale
MILLDALE ¼
layby fold
Wetton Low 1056'
Dale Bottom
Hope
Watts Russell Arms
Ashbourne Lane
ruinious barn
N.P. car park/ toilets
wells
football pitch
Stream!
Football pitch
mere
Ye Olde Royal Oak
Memorial Hall
Hope Marsh
Windledale Hollow
Wetton
George Inn
National Park car park & toilets
HULME END 2½
Alstonefield
Permissive Footpath via lane to Thor's Cave SEE WALK 5

continued from page 54

Brunister, which on first acquaintance appears to have a similar origin to Bunster (Hill), may derive from 'thorn scrub cleared by burning'. Reaching the foot of the lane cross the Hopedale road (cafe R in Milldale) to a stile. The apparent place-name tautology of Hopedale (valley, valley) can be explained by qualifying the two elements. Hope implies a narrow valley, and dale refers to the low ground itself (a useful parallel being found in the Swiss Alps, where one finds 'high level pastures'), so we have 'a narrow valley with little pastureland'. Follow the path rising steeply by the wall to reach a stile next to an interesting old quarried hollow, with its exposure of thinly bedded limestone - nature's walling! Pass through the small funnelled enclosure to a constriction focussed upon a sycamore tree. The path keeps company with the wall L up to a gate, here entering a lane ❹, which is immediately left R over a stile, passing to the L of the abandoned manual well pump. This pump has lost several necessary functional features such as the down pipe and winding handle, a similar pump in almost working condition can be seen in a roadside farmyard at Upper Town, Bonsall. Two stiles lead by a garden wall to a humble farmyard with its quaint, but evidently still operative, shippon. At a gate the tidy green at the heart of Alstonefield is reached; go L by the George Inn (quite to be recommended for a hearty walker's lunch). Passing the Cottage Studio of Jean Goodwin and the village shop, advance along the short lane by the Memorial Hall and Old School House.

continued on facing page

Shippon in Alstonefield

continued from facing page ──────

After crossing the first of many stiles beside a barn, walk across the recreation ground (a game of football played here in the depths of winter must be a Siberian experience!) to a stile. The prominent wooded peak R is Steep Low. Descend on a R slant to another stile (by the mere) giving onto the Hope Green road. The stile facing leads to another, where keep on straight beside the hedge to yet another stile. Soon veer R over a stile, crossing a paddock to a recently erected hedge-stile, then to a double-stile and plank footbridge (thank goodness for the variety!), reaching the minor road off Hope Marsh by climbing the pasture to a you-know-what. Again, cross the facing stile to a gate/stile ❺. Only four stiles to go, the first two switching the path over the wall before a final stretch of field path leads to the others, the final one being the waymarked stile onto the Wetton road. Go R into the village to complete the walk in style.

Ye Olde Royal Oak, Wetton

Manor House Farm, Wetton

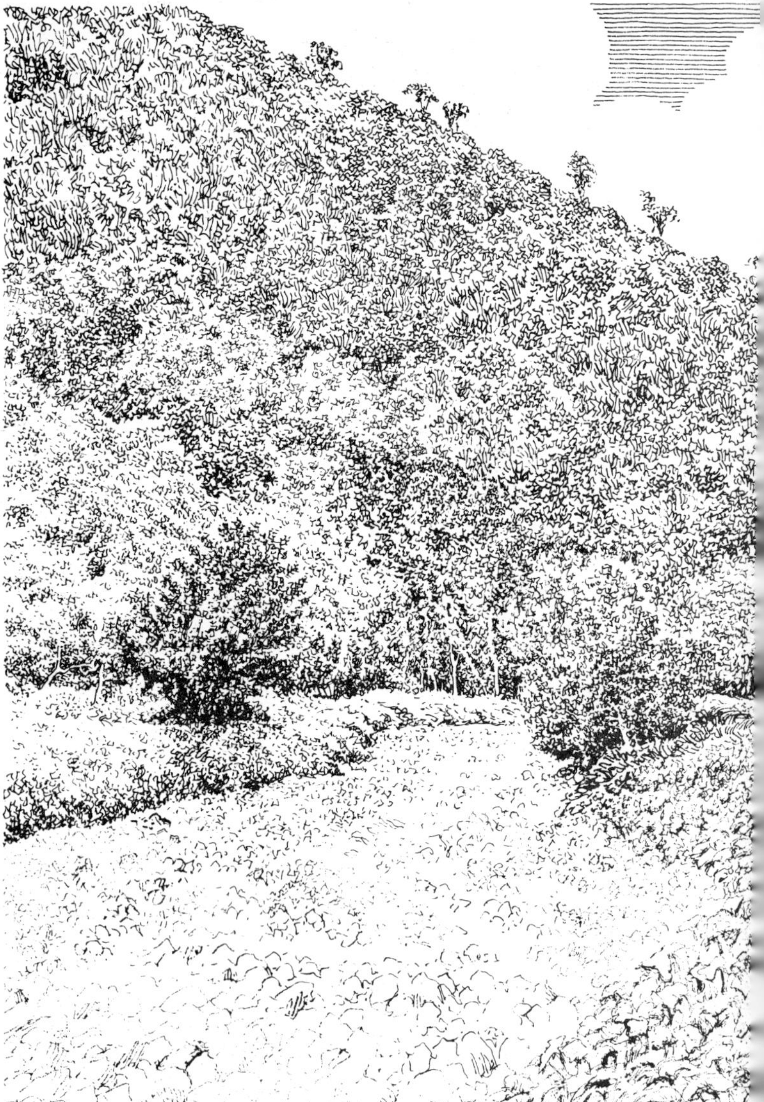

The summer-dry Hamps and Manifold Track

WALK 7   HAMPS VALLEY
from Grindon   6 miles

This easy-going walk through choice Peakland scenery at your own relaxing pace with the contrasting characteristics of the Hamps' wooded depths and the spacious views from the high lane above Back o'th' Brook visits two of the quiet unsung village delights of the Staffordshire Moorlands.

The White Peak is rightly famed for the quality of its valley walks; who for instance could not delight in Lathkill Dale, Chee Dale or Dove Dale? But perhaps the most amazing experience awaits those new to the Manifold and Hamps valleys. Each a beautiful pageant of woodland-shaded sinuous valley, with shapely ridges rising to greet the traveller at every turn. Yet where is the water? For except during periods of consistent rainfall, the rivers flow discreetly through faults in the limestone strata. The Hamps plays the disappearing act just below Waterhouses, making the walk beneath Old Soles Wood something of a strange experience. Therefore, whilst this is a large valley you might only encounter water in the occasional pool or simply reflect on the drought at the Red Lion or Cavalier!

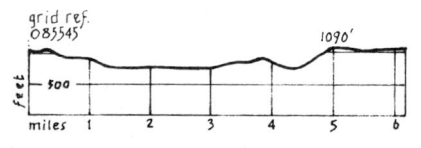

S From the car park on the W side of Grindon churchyard, go S following the road from the Green to The Cavalier junction. Turn L into the village then R after Porch Farm into a lane. Branch L at first lane junction taking the stile R before Buckfurlong Farm. A series of stiles facilitate progress down the valley and past two substantial meres, inscribed with the name of their maker 'E. ALLEN'. **1** From the stile by the lower mere, the path keeps to the L side of the narrowing valley, contouring L where the stream bed slips steeper R towards the Hamps glen. Follow the natural line sweeping down and alongside the Manifold Track to a gate.

——— *continued on page 62*

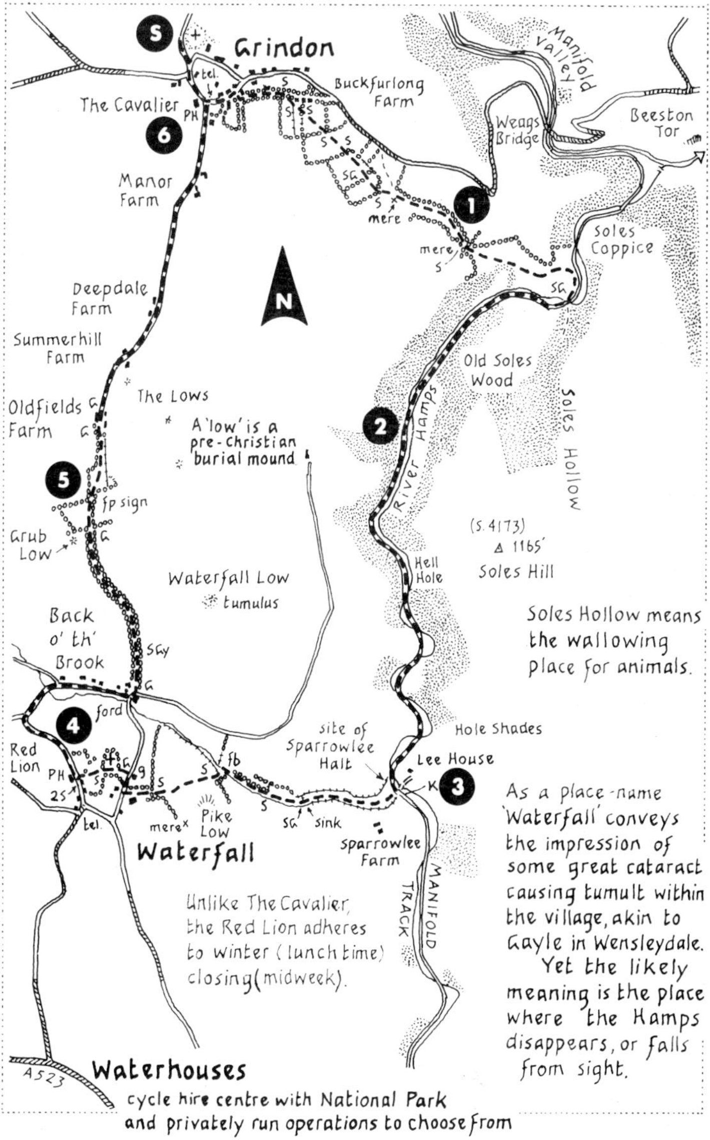

Grindon
S
tel.
The Cavalier
PH
6
Buckfurlong Farm
Manifold Valley
Weags Bridge
Beeston Tor
1
mere
Manor Farm
Soles Coppice
SG
Deepdale Farm
N
Summerhill Farm
Old Soles Wood
The Lows
Oldfields Farm
2
River Hamps
Soles Hollow
A 'low' is a pre-christian burial mound
5
fp sign
Grub Low
(S.4173)
Δ 1165'
Soles Hill
Hell Hole
Waterfall Low
tumulus
Soles Hollow means the wallowing place for animals.
Back o' th' Brook
SGy
ford
4
Hole Shades
Red Lion
PH
site of Sparrowlee Halt
Lee House
3
fb
As a place-name 'Waterfall' conveys the impression of some great cataract causing tumult within the village, akin to Gayle in Wensleydale. Yet the likely meaning is the place where the Hamps disappears, or falls from sight.
2S
tel.
mere
Pike Low
sink
Sparrowlee Farm
Waterfall
MANIFOLD TRACK
Unlike The Cavalier, the Red Lion adheres to winter (lunch time) closing (midweek).
A523
Waterhouses
cycle hire centre with National Park and privately run operations to choose from

continued from page 60

Joining the Manifold Track go R, retaining its company as it switches over the normally silent river eight times within the gorgeously secluded dell ❷ to reach Lee House. At the kissing gate R ❸ enter the valley pasture, proceeding W to a stile/gate next to the swallet where this Hamps tributary running upon a gritstone bed meets the pervious limestone strata and is 'lost'. Accompanying the surface brook closely, cross a stile; the path, initially clearly defined, diminishes as the end of the wall is approached. Cross the single slab footbridge, rising to a stile and trending uphill out of the shallow valley to another stile. Cross the farmyard approach, carefully picking your way through the mire — squelch — (if, like the author, you come this way during the wetter season - which contary to cynical belief does not extend from January to December!). Reaching the road in Waterfall, go R and turn L to enter the churchyard. The church is set back from the road and is almost completely surrounded by fields. Once, presumably, it was more centrally located in the community.

continued on facing page

Waterfall Church — this delightful little three cell building boasts a Norman chancel arch, a classicised nave and tower and post-Reformation woodwork in the chancel — a pleasure to peruse.

Red Lion Inn

continued from facing page ———
Pass out of the churchyard, crossing the pasture. Keep to the S side of the short length of wall, to two stiles adjacent to the barn opposite the Red Lion Inn. Go R following the minor road ❹ down to Back o'th' Brook; it would appear that the brook formed an important division of the community, given the use of 'back' in the sense 'beyond'. At the road junction beside the ford (no footbridge), go L, entering the rising lane at a gate. This recently concreted track deteriorates into what can be a muddy passage, but thankfully improves again after the intervening stile/gateway. Through the commendable efforts of an M.S.C. team in 1985, this upper section of lane to Grub Low was cleared of dense thorn scrub. Advance to the footpath sign, beyond which join the track ❺ to Oldfields Farm; the imposing three storey farmhouse dates from the C18th. Pass through the farmyard and along the minor road to re-enter Grindon ❻ by The Cavalier - how convenient! Do take the opportunity to saunter around this attractive upland village, so perfectly poised above the Manifold and Hamps Valleys. The church, dating from 1848 is elegantly proportioned in Early English and Decorated styles - a commendable product of the Victorian age (so prone to excesses).

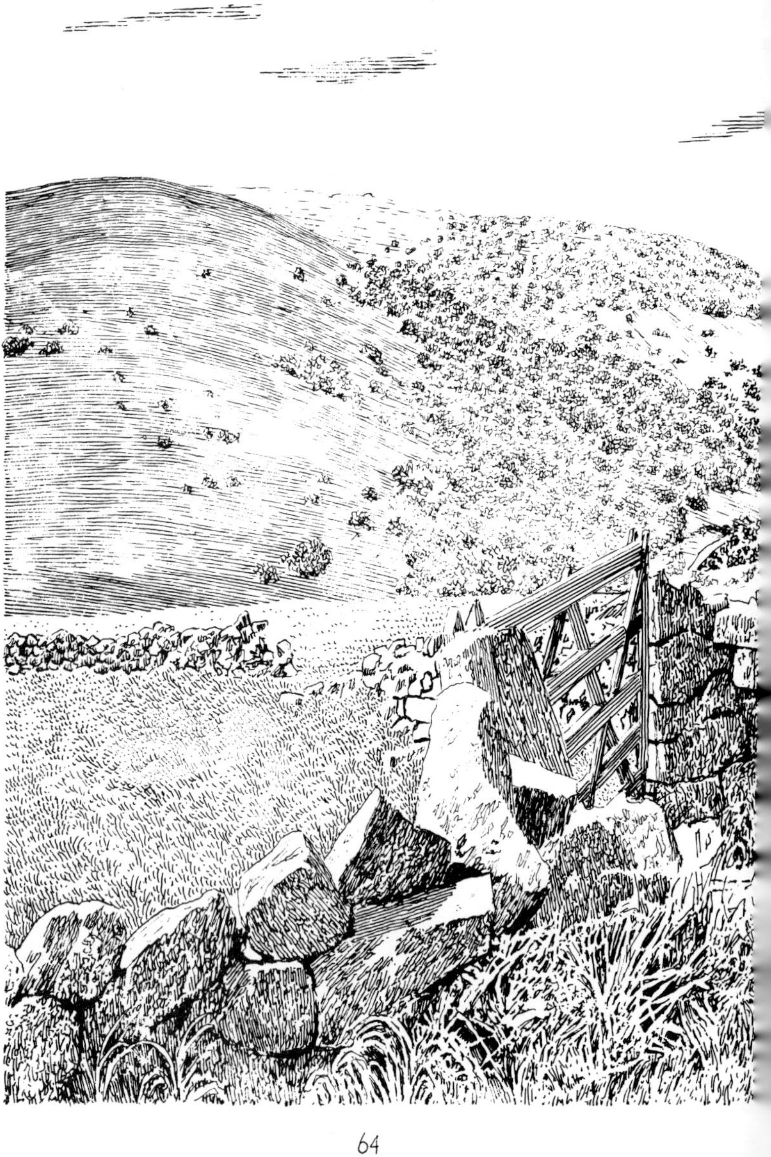

The Hamps valley from Larkstone Lane

WALK 8   THROWLEY MOOR
from Weag's Bridge   5¼ miles

The Manifold valley, though not as impregnable a barrier for cross-valley communication as Dovedale, still poses spectacular adventures for motorists travelling between Grindon and Alstonefield or Wetton. Once in the depths of the valley at Weag's Bridge, the walker has every reason to bless the fact that cars cannot career along the tarmac'd trackbed to N or S. During the early years of this century from 1904 until 1934, there was a railway station at the car park site serving the Grindon neighbourhood. Presumably this is an ancient bridging point over the erratic Manifold stream, in Saxon times associated with a certain landowner name 'Weag'.

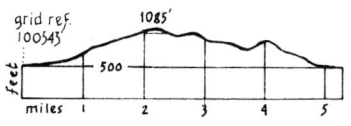

S Walk S along the Manifold Track to enter the Hamps valley. The name Hamps means 'summer dry' and despite walking this way three times in winter, I have yet to see the merest hint of water. Certain areas of the riverbed are colonised by burdock whilst elsewhere large boulders are strewn. Immediately after the third Hamps bridge branch L (at the point where the Grindon path enters from the R) through the kissing gate. The path rises steeply up the narrow trod **1**. Walkers may experience the weird sensation of hearing cattle bellowing from various angles overhead, yet it is a delightful ascent - for all the 'background' noises. The path keeps within the narrow valley of light scrub to emerge at a devious stile into the pastures of Soles Hollow. Pass through two gates heavily poached by cattle, no doubt the original wallowing place for livestock obscured in the Old English word 'Soles'. Notice the walled mere with no apparent point of access for livestock. Continue beyond a second, even larger walled mere to reach the Throwley Moor road. Go over the stile/gate opposite, keeping near to the wall **2** to a stile/gate. Pass round the

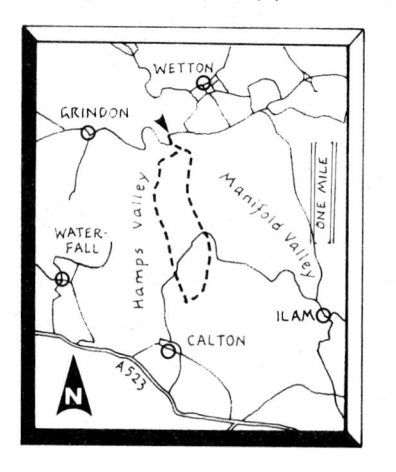

continued on page 68

66

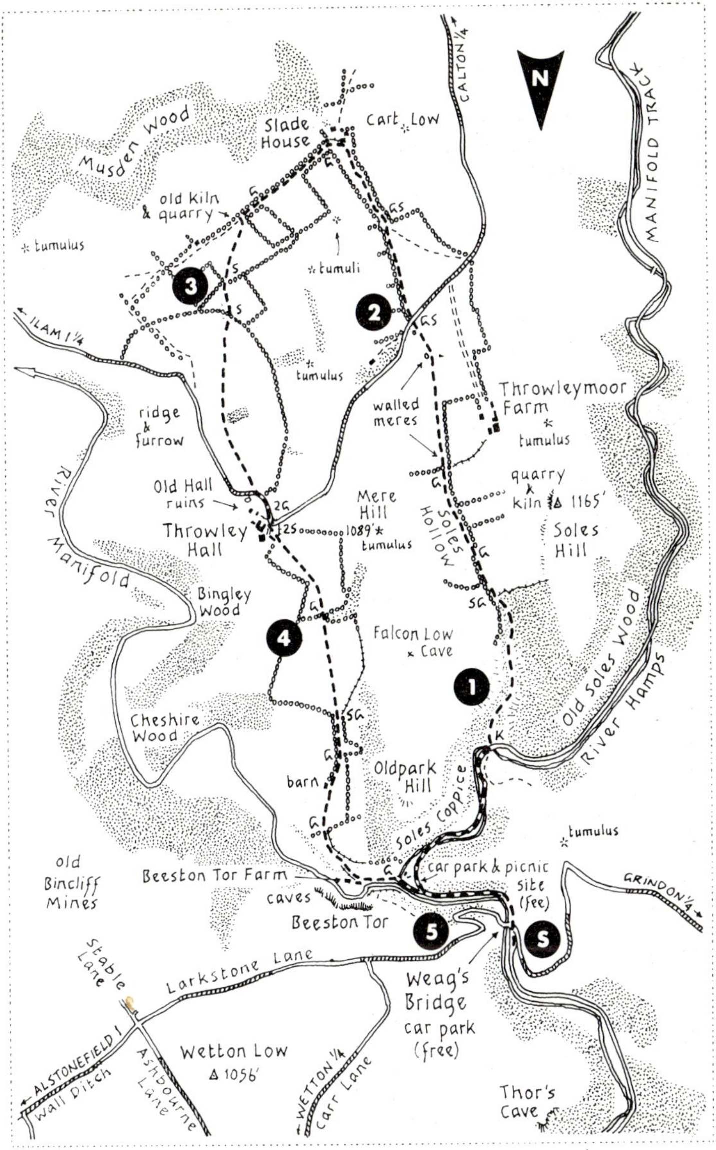
N
CALTON 1¼
MANIFOLD TRACK
Slade House
Cart Low
Musden Wood
old kiln & quarry
tumulus
tumuli
ILAM 1¼
tumulus
ridge & furrow
walled meres
Throwleymoor Farm
tumulus
River Manifold
Old Hall ruins
Throwley Hall
Mere Hill
1089'
tumulus
Soles Hollow
quarry & kiln
1165'
Soles Hill
Bingley Wood
Falcon Low Cave
Old Soles Wood
River Hamps
Cheshire Wood
Oldpark Hill
Soles Coppice
barn
tumulus
old Bincliff Mines
Beeston Tor Farm
car park & picnic site (free)
GRINDON ¼
caves
Beeston Tor
Stable Lane
Larkstone Lane
Weag's Bridge car park (free)
ALSTONEFIELD 1
Wall Ditch
Ashbourne Lane
Wetton Low
1056'
WETTON ¼
Carr Lane
Thor's Cave
1
2
3
4
5
S

continued from page 66

mere enclosures in the depression, descend on the track to Slade House (sadly derelict). The right of way is marked through the farmyard, though walkers may find it sensible to skirt L on the track rather than enter the muddy yard. Leading N.E. from the gate, the track, which provides open views over the Musden valley towards Ilam, Bunster Hill and Thorpe Cloud, is twice confined by walls as a lane. At the end of the second length of lane, skirt L above the well-preserved limekiln and source quarry. Aim diagonally across the pasture to a ladder stile; ❸ descend the next field to another substantial ladder stile. At this point there are views of the great wooded sweeps of the Manifold valley looking towards Bincliff. The walk now follows a thin, but discernible, path gently declining towards Throwley Hall. Keep below the plantation strip. From here the path becomes less distinct, especially near the foot of the slope, slant down to the unenclosed road at the pond.

The present early C19th Hall replaced the Old Hall, now in ruins, can be clearly seen from this spot.

Throwley

Throwley Old Hall, built in 1603 by Sampson Meverell, replaced an earlier house on the same site. The Elizabethan mansion consisted of a two-storey wing attached to a tower one floor higher. Follow the road L to the range of substantially built outbuildings: the stable block, L of the road gate, is known as the Barracks since tradition holds that soldiers were billeted here during the Civil War. The place-name Throwley aptly (in topographical terms) means 'homestead in a trough shaped valley', clearly alluding to the deep Manifold valley.

Pass through two gates leaving the road R by an enclosed mere. Cross the stile, proceed through the spinney to a fence stile, then ascend the field to the brow to the stile/gate next to a largely felled grove. Passing over the ridge ❹ go straight down the field, with fine views ahead, to reach a stile/gate joining a track. Go through two gates, past a barn, to reach the access road to Beeston Tor Farm. ——— *continued on facing page*

continued from facing page ─────

The impressive sight of Beeston Tor, clearly seen during the latter part of the descent, is a favourite crag of rock-climbers and is also the last great reef limestone buttress of the Manifold gorge.

Beeston Tor

St Bertram's Cave, concealed at the foot of the crag, gives access to a system of phreatic (underground water flow) tubes, joints and rifts and was excavated in 1926 and 1934 when a hoard of Saxon coins was discovered, together with evidence of Iron Age and even Romano-British occupation - the finds are deposited in the Buxton and British Museums.

Of interest to rock-climbers, Jackdaw's Hole, a cleft high on the face below the overhang, can be reached from within St. Bertram's Cave via a 30' rift chimney emerging through a squeeze window. There can be a problem of access to the crag when the river is flowing strongly: hen the stepping stones, W of the farm buildings, are likely to be submerged!

Incidentally, if you are wondering where the Hamps enters the Manifold whilst careering underground, all will be revealed by visiting Ilam Estate Country Park (WALK 14) 2½ miles S.E. where the resurgence bubbles to the surface in the Manifold riverbed (clearly viewed on the Paradise Walk).

The walk concludes **5** as it began, retracing the Manifold Track back to Weag's Bridge. Walkers may relish the opportunity to add to their enjoyment of their day out by wandering N with the Manifold Track to view Thor's Cave (see WALK 4), only ½ mile distant.

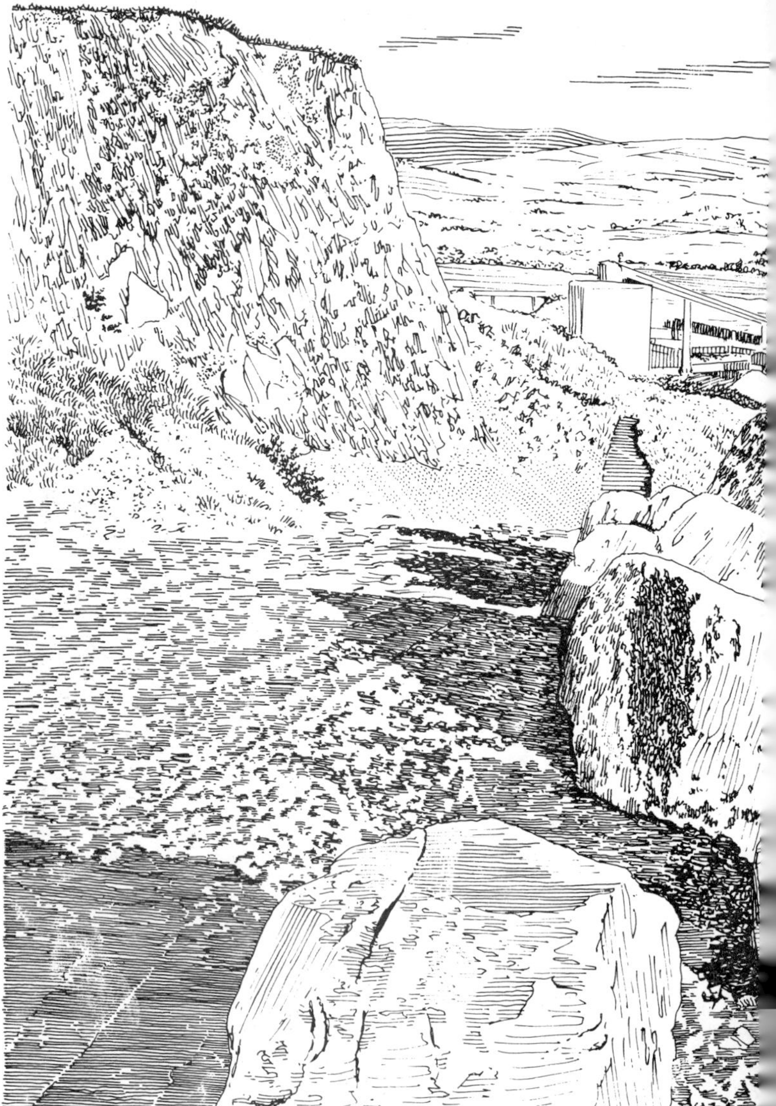

Blue Circle Cement Works, Cauldon Low

WALK 9   The WEAVER HILLS

from Waterhouses   6¾ miles

To appreciate beauty it is necessary to first witness ugliness; to distinguish an eyesore it is necessary to know nature's way; to enjoy hills there is need to survey the plain. Such landscape comparisons come into stark relief on this rather special outing.

The Old Station car park, established by the Peak Park Authority, will be seen by the majority of active visitors as a means of access to explore the gorgeous final miles of the Hamps valley to its meeting with the Manifold at Beeston Tor, achieved most efficaciously with pedal power along the Manifold Track.

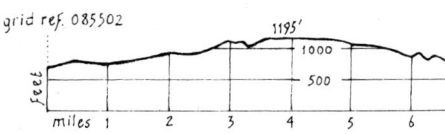

grid ref. 085502

Yet to ignore the Weaver Hills and Cauldon Low would be a mistake.

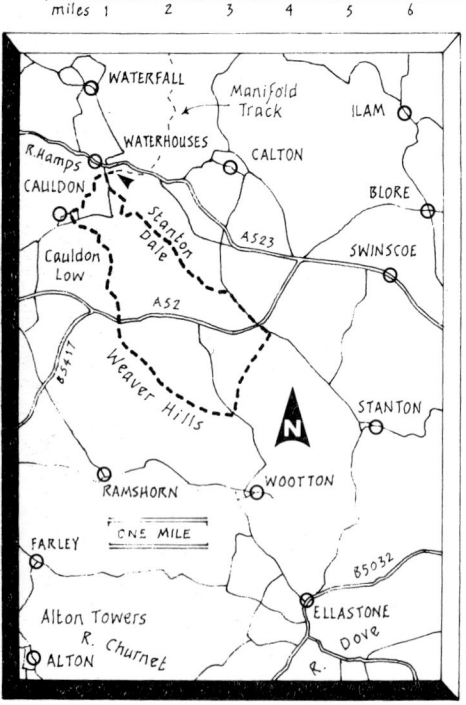

Approaching the Peak District from the south, the first swell of high ground to catch attention as one nears Ashbourne is the Weaver Hills, and soon after, on the descent to Clifton, that splendid view up the Dove valley reveals Bunster Hill and Thorpe Cloud at the very jaws of Dove Dale. For all the wonders secreted there, the first-time visitor would do well to consider a walk along the breezy Weaver Hills, from which promenade they may set their sights on the contrasts that make the White Peak so special and mark it out as a place to wander for sheer pleasure's sake.

72

The view south is agreeably wooded beyond Alton Towers to Needwood Forest and the distant Cannock Chase. To the north, an intriguing mix of wall-enclosed upland country, rising and falling before one's eyes like a storm-tossed sea. This is unquestionably Pennine country arisen from the Midland lowlands in sudden rapturous glee. This southernmost bulwark, of oft bleak and wet climate, nurtures a different kind of Englishman; resilient, hardy, cautious and canny, he is attuned to fighting the elements and surviving with pride. Long let us uphold the independent farming people who continue from generation to generation that unique livestock based farming tradition which has bequeathed to us the characteristic White Peak landscape we treasure today.

The sympathetic continuity of pastoral farming practice cherished within the National Park is easily forfeit without. Sensitive herb-rich pastures, sturdy barns and the beautiful drystone walls which reflect the simple tactile relationship of man with the mother rock are swept aside and counted as nought when big industry moves in. Locals know the dusty complex of Cauldon Low as 'Smoke City'. Everything comes on a giant impersonal scale, as walkers will know who wander cautiously down the footway through the main quarry en route for the delightful little community of Cauldon, an oasis enveloped in a desert cauldron of heavy plant.

Beauty may be in the eye of the beholder, but eyesores impact on all casual observers. Nonetheless, the perceptive walker will quickly realise that real countryside stubbornly survives close at hand, held remote and seldom trodden exactly because the quarrying activities repulse recreational attention.

Staffordshire Peak Arts Centre

(S) From the Old Station car park (off the Cauldon road in Waterhouses) follow the road L from the vehicular access towards the towering Blue Circle Cement Works. After approximately 250 yards, seek a stile L and advance diagonally across the pasture, keeping R of the pond by Middlehills Farm, to reach the farm access track. Go R with the lane, and at the lane junction turn L. At a gate, Stanton Dale is entered, the stroll up this quiet retiring dell a welcome simple pleasure enhanced by the rapidly retreating clamour of the quarries. **(1)** A stile is negotiated just after a small shippon, where cows will no doubt in the past have been tethered, fed and milked. The hill to the N would confirm the locality as traditional cow pasture, to judge by its name, Milk Hill. Take the lane forking R, thereby remaining in Stanton Dale (The Dale on O.S. maps). Shortly after a gate, the lane is impeded by hurdles. Do not be dismayed, continue beyond in the more confined, seldom trodden, Dale Lane. A few nettles may need trampling at this point but no doubt with a little more use (from readers of this guide) this mildly intimidating rash will soon be tamed! Thereafter the lane, though constricted by blackthorn in places, never encroaches too much, emerging after Dale Tor onto Common Lane. **(2)** Follow the minor road R to the crossroads where an attractive toll booth of 1845 stands, marshalling still (in spirit only now) the speeding traffic along the A52. Go forward with the minor road ultimately bound for Stanton; however, after approximately 200 yards diverge R through a gate onto Wetside Lane (track) - illustrated below. The track rises via three gates to enter a pasture, where evidence of a **(3)** track is lost. However, maintain company with the wall, climbing a fixed gate. Notice the old lime quarries R which supplied material for the long redundant kilns L.

After a gateway the right of way (which incidentally is a RUPP - road used as a public path - some road!) descends and rises to a gate onto an unenclosed public road. The sign affixed to this gate is designed to inhibit casual parking and in no way affects the status of the path just followed - the land, of course, is private.

Go R, slanting L off the road with the fence to a stile/gate.

Keep with the wall on the R to a hurdle gate; thereafter the wall is on the L. Pass through the gate where a fence links the two walls together.

—— *continued on page 76*

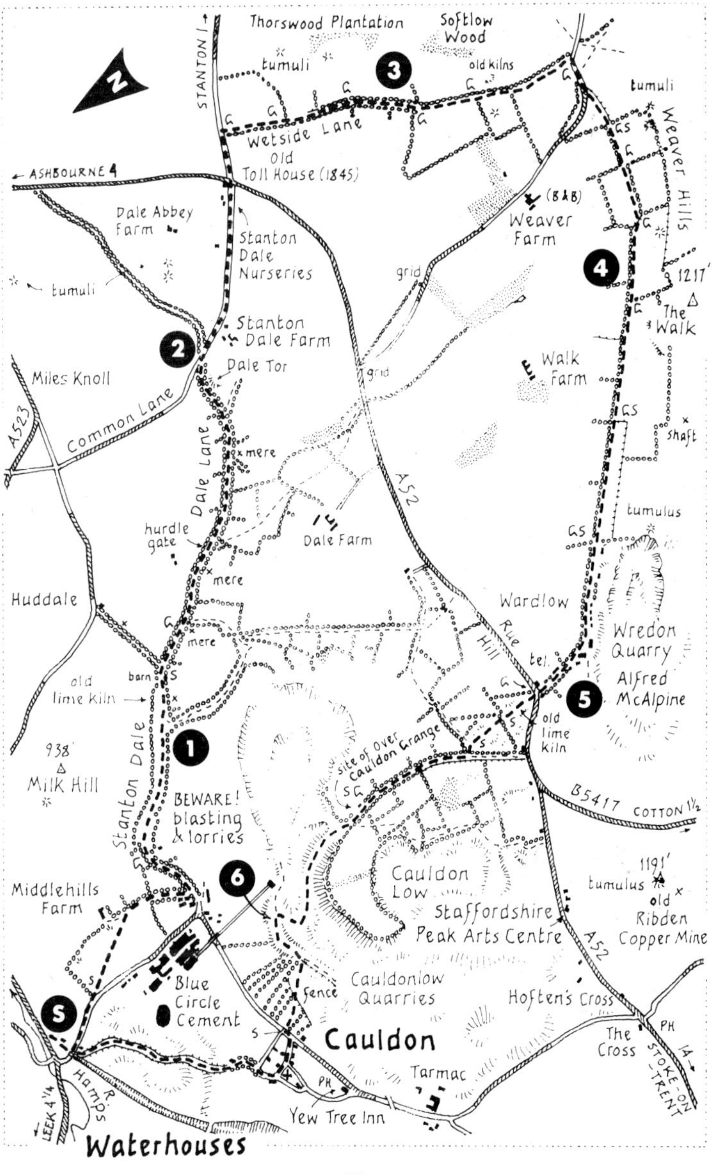

Thorswood Plantation
Softlow Wood
STANTON 1
tumuli
old kilns
tumuli
Wetside Lane
Old Toll House (1845)
ASHBOURNE 4
Weaver Hills
(B&B)
Weaver Farm
Dale Abbey Farm
Stanton Dale Nurseries
tumuli
grid
1217'
The Walk
Stanton Dale Farm
Dale Tor
Miles Knoll
Common Lane
A523
Walk Farm
grid
GS
shaft
mere
Dale Lane
A52
tumulus
hurdle gate
Dale Farm
GS
mere
Huddale
Wardlow
Rue Hill
Wredon Quarry
mere
barn
tel.
Alfred McAlpine
old lime kiln
old lime kiln
site of Over Cauldon Grange
938'
Milk Hill
Stanton Dale
BEWARE! blasting & lorries
B5417
COTTON 1½
1191'
tumulus
old Ribden Copper Mine
Cauldon Low
Middlehills Farm
Staffordshire Peak Arts Centre
A52
Blue Circle Cement
Cauldonlow Quarries
fence
Hoften's Cross
Cauldon
The Cross
PH
STOKE-ON-TRENT 14
Tarmac
R. Hamps
LEEK 4¼
PH
Yew Tree Inn
Waterhouses

South from the Weaver Hills

Labels (top panorama): Needwood Forest · Cannock Chase · Brookleys Lake · Churnet Valley · Alton Towers · Canada Lake · Wootton Lodge · Wootton Park · 'tid Low Farm · Hole Brook Valley

Two views from the tumulus near mile four

Labels (second panorama): The Wrekin · Whiston · Three Lows · The Walk · Kevin Quarry

continued from page 74 ———

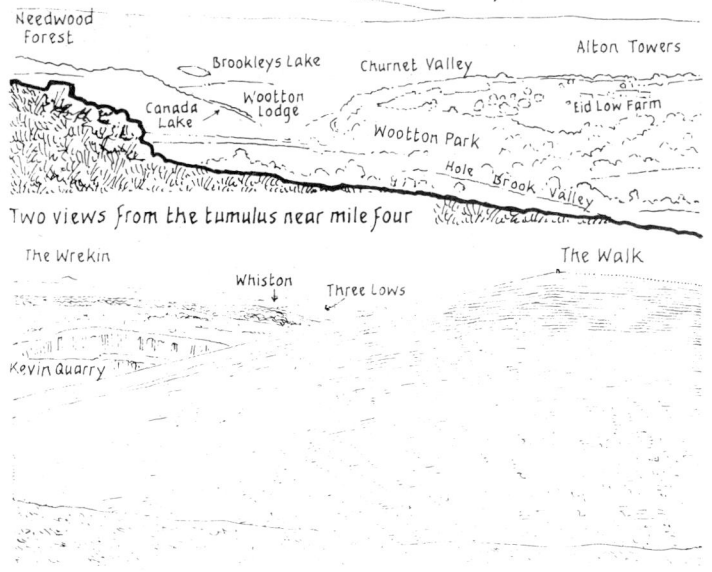

④ A brief digression L to an evidently robbed tumulus mound reveals a splendid southerly prospect, partially illustrated above. The October day on which I surveyed this scene was marked by a keen south-westerly breeze racing the clouds up from the far-off Wrekin, squally showers sweeping across the undulating vale creating startling shadows and streaks of light. The prominent bald summit of The Walk across the combe stands proud as if addressing the lowlands low, for not merely is this where the Pennines begin but does no piece of English soil, to the Channel, equals its altitude (nor for that matter the ground you presently stand).

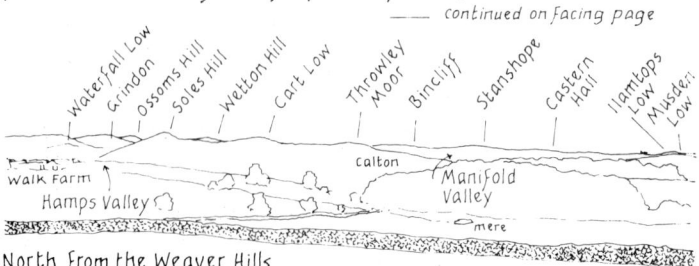

——— *continued on facing page*

Labels (bottom panorama): Waterfall Low · Grindon · Ossoms Hill · Soles Hill · Wetton Hill · Cart Low · Throwley Moor · Bincliff · Stanshope · Castern Hall · Ilamtops Low · Musden Low · Walk Farm · Hamps Valley · Calton · Manifold Valley · mere

North from the Weaver Hills

76

continued from facing page ———

The Weaver Hills would appear to derive their name from 'winding', an ancient word normally applied to rivers: presumably this is a transposed name alluding to their paternal bearing upon the Churnet valley. The slightly odd singular 'The Walk', whilst tempting to ally with the grand promenade afforded by this prominent ridge, may in fact have been corrupted from an earlier form perhaps relating to quarrying (hence the village name Stanton, obviously an early stone built community).

The bridleway advances beside the wall via gates/stiles (later beside an embankment of dubious stability composed of topsoil from the expanding Wredon quarry). The view all along this section of the excursion is introversively Peakland, particularly of the hills cradling the Hamps, though Minninglow spotters will not be disappointed nor yet Congleton folk, for The Cloud raises its cheeky head NW. Alfred McAlpine's Wredon Quarry, source of Redland Aggregates (roadstone) is growing at an alarming rate. Indeed, when I passed during the autumn of 1986 a small dusty cluster of tents stood beside the track not the encampment of quarry staff but archaeologists racing against time to salvage details of a Bronze Age barrow about to be consumed by the inexorable advance of stone extraction. The tiny community adjacent to the quarry bears the name Wardlow, which as with Warslow in WALK 3, means 'lookout mound', perhaps indeed the very tumulus under investigation!

Pass on beyond the workshop sheds, alert to speeding lorries, **5** to reach and cross once more the A52. Enter the old shallow quarried field by the facing gate. The partially obscured lime kiln in a depression L of the footpath gives the likely clue to the pockpitted nature of the quarrying undergone in this enclosure. Seek a stile at the top of a bank, maintain direction skirting round a hollow to join a lane at a stile/footpath sign. Go R down to a stile/gate near to the site of Over Cauldon Grange. The expansionist activities of the Blue Circle Cement Company has brought about the demise of this remote farmstead and also necessitated the diversion of several paths. NB-For the benefit of walkers wishing to shorten their circuit, the modified footpath network between Stanton Dale and the A52 has been plotted on the route map.

To the credit of the company, they have made strenuous efforts to retain the (important to this walk) path down to Cauldon. Supported by meticulous signposting, they have done their level best to keep walkers and heavy plant apart, laying a carefully contrived path that keeps L under the cliff before sweeping down and up a rise, **6** going L finally branching R down the reconstituted bank to the village.

——— *continued on page 78*

77

Blue Circle Works (SOLES HILL, THROWLEY MOOR)

continued from page 77

The steep hillside has a thin vegetative cover nothing like the dense sheep cropped pasture it replaced, the one redeeming grace of this descent being the view both comprehensively of the Blue Circle complex and, in total contrast, charmingly upon Cauldon. Cross the barbed fence (no stile at present) close to the rank hedge/wall line, using the convenient boulders, and descend the field diagonally to join the road at a stile. Go L passing a fountain of 1878 with its tap, horse trough and peculiar, and obscure, inscription 'Thy Clouds Drop Fatness'! Follow the village lane up R to visit the church exuding a quiet dignity expressed, as with so many local churches rebuilt during the latter half of the C18th, in Classical style. The place-name Cauldon comes from 'calves' hill,' and whilst cattle still graze close to the present village, the great pastures of Cauldon Low have long since been lost to the needs of the motorway age - reflect on Cauldon's sacrifice as you speed along the M6! ———— *continued on facing page*

Yew Tree Inn, Cauldon

78

continued from facing page ———

Pre-eminent of Cauldon's attractions is a place of refreshment, The Yew Tree Inn (the yew tree shading the entrance was planted three hundred years ago when the hostelry itself was built). Whether you are a CAMRA devotee or enjoy the genuine article in terms of bygone atmosphere, this quite superb pub should not be missed. The family room and entrance lobby housing 2p slot polyphons and symphonons a delight for young and old. The walk concludes by following the byway R at the junction between the church and a fine venacular farmhouse (see above), this leads onto a tarmac path leading down via a sturdy footbridge to the Waterhouses Old Station entrance.

Stanton Dale

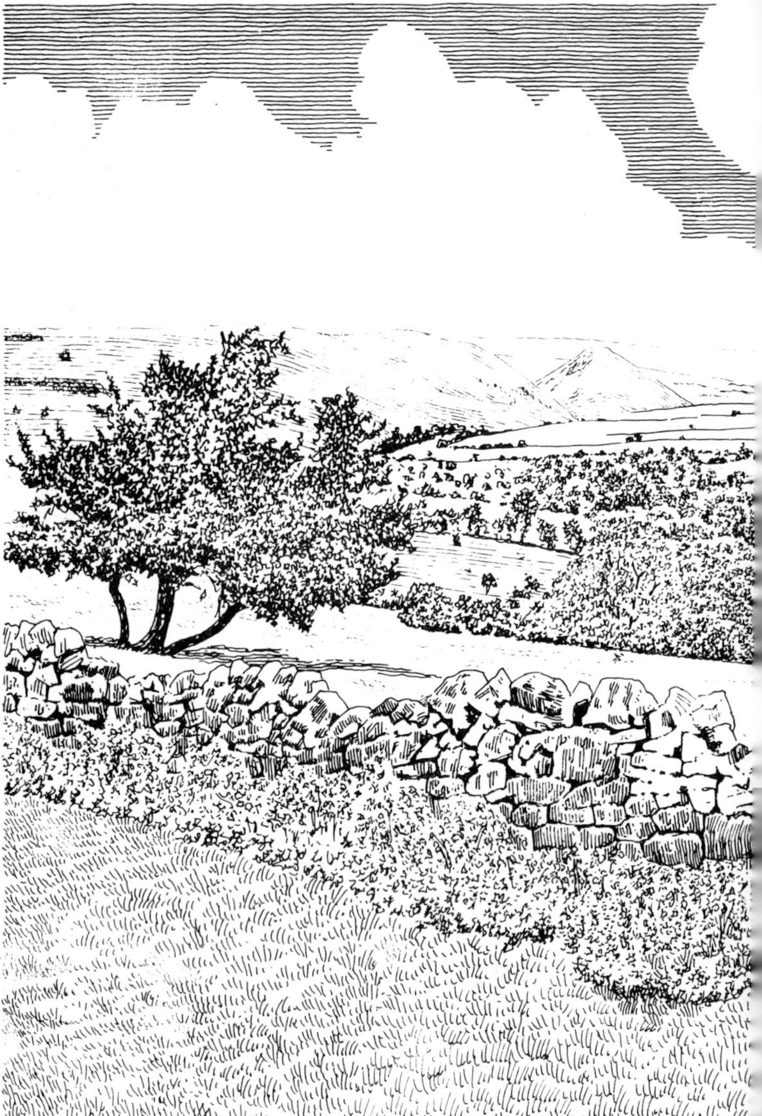

Thorpe Cloud and Musden

WALK 10   MUSDEN
from Ilam   5 miles

Whilst Ilam Hall may seem an overstatement of affluence (and this despite the loss of an entire front wing), and the model Alpine-style estate village a trifle misplaced, there can be little denying this a fine setting for a man with a grand plan. In the decade before 1830, it would seem Jesse Watts-Russell set to work to steal the show from the Earl of Shrewsbury's Alton Towers (then no frivolous fairground, but a stately home of some pretention). The first Ilam Hall which it replaced was built in 1546 by John Port, who had received the manor from Henry VIII's confiscation of the Burton Abbey lands. The Victorians' excesses did not completely extinguish Ilam's earlier landscape fabric, although they had a good try! In fact, what is left is easier to translate because of the freedom from tight enclosure by the creation of the park.

The church, victim though it was to the flights of fancy of the Watts-Russell dynasty, does retain genuine and substantive Saxon and Norman influences with subsequent additions, of which possibly the seventeenth century St Bertram's Chapel ranks as the finest portion. Of the Victorian period, Francis Chantrey's sculpture of David Pike-Watts on his deathbed blessing his daughter and her three children has a touching charm.

This walk reveals a beautiful and seldom seen aspect on the Ilam locality, making the breezy traverse of Musden Low and returning within the sinuous wooded valley of Musden, far removed from the popular tourist haunts.

Ilam (is not one hour before noon!) it is the archaic river-name of the Manifold, meaning 'hill stream'.

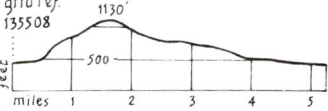

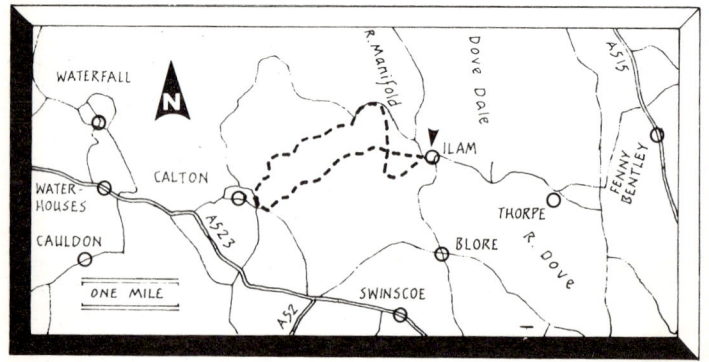

grid ref. 135508

Bunster Hill

(S) The walk may begin from the National Park car park upon Blore Pastures overlooking Ilam, or in the National Trust car park in front of Ilam Hall (parking fee). For convenience and compromise, the description begins at the roadside near the Watts-Russell Memorial (the choice is yours, but at busy times avoid congesting the village thoroughfare).

Proceed along the road towards, and beyond, the entrance to Ilam Hall, finding a gate L into the parkland. Take a W course across the Country Park, without the aid of a visible path. Notice the extensive areas of ridge & furrow. These were associated with the former village of Ilam, which was demolished and re-sited in the 1820s when the park was laid out to beautify the Hall's romantic setting: they are certainly uncut by the plough since. The footpath descends to the Manifold footbridge: cross the meadow beyond to a wall stile, rising to a further stile, thereon more steeply guided by waymark posts. Cross the Upper Musden/Musden Grange track (followed on WALK 11) at a signpost to pass through a wall gap, then accompany the wall to where another waymark post directs L to a squeeze-stile (gritstone uprights). The path slants slightly R to a further stile **(1)** beyond which it reaches a muddy passage running beside a largely derelict group of barns (gate). Continue beside the wall, rising gently over the shoulder of Musden Low. This large enclosure, recently enlarged further by the removal of an intermediary wall, is, nonetheless, typical of Grange fields, intended purely for the grazing of large flocks of sheep in monastic times (established when there was no scope for the wool economy in the fertile lowlands). At the top, a stile marks the beginning of the descent, beside a hedge, to Dog Lane, entered at a stile. Old references to dogs such as this invariably mean hunting hounds, perhaps inferring a long-lost kennels. Go R to enter Doglane Farm, take the step stile L out of the farmyard (do not be lured down the inviting, short cutting, lane through the farmyard gates, which is not a right of way). Traverse the pasture, aiming for the far R corner. Cross the stile, and a second one some 80 yards on the R, to reach the Green Lane (road). By implication a 'green lane' served as an enclosed drove way (prior to the wholesale enclosure of Calton parish) linking to a main trackway (now the A52).

—— *continued on page 84*

continued from page 83

2 Go R to the crossroads, no doubt, like my companions of the day, taking the weight off your feet for a few moments on the bench so thoughtfully sited.

The prescribed route now takes the Throwley road, Back Lane, but if latitude of time is at your disposal, a stroll around the delightful little upland village of Calton is recommended. The name Calton, similar to Cauldon, derives from 'farmstead where calves were reared'. It is very likely that a community has long held this high ground at the neck of the Throwley Moor ridge, at the meeting point of ancient trackways. If the village can offer no public house or shop (other than the Post Office), its compensations lie in the pleasing array of cottages and grand farmhouses, notably at the W end of the main street. St Mary's church contains some interesting charity boards associated with Catherine Port of Ilam Hall and two clocks, one of which is double faced, with both interior and exterior faces. The walk follows Back Lane for about 200yds from the crossroads; branch R at a stile into the shallow upper valley of Musden. Hereon navigation is determined exclusively by the need to keep to the valley floor, initially via stiles and later, within the deep sequestered wooded glade, gates. **3** Muddy patches and thorn scrub hamper progress only minimally in the upper wooded section of the valley but generally the going is good. Musden (which means 'mouse infested long sinuous valley') is, rather surprisingly, not protected as a Nature Reserve, yet this is precisely the sort of enclosed habitat that needs such respect. The pungencies of wild garlic (ramsons) fill the air during the descent. Two interesting bedded outcrops of carboniferous limestone are passed en route, the first thin layered and corrugated (near the gate beyond mile three), and the second, at the foot of the valley, acting like a sentinel. Passing through a gate, the footpath slips by sheeppens to a stile and onto the Musden Grange access track. Turn L through Rushley Farm to join the Throwley road, continuing downhill to cross Rushley Bridge. The riverside scenery is quite beautiful, though the Manifold stream is not always in attendance.

continued on page 87

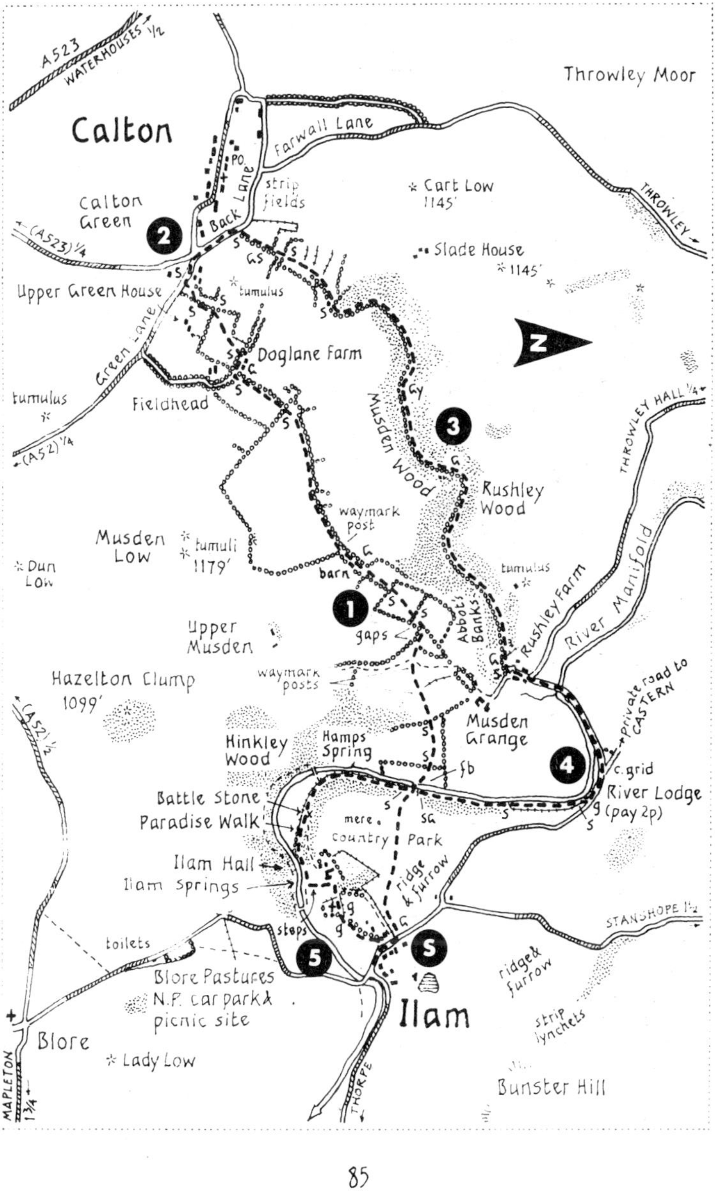

A523
WATERHOUSES 1/2
Calton
Farwall Lane
Throwley Moor
PO
Back Lane
strip fields
Cart Low 1145'
Calton Green
(A523) 1/4
Slade House
1145'
THROWLEY
Upper Green House
tumulus
Green Lane
Doglane Farm
tumulus
Fieldhead
(A52) 1/4
Musden Wood
THROWLEY HALL 1/4
Rushley Wood
waymark post
Musden Low
tumuli 1179'
Dun Low
barn
tumulus
Abbots Banks
Rushley Farm
River Manifold
Upper Musden
gaps
waymark posts
Hazelton Clump 1099'
(A52) 1/2
Private road to CASTERN
Musden Grange
Hinkley Wood
Hamps Spring
fb
c. grid
River Lodge
g (pay 2p)
Battle Stone
Paradise Walk
mere
country Park
Ilam Hall
ridge & furrow
Ilam Springs
STANSHOPE 1 1/2
toilets
steps
ridge & furrow
Blore Pastures N.P. car park & picnic site
Ilam
strip lynchets
Blore
Lady Low
Bunster Hill
MAPLETON 1 3/4
THORPE

Musden

continued from page 84

In summer months, the river prefers to slink a devious subterranean course to emerge at the Boil Holes immediately S of Ilam Hall, as we shall see. Following the road via a cattle grid to River Lodge ❹ enter the gate R, paying, with good grace, the humble courtesy fee of 1p, before stepping over the stile out of the garden and along the riverside path. The narrow strip of meadow is replaced by a more confined path at a stile; thereafter two more stiles are crossed to enter upon the Paradise Walk. Strolling this way on an autumn evening when Hinkley Wood (clearing of the stallion) a blaze of golden rays and the rooks and jackdaws are congregating, raucously sharing their news of the day, one is in quite a memorable arena. The Hamps Spring resurgence can be seen, though access to the riverbank to get a closer look is not encouraged. The river Hamps disappears during summer months below Waterhouses, running beneath Musden Low at the base of the limestone strata to gush forth here, giving what can be an empty riverbed a surprise re-charge.

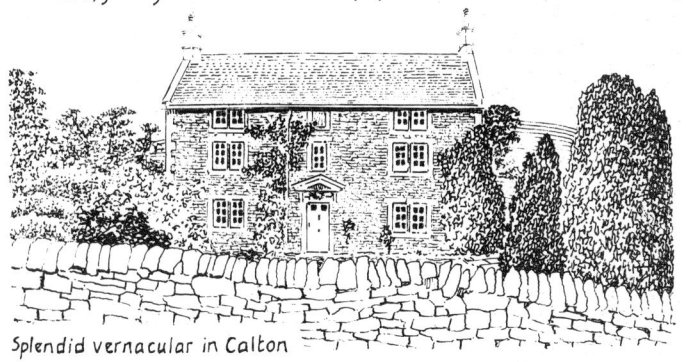

Splendid vernacular in Calton

Passing the Battle Stone, the Paradise Walk arrives at the outcrop where the subterranean Manifold debouches into the main riverbed, the Boil Hole being the spring to the L of the path behind safety rails. Ahead, the serenity of the river is broken over two weirs, passing under St Bertram's Bridge on course for its confluence with the Dove. This graceful single-arched bridge, which served the old Ilam community, gives access to the Trust's Hinkley Wood Trail. NB: The N.T. restrict access to this path, therefore, if you wish to follow it, enquire at Ilam Hall. The steps near the Boil Hole rise to the car park in front of Ilam Hall. In season, a most welcome tea room, National Trust shop and a large Youth Hostel mean that visitors are well catered for: there are also toilets, and gentlemen may discover that their facilities, within a 'pepper-pot' have some novelty value! The walk concludes down the church path ❺ via gates to the village street.

The portals of Dove Dale from Blore Pastures

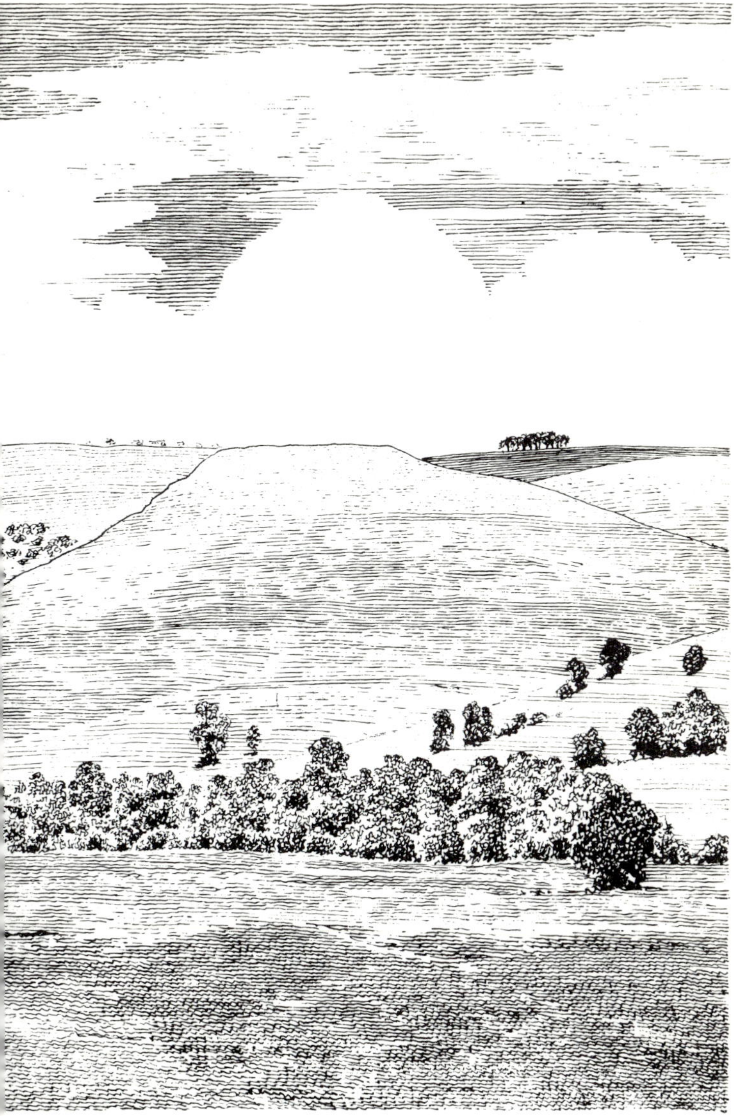

WALK 11   ILAM

from Blore Pastures   4 miles

It is a curious fact that though the Dove and Manifold run south side by side from their source to confluence, they react to the reef limestone massif in startlingly different ways. The Dove charges headlong within a deep 'v' shaped gorge, permitting of precious little meadow and therefore no settlement. In contrast the Manifold meanders, hence its contemporary name, with scope on its near banks for historic settlement and land use e.g. strip lynchets. Its not having been distinguished by the suffix 'dale' which like 'hope' implied a secretive fold in the hills, suggests it has long been a place of ribbon access: a lifeline rather than (as in Dove Dale's case) a hostile barrier.

But quite the most remarkable feature of the river is its strange ability to disappear during dry seasons, running the four-mile section from the vicinity of Wettonmill to the Boil Hole in the grounds of Ilam Hall unseen in silent career below ground. It shares this feat with the Hamps, which also bubbles to the surface near the Paradise Walk, having short cut its natural valley course to Beeston Tor by slipping impishly under Musden Low.

This walk is designed to give visitors the opportunity to visualise Ilam in its whole landscape setting, sheltering on a gently rising bank within a giant loop of the river just as it breaks free of the hills. On a prime site for a community to take deep root and flourish, who can doubt that the ridge & furrow preserved in the parkland and above at Blore stems from ancient tillage? Notice the thinly disguised reference to the grazing of the oxen plough team surviving in the farm-name Oxleisure, which translates to 'the ox meadow'.

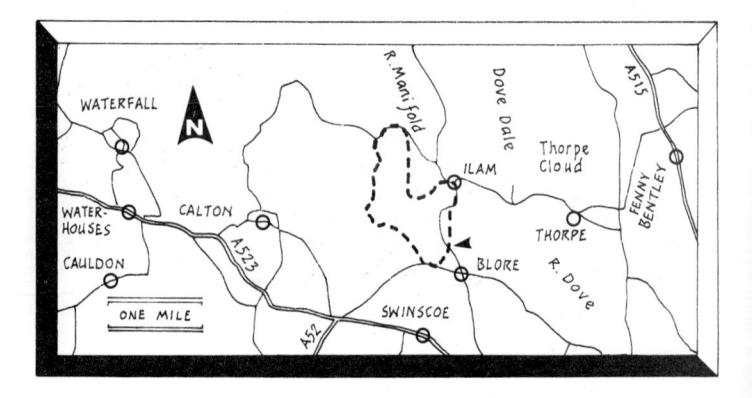

S Walk N from the Blore Pastures National Park car park through the picnic enclosure and via stiles down the parkland pasture to join the unenclosed road above Oxleisure Farm. The prospect of Bunster Hill and Thorpe Cloud marshalling the entrance to the Dove Dale gorge witnessed on this descent must confirm its rightful place as the true dramatic beginings of the Pennines.

Follow the road over the cattle grid and go with care, along the narrow road to cross Ilam Bridge. From the monument to Mary Watts-Russell, approach the entrance to Ilam Hall, branching L by a gate at Dovedale House, whence following a footpath to the church.

Dedicated to the Holy Cross, Ilam church is a fascinating mixture of styles; Saxon, Norman, Early English and Decorated, a magpie collection of historical influences that makes this a most worthwhile building to admire. The most tangibly Saxon artefact is the font (seen here): it has been suggested that it depicts scenes from St Bertram's life. The partial remains of two Saxon crosses also stand in the churchyard. St Bertram's Chapel was built in 1618, and contains his C9th tomb cover and shrine circa 1386. On the outside of the chapel, set in the lintel of the door, are the initials of the three landowners who funded the re-building: Richard Meverell of Throwley (Old) Hall, Nicholas Hurt of Castern Hall and Robert Port of Ilam Hall. Within the church again, the last of the Meverell line, Elizabeth, who married Lord Cromwell, is seen sculpted with her children above the family tomb.

———— *continued on page 92*

Ilam Church

Ilam Hall

continued from page 91

Passing through the kissing gate, follow the path to Ilam Hall; either go L down the bank via the well enclosure (water supply of the village before it was uprooted by Jesse Watts-Russell) to St Bertram's Bridge, an old bridging point, or descend the steps near the Hall to reach the Manifold resurgence. Parade sedately along the Paradise Walk, noticing the oddly coupled sycamore and the Battle Stone (plaque). **(1)** This point can be reached from the terraced gardens down a gently inclining path. Follow the Walk through to River Lodge or (as in WALK9) cross the Manifold footbridge and climb the steep grass bank S of Musden Grange.

Having paid your dues at River Lodge (which will be remembered in Spring for its abundance of snowdrops), follow the road L, **(2)** crossing Rushley Bridge, to diverge from the Throwley road at Rushley Farm. Continue up the track to Musden Grange, all trace of the monastic cell, associated with this Burton Abbey grange, having long since been extinguished. Do not enter the farmyard, remaining with the track just a few yards before branching L to keep, the rising wall to the L. At the top, slant L on the tractor-rutted track through a wall gap rising diagonally up the slope. A footpath sign is passed at the point where the direct route up from the Manifold footbridge meets the track. Advance to an oft 'times muddy gateway/stile (due to the poaching of cattle - poaching in this guise means 'to churn-up with the hooves'). Keep alongside the wall to the corner, where veer R

continued on page 94

The Boil Hole at Ilam Spring, the Manifold resurgence below Ilam Hall

continued from page 92

rising to a stile, cross the succeeding field to a stile L of the derelict barn. Upper Musden must be one of the best sited rural retreats in Staffordshire, commanding a memorable view over the Manifold valley. The farmhouse, sheltered by tall trees, nestles next to a mere and stock buildings, but being so remote from services, it has been cast off and fallen prey to the ravages of the elements. No sooner has the farmyard been entered than it is quit, over a stile immediately L, sweeping down ❸ by the old hedgeline to the gate/horse barrier at the bottom of the unnamed re-entrant valley. An obvious bridleway track leads up to a gate and continues beneath the eye-catching Hazelton Clump and above Hinkley Wood (which means 'the clearing where stallions were kept'), via a further gate/cattle loading baffles, eventually reaching the Blore road at a fence stile. Go L, finding a stile/gate L where the road curves L. A thinly-disguised track descends the old ridge & furrowed pasture ❹ conveniently to a stile opposite the Blore Pastures car park.

Congreve's Grotto

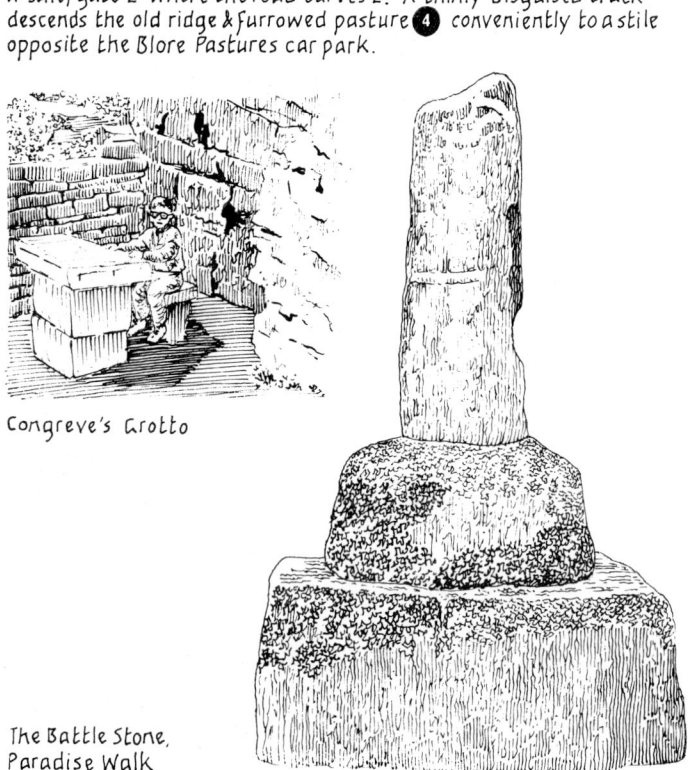

The Battle Stone, Paradise Walk

Map labels (approximate, as drawn):

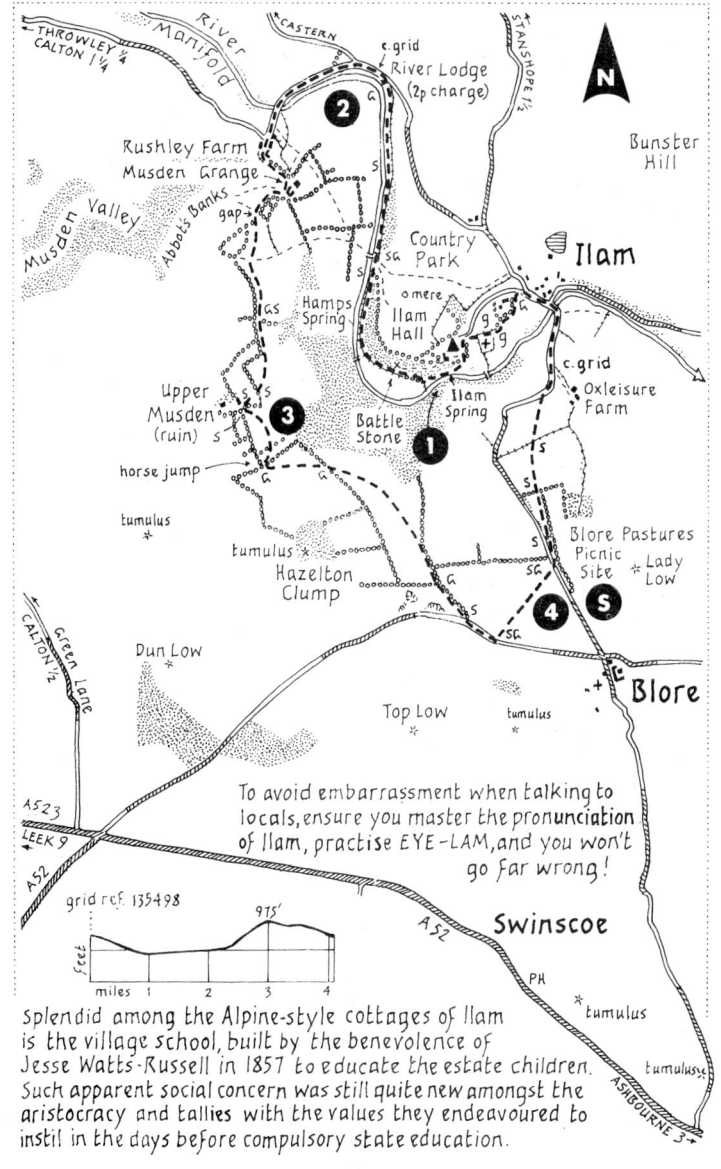

- THROWLEY / CALTON 1¼
- River Manifold
- CASTERN
- c. grid
- River Lodge (2p charge)
- ❷
- STANHOPE ½
- N
- Rushley Farm
- Musden Grange
- Bunster Hill
- Musden Valley
- Abbot's Banks
- gap
- Country Park
- Ilam
- Hamps Spring
- o mere
- Ilam Hall
- Upper Musden (ruin)
- ❸
- Battle Stone
- Ilam Spring
- ❶
- c. grid
- Oxleisure Farm
- horse jump
- tumulus
- tumulus
- Hazelton Clump
- Blore Pastures Picnic Site
- Lady Low
- ❹ ❺
- Dun Low
- Blore
- Top Low
- tumulus
- Green Lane
- CALTON ½
- A523
- LEEK 9
- A52
- Swinscoe
- grid ref. 135498
- 915'
- feet
- miles 1 2 3 4
- PH
- tumulus
- ASHBOURNE 3
- tumulus

To avoid embarrassment when talking to locals, ensure you master the pronunciation of Ilam, practise EYE-LAM, and you won't go far wrong!

Splendid among the Alpine-style cottages of Ilam is the village school, built by the benevolence of Jesse Watts-Russell in 1857 to educate the estate children. Such apparent social concern was still quite new amongst the aristocracy and tallies with the values they endeavoured to instil in the days before compulsory state education.

River Dane at Three Shire Heads

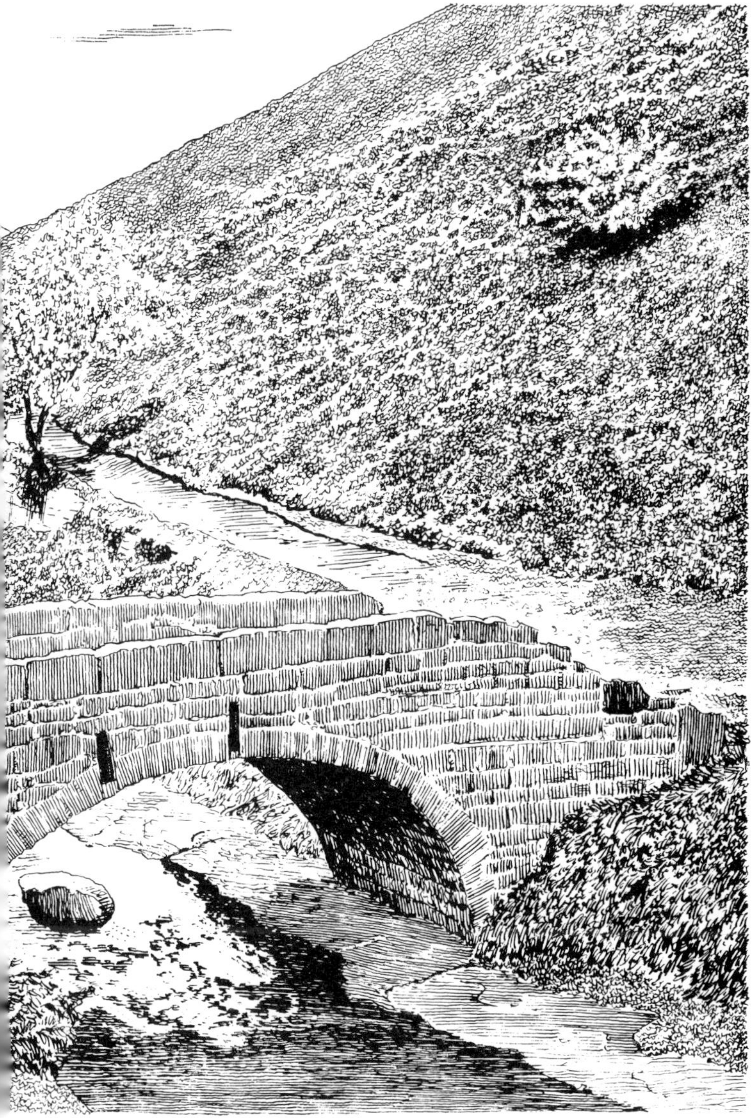

WALK 12   FLASH
from Cistern's Clough   7½ miles

Although the name Cistern probably means 'thorn in a bog', it does not follow that Axe Edge had anything to do with the hacking of trees. Indeed, this old name meant, quite appropriately, 'water source'. Coinciding with the main watershed of England, this gritstone upland of soggy peat bog parents five notable rivers. Flowing W to the Mersey and Irish Sea are the Dane and Goyt, with the E flowing waters of the Dove, Manifold and Wye on course for the Trent and North Sea. Here is described a most satisfying and varied walk, visiting the lonely, romantic packhorse bridge at Three Shire Heads, Flash, the highest village in England and several commendable viewpoints, with Wolf Edge arguably the pick of the bunch.

The re-aligned A53 at Cistern's Clough provides walkers with an admirable car park from which to explore the wild country at the head of the Dane, Manifold and Dove. At 1590', the highest starting point in this guide, this is a fine beginning to a day in hills, with refreshment conveniently placed at Flash and Flashbar.

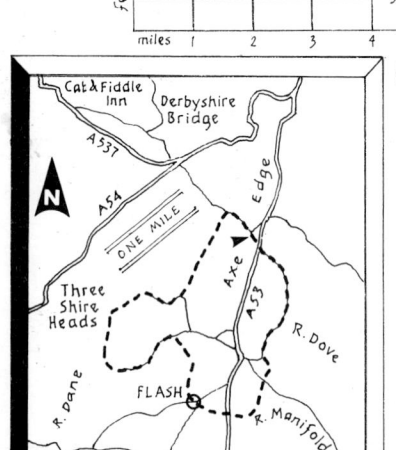

grid ref. 035697.

S From the fence stile above the car park, join the track ascending the clough to meet the minor road. Follow the road, eschewing the tempting shooters' track. At Dane Head, a heather path diverges to wend through the grough landscape over the spongy shoulder of Cheeks Hill — no hardship as the path is never in doubt. A fence and wall mark the county boundary; crossing the stile, notice several capped shafts close by. Follow the track **1** downhill beside the clough and go through two gates below Orchard Farm — an unlikely place for an orchard and

—— continued on page 100

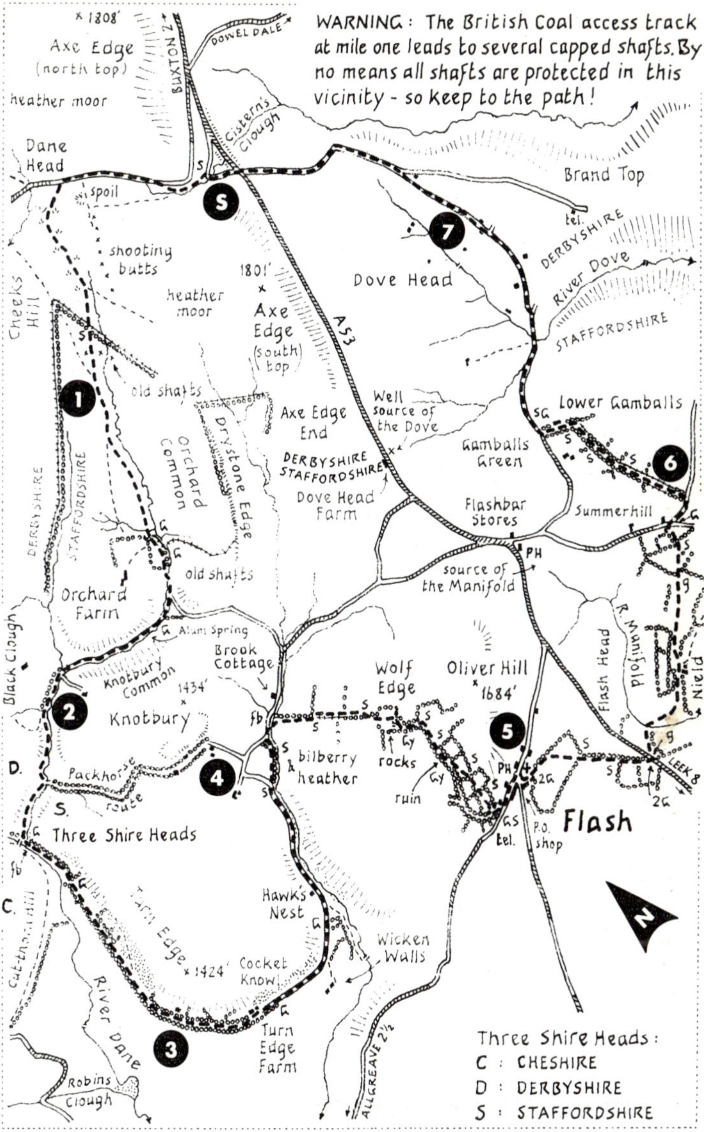
WARNING: The British Coal access track at mile one leads to several capped shafts. By no means all shafts are protected in this vicinity - so keep to the path!
1808'
Axe Edge (north top)
heather moor
BUXTON
DOWEL DALE
Dane Head
Cistern's Clough
spoil
Brand Top
DERBYSHIRE
River Dove
STAFFORDSHIRE
shooting butts
1801'
Axe Edge (south top)
Dove Head
A53
Cheeks Hill
heather moor
old shafts
Orchard Common
Drystone Edge
Axe Edge End
Well source of the Dove
DERBYSHIRE STAFFORDSHIRE
Dove Head Farm
Lower Gamballs
Gamballs Green
Flashbar Stores
Summerhill
PH
source of the Manifold
old shafts
Orchard Farm
Alum Spring
Brook Cottage
Black Clough
Knotbury Common
1434'
Knotbury
Wolf Edge
Oliver Hill
1684'
R. Manifold
Flash Head
Nield Bank
bilberry & heather
rocks
ruin
Packhorse route
D.
S.
Three Shire Heads
Flash
P.O. shop
tel.
LEEK 8
Hawk's Nest
C.
Cut-thorn Hill
Turn Edge
1424
Cocket Know
Wicken Walls
River Dane
Turn Edge Farm
Robins Clough
ALLGREAVE 2½
Three Shire Heads:
C : CHESHIRE
D : DERBYSHIRE
S : STAFFORDSHIRE

continued from page 98

apparently a refuge for T20 Ferguson tractors! Where the access road forks, go R to a road gate. Stay on the metalled road within the narrow clough; where this switches back onto Knotbury Common, **(2)** continue along the clough track, passing a packhorse bridge, to arrive at Three Shire Heads.

Here, at the meeting of three counties, packhorse routes converged on the Dane gorge. The focal bridge, now widened from its earliest structure, overlooks the Panniers Pool where jaggers (men in charge of the packteams) will have gained refreshment, washed and encamped. This place, steeped in folk legend, was the resort of rogues and outlaws in days of yore: they could slip nimbly from one county to the next, by so doing eluding the agents of law enforcement. Today the bridges and waterfalls are popular with walkers who idle awhile in this beautiful setting. Hemmed in by bracken clad hillsides, the place has a timeless air, a sanctuary, a place to cast the imagination back to a time when journeys were measured in days not minutes.

From the gate go immediately R, cross the Black Clough packhorse bridge, glancing back to admire the scene with the River Dane, last seen at its source, tumbling into the Panniers Pool (see drawing above).

—— *continued on facing page*

100

continued from facing page ———

 Heading S along the prominent bridleway, the route proceeds via a gate and under Turn Edge. The name Turn Edge meaning 'thorn-covered hillside', though oaks are more prevalent today. Hen Cloud and the Roaches massif form the landmarks in the views ahead, whilst the undulating country S to Goldsitch Moss is composed of productive outcrops of coal. A similar pocket was also formerly exploited on Goyt's Moss above Derbyshire Bridge. ❸ Beyond Turn Edge Farm the track changes to metalled road, passes Hawk's Nest (cottage) and rises up the clough to a stile R at the head ❹. The stream has evidently been modified, the dyke enlarging the area of quality pasture—which is at a premium in this vicinity. Another stile is crossed before reaching the unenclosed road; go R, branching R again at the sign and single slab stone footbridge.

 Ascend the heather moor to a stile, keep close to the fence (path is well waymarked) rising to a stile R, thereafter completing the ascent to the summit outcrop of Wolf Edge. There are several isolated references to wolves in Peakland, confirming this bleak upland region as a last refuge for a persecuted predator. Before the wholesale agricultural clearances of the Dark Ages, they were as common as foxes in the forested vales of England. Wolf Edge is certainly a place to relax for a few minutes, absorb the view and listen to the plaintive cry of the curlew. The rocks appear to have been quarried a little, which perhaps explains the gap or nick feature in their midst.   The view extends from Axe Edge to the N round the western arc by Drystone Edge, Dane Bower, Shutlingsloe, Tagsclough Hill, The Cloud (near Congleton), Back Forest and The Roaches S. The nearby and featureless rough grazings of Oliver Hill (highest ground in Staffordshire), closes off the view E to the White Peak, ensuring attention is maintained towards the western horizon.

continued on page 102 ———

SHUTLINGSLOE　　　　　　　　　　　WHETSTONE RIDGE
DANE BOWER
KNOTBURY

View NW from Wolf Edge

summit rocks on Wolf Edge

continued from page 101

Slant R, through a gateway and down the lane to a fence barrier. Go R again entering a lane at the stile. Pass a ruin then branch L through a gateway. Cross two pastures via stiles to re-enter the lane, turning L via a gate/stile into Flash main street.

Flash church

continued from facing page ———

Go L, past the former chapel, the New Inn and village stores/Post Office. The notice on the end wall claims this to be the highest Post Office in England - at 1518'. Quarnford, the parish name, means 'mill by a ford', presumably located on the Dane: 'Flash' possibly derives from 'fleot' meaning sudden stream. This exposed village gained notoriety as a source of forged 'Flash' money. The offenders were aided by the proximity of the Three Shire Heads which helped as a means of evading arrest, police being unable to cross county boundaries. Hence the scattered community became a popular refuge for shady characters. However the district has long rid itself of men of such dubious virtue. Originally dating from 1744, but sturdily rebuilt in 1901, Flash church (see above) adds greatly to the charm and dignity of this oft-times bleak resort, exposed as it is to the rigours of the Peakland winter, with little natural shelter except Oliver Hill to the N.

Advance to the road junction, go R down the access lane to Northfield Farm, turning L and passing through two gates enter a pasture. **5** Angle R to a stile, follow the field boundary via the

——— *continued on page 104*

continued from page 103 ─────

second stile to two gates and onto the busy A53. Go directly across this highway to a narrow gate, descend into the depths of the first of the Manifold's many folds (meanders). An obvious track leads round to Nield Bank (cottage).

HIGH EDGE   HOLLINS HILL

From the cottage rise to the brink following the bank top to an odd fence gate at the wall corner. Advance over a broken wall to a low barbed wire fence (no stile) follow the wall to a gate onto the minor road at Summerhill (a recognition of the hard winters, when this house was built it will only have served as summer accommodation, 'hafod' in Wales, for a shepherd). To the R, up the ridge road, the Traveller's Rest adjacent to Flashbar Stores is handily placed.

Dove Head Spring may be visited by crossing a stile opposite Dove Head Farm, secreted within a rude stone-built portal inscribed with the intertwined initials CC IW.

These were cut into the lintel in the C19th and refer to the two C18th anglers most closely associated with the river — Charles Cotton and Izaak Walton. Cotton, in poetic mood wrote;
'O my beloved Nymph, fair Dove! Princess of rivers! How I love Upon thy flowery banks to lie!'

Dove Head Spring

───── *continued on facing page*

104

continued from facing page ——

Turn R, then fork L along the lane for Colshaw, branching L down the green lane ❻ to the delightfully and sympathetically restored cottage Lower Gamballs, reached via three stiles. The lower part of this lane is prone to run as a stream, though this does not constitute a hazard. Emerge onto the minor road via a stile/gate turning R, downhill, to cross the infant Dove and, of course, thereby leave Staffordshire and re-enter Derbyshire. The walk concluding up the road to Cistern's Clough. ❼

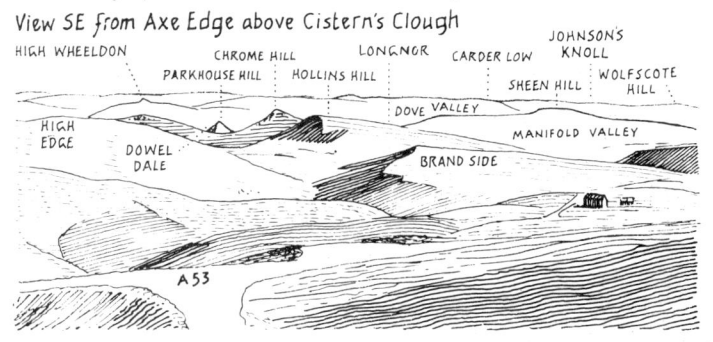

View SE from Axe Edge above Cistern's Clough

HIGH WHEELDON — CHROME HILL — LONGNOR — CARDER LOW — JOHNSON'S KNOLL
PARKHOUSE HILL | HOLLINS HILL — SHEEN HILL | WOLFSCOTE HILL
DOVE VALLEY
HIGH EDGE — DOWEL DALE — MANIFOLD VALLEY — BRAND SIDE
A53

Walkers who have revelled in the peat whilst sampling 'High Peak Walks' will certainly enjoy the brief encounter with the groughs of Dane Head. However, you should be mindful that access is not encouraged on the summits of Axe Edge Moor.

WHETSTONE RIDGE 1795'

CAT & FIDDLE INN

Dane Head

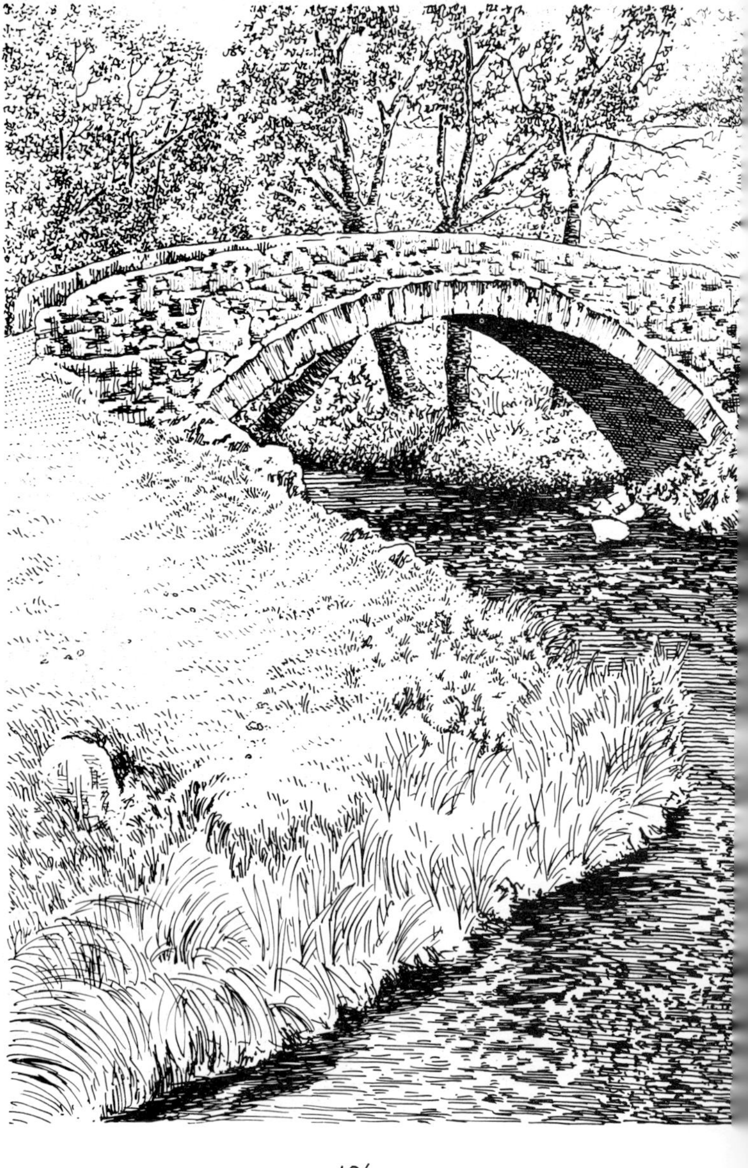

Washgate Bridge

WALK 13   DOVE and DOWEL
from Hollinsclough   4¼ miles

In presenting this superb excursion, I console myself for sharing its sustaining beauty by the realisation that I am in no way 'discovering' and therefore committing the unforgiveable sin of 'popularising' a rare and precious gem. Discerning walkers come this way frequently, seeking the old ways of jaggers and the stunning reef limestone hills of Dowel Dale. Packhorse bridges have an unfailing fascination and Washgate may lay claim to pre-eminence because it has only ever served pedestrian traffic not even tractors can come this way. So the setting is held in time to a remarkable extent, the meeting place of several rough country routes. The zig-zagging lane leading up to Leycote with its cobbles further enhances the authenticity and romantic imagery.

Leaving the upper Dove shales for the limestone uplands above Booth Farm, walkers are treated to scenery not far removed from the Yorkshire Three Peaks district, with scars, sinks and resurgences. Don't rush this walk and, in deference to the landowners' wishes, please keep off Chrome and Parkhouse Hills.

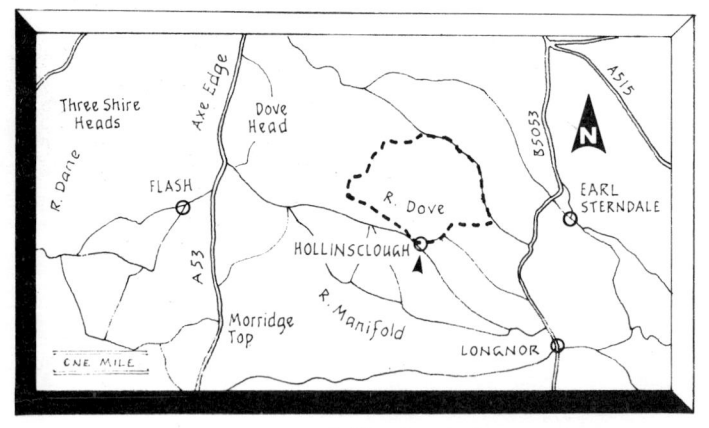

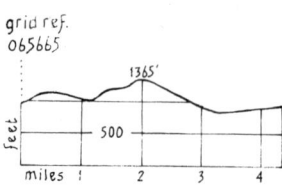

grid ref. 065665

Hollinsclough, formerly famous for its silk weaving cottage industry, has no more than a dozen houses to rub together, yet, especially when seen with the daffodils in full bloom, it is a charming little place smiled upon by Chrome Hill, here known as the Dragon's Back.

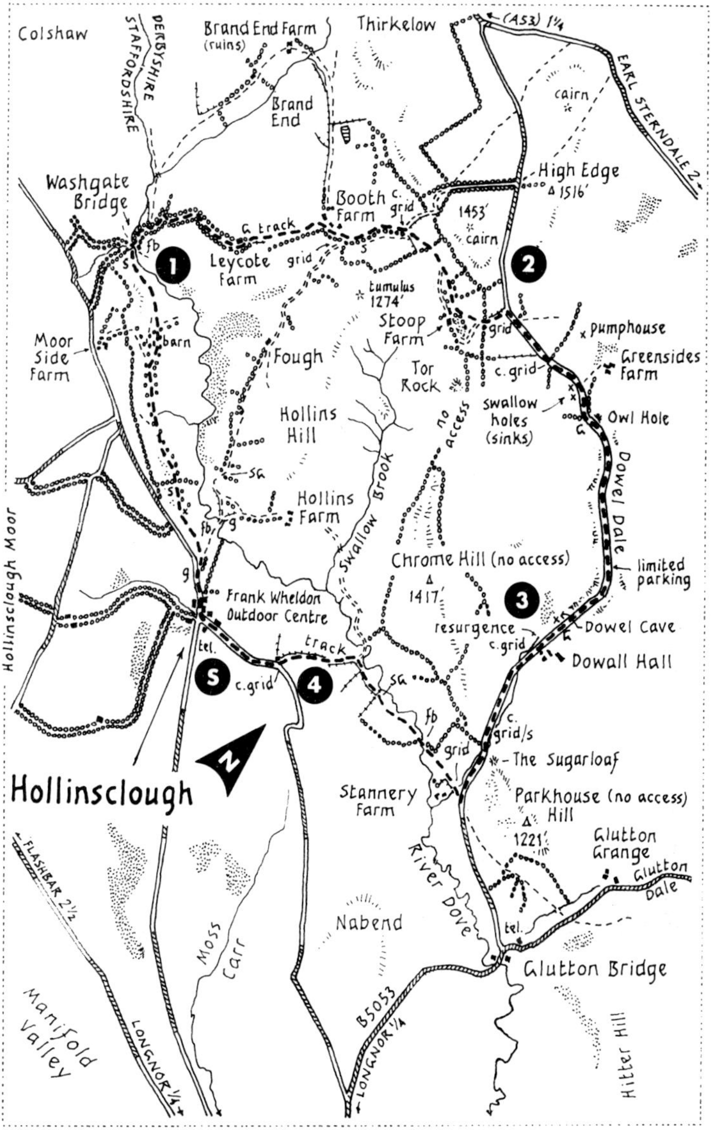
Colshaw
DERBYSHIRE
STAFFORDSHIRE
Brand End Farm (ruins)
Thirkelow
(A53) 1¼
Brand End
cairn
EARL STERNDALE 2
Washgate Bridge
High Edge
1516'
Booth Farm
c. grid
G track
fb
1453'
cairn
Leycote Farm
grid
tumulus 1274'
Stoop Farm
grid
Pumphouse
Moor Side Farm
barn
Fough
Tor Rock
c. grid
Greensides Farm
swallow holes (sinks)
Owl Hole
Hollins Hill
no access
Dowel Dale
SG
Hollins Farm
Swallow Brook
Hollinsclough Moor
fb
g
Chrome Hill (no access)
1417'
limited parking
g
Frank Wheldon Outdoor Centre
resurgence
Dowel Cave
tel.
track
c. grid
Dowall Hall
c. grid
SG
fb
c. grid/s
grid
The Sugarloaf
Hollinsclough
Stannery Farm
Parkhouse (no access) Hill
1221'
Glutton Grange
Glutton Dale
FLASHBAR 2½
River Dove
Nabend
Moss Carr
tel.
Glutton Bridge
Manifold Valley
LONGNOR ¼
B5053
LONGNOR ¼
Hitter Hill

S Park along the verge beyond the telephone kiosk in Hollinsclough. Follow the road N from the centre of the village, rising for about 100 yards to a bridlegate R; go through and down beside the wall. Instead of completing the descent to the packhorse bridge, follow the obvious shelf path L, contouring through the light birchwood. Cross a wall stile, keeping above the broken wall for 200 yards before drifting below it, without losing height. Notice the dark coal measure exposure in the shale bank of the Dove below. Where the Moor Side track angles uphill L, continue through the gateway and follow the path below the redundant barn. The path declines **1** to a fence stile, ford the side stream to arrive at Washgate Bridge.

continued on facing page

Cobbled packhorse path above Washgate Bridge

Washgate Bridge

continued from facing page
This packhorse bridge is, remarkably, the focus of eight paths. The setting is both exquisitely romantic in modern terms and quintessentially poignant, for it is easy to cast the imagination back to the time, perhaps two centuries ago, when travel-torn jaggers coaxed their pony teams laboriously this way. The going was hard through these hostile hills, and maybe they would halt awhile at this point, seeking refreshment for man and beast. The name Washgate tells of the river's use as a sheep wash, by this means cleaning the fleece before clipping in late Spring, a practice no longer carried out in rivers, with the advent of specialised dipping and penning facilities on all sheep farms. The ruins beside the cobbled lane, beyond the barn, may either be shepherd's quarters, or a refuge for pack teams. The zig-zagging lane rising N from the bridge is every bit as pleasing as the single-arch bridge: unadulterated by wheeled traffic (cross-country motorcyclists please note), it remains as functional as when first laid - a real joy to tread. The lane loses its cobbles higher up on the approach to Leycote, but walkers have open views in compensation. Leycote farmyard, rustic though it may be, poses no problems (barking dogs excepted) and from the gate, a firm track continues past Booth Farm. The name 'booth' implies that several centuries ago some form of corral existed here, providing a secure fold as protection for domesticated stock against wild animal (wolf, perhaps) attacks, or simply theft.
—— *continued on page 112*

continued from page 111 ———

Picking up the access road beyond Booth Farmhouse, walkers are at liberty to curtail their outing R at the cattle grid, following the steadily declining track via Fough (pronounced 'foo'). This course of action has an integrity with the shale scenery and, whilst this gives fine views of the Dove headwater hillscape, why deny yourself the enduring pleasure of striding into the spectacular limestone amphitheatre of Dowel Dale?

Despite the footpath stile by the mere R, it is better to keep to the road branching R at the cattle grid giving access onto the Stoop Farm track. After an intervening wall is passed and the track begins to curve R, depart L holding a line above the trees. Do not enter the Stoop farmyard nor contemplate finding a devious ridge route onto Chrome Hill: your way is barred, so forget it! A stoop was a stone wayside marker so perhaps the farm name is a recognition of an old regular way to Washgate. Rejoin the Stoop access road at the cattle grid, shortly reaching the open public road.

❷ Going R, the route remains faithful to this minor road for nearly 1½ miles. Beyond the next cattle grid, notice the dry valleys L, and soon R, sinks, shack holes or water swallows: there are various names for them but the effect is the same. The deep hollows consume surface water which percolates by devious means underground to reappear at Dove's well (the Dowel resurgence).

——— *continued on facing page*

112

continued from facing page ———

Go through a gate and pass Owl Hole, a sink feature that, were it not so abused as a dump, would be most dramatic to behold. The dale constricts hereon and is an unquestioned delight to wend through.

③ Just short of the cattle grid at the foot of the dale, glance up R to Dowel Cave (no access). Excavations within revealed animal remains associated with Neolithic funerary customs, principally the charred bones of a large ox, a species which lost favour and became extinct in the subsequent Iron Age. The Dowel resurgence next claims attention, again to the R, a normally strong current issuing forth. The adjacent Hall Farm must have its roots far back into history, this being a well-watered sheltered spot, the perfect location for a small durable settlement. Not surprisingly, the present farmer (Mr Etches) relies on his dairy herd to eke out a living, this has for many years been the practise locally, formerly supplying a Cheshire Cheese factory at Glutton Bridge. Follow the tiny Dowel stream (exactly why this side stream should hold the Dove's source in its name is not clear), beyond the Sugarloaf, keeping its ennobled watch on the passage of travellers.

Leave the road R along the track, over a cattle grid, advancing to a Dove footbridge.

Follow the meandering banks of the river to a fence stile/gate to join the Hollins Farm access track going L

④ At a final grid, turn R along the road, re-entering Hollinsclough past the former school house, now an outdoor centre.

Dowel Dale

The upper Dove valley and Chrome Hill from Parkhouse Hill

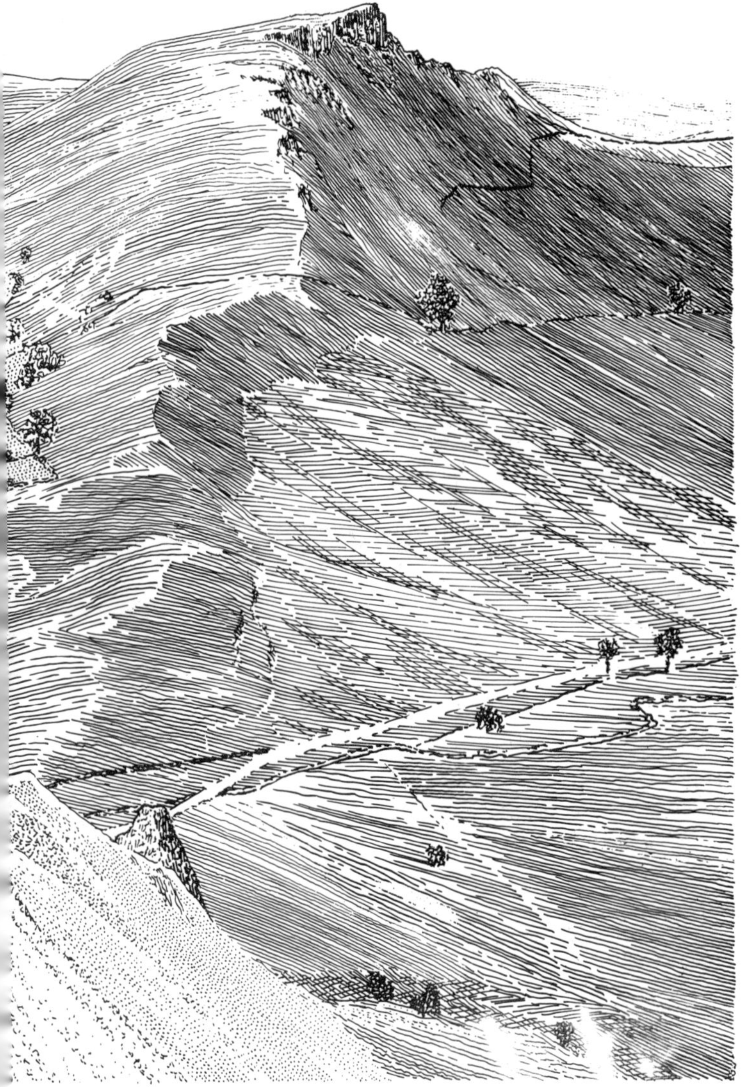

WALK 14   HIGH WHEELDON

from Longnor   5½ miles

The compact gritstone village of Longnor rests securely upon a saddle of the dividing ridge between the upper Dove and Manifold valleys. Cryptically concealed within its place-name is a reference to a 'long alder copse', a now lost shelter belt fringing the escarpment.

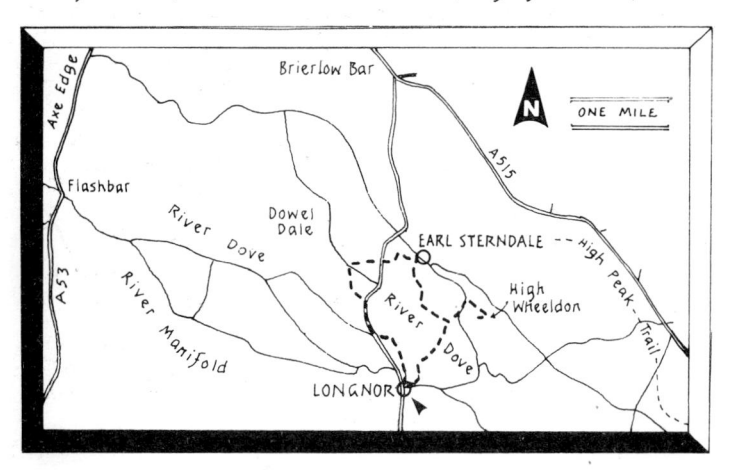

From the time when Longnor was a humble chapelry in the huge parish of Alstonefield, the community has grown steadily, the major expansion occuring during the urban revival in the late 18th and early 19th centuries. This development, upon a turnpike crossroads, coincided with the colon- ization of the vast waste of the gritstone moorland to the west, around the headwaters of the Manifold and Dove. These farmsteads, needing a market centre, focussed on Longnor, though its growth was stifled by its isolation from the railway system and the dominance of Buxton.

Travellers have always seen Longnor as an oasis in a lonely rolling hill country betwixt the verdant Derbyshire limestone and sombre Stafford- shire gritstone landscapes. The walk belongs to the limestone world beyond the brink of the scarp which effectively hides the Dove valley from the dip-slope 'town'. Walkers are treated to a sumptuous bill of fayre, advancing beyond Nab End to admire the stirring amphitheatre of Dowel Dale prior to criss-crossing the reef limestone spine via Earl Sterndale to claim the prize scalp of High Wheeldon. Seen from Earl Sterndale this is the perfect 'conical' hill and ascendees will be richly rewarded for their undoubted effort with a splendid all round panorama.

grid ref. 089649   1383'

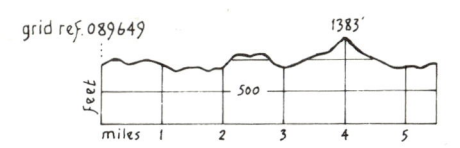

feet — 500

miles 1 2 3 4 5

S Currently there is no alternative car parking to the cobbled Market Place in the whole of Longnor. When the projected car park off the Crowdicote road is completed, this should be used by all walkers, thus permitting short-stay visitors liberty to park in the village centre. The walk must begin, but remember to save some time at the end to look in at 'Sculpture', the remarkable craft workshop within the old Market Hall. Quite the most endearing way in Longnor is Chapel Street, a narrow paved alley: an old walk possibly the earliest road within the township. Restorations here include the Parrots Restaurant, charmingly in keeping and lending a touch of much needed class to attract tourists to a community gaining new purpose from contemporary arts and crafts.

―――― *continued on page 118*

Longnor's cobbled Market Place featuring the Market Hall and Church

continued from page 117

Follow Chapel Street up the steps, angling L across Church Street into the narrow tarmac'd lane, watching for the footpath signs that direct R. Follow the scarptop wall by a bungalow development, through a wicket gate to reach a stile. At this point, enjoy the fine prospect into the Dove valley and across to the shapely objective of this walk, High Wheeldon. A clear path descends the scrubby bank to join the Underhill Farm access track, going L, rising steadily to the road junction. Go R with the B5053, the superb views amply compensating the need for traffic vigilance.

1 Just prior to the road's sharp descent to Glutton Bridge, branch L with the lane to Dove Bank. Do not enter the premises but cross the facing stile at the end of the straight lane and a further stile before descending through a rank hedge down to a footbridge over the River Dove. This small stream, twisting with excitement upon release from the deep folds of the shale hills of its source, has many ox-bows and abandoned banks in the making. Passing this way in March, the author noticed frog spawn in the pool beneath the old river bank L and dippers flitting in lively accompaniment to the chattering stream; walkers should always be alert to witness nature.

continued on facing page

Parkhouse Hill featuring the Sugar Loaf

continued from facing page

Geological timescales are, in all honesty, impossible concepts to grasp. Yet the hills rising so tantilisingly ahead do give a rare opportunity to visualise a 300 million year old fossilised seascape. The route rises, rounds the wall corner to cross a stile onto the minor road beneath the towering Parkhouse Hill. Both Chrome and Parkhouse Hills are composed of reef limestone, living examples of which occur worldwide in warm shallow seas like the Great Barrier Reef off the Pacific coast of Australia. The gap through which the road and tiny Dowel Dale stream pass is an original inter-coral reef channel. This helps to explain why the hills rise so abruptly from the meadow strath.

Chrome Hill derives its name from the Old English word 'crumb' meaning 'curved or sickle-shaped'; an obvious allusion to the shape of the ridge (to which there is no access). Parkhouse Hill derives its name from the former monastic grange estate of Glutton. Prudently the owner (Glutton Grange) discourages access to this remarkable peak, ostensibly to reduce the damaging effects of geologists chipping away specimens. It is to the farmer's credit that unsightly fences have not been erected, resorting instead to polite notices.

The reef was formed during Carboniferous times and arose at the fringe of a vast lagoon to the E which stretched from Castleton in the N to Brassington in the S with Eyam, Bakewell and Matlock the E limits. The line of fringing reefs continue S through Hitter Hill and High Wheeldon, outcropping frequently down Dove Dale. A deep water basin existed to the W wherein the sandstone of the Staffordshire Moors was laid. Readers unversed in the continental drift factor will wonder how it is that such hot sea conditions could prevail in chilly old England. The fact is, we've moved from the Equator to our present temperate latitude during those intervening 300 million years and for that matter must still be heading for the even chillier North Pole!

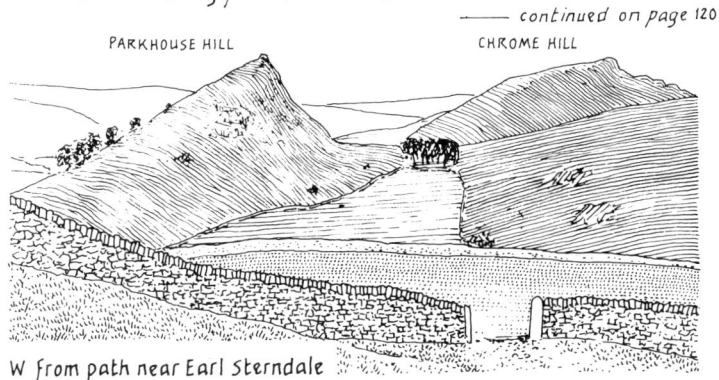

continued on page 120

PARKHOUSE HILL   CHROME HILL

W from path near Earl Sterndale

continued from page 119

The route crosses the S flank of Parkhouse Hill to a wall stile, thereafter declining to a gate/stile and stream ❷, then rising to a stile onto the B5053. Glutton Grange farmhouse (seen to the L) has a datestone 1675 and stands attractively beside the road at the entrance to Glutton Dale. The less than flattering place-name does not, I believe, come from association with Friar Tuck (despite monastic links and other Robin Hood-type names in the locality)! It was first recorded in 1415 as Gloton, and is taken as some obscure personal nickname.

Glutton Grange

The yellow daubed slab stile directly opposite gives access into the field, where a footpath angles L up to another vividly waymarked stile. Ahead, the path follows a distinct groove, rising quite steeply to the brow of Hitter Hill (an apparent reference to some long-lost blacksmith's shop. From the wall stile at the top, where the view of Parkhouse and Chrome (pronounced 'croom') Hills is quite startling, the footpath advances via a gateway across two enclosures to reach the street in Earl Sterndale at a stile/gate.

Earl Sterndale corresponds with King Sterndale beyond Brierlow Bar, presumably linked by family association way back in the Dark Ages. The Old English stæner for 'stony ground' is rare in the district: the early Medieval separation of the lands between the crown and William de Ferrars, Earl of Derby (known to have held the estate in 1244) explains the prefix. The grey-stoned village may not draw forth accolades regarding its charm; nonetheless the village pub is a friendly enough refuge and the small green across

continued on page 122

Reef limestone peaks of Dowel Dale

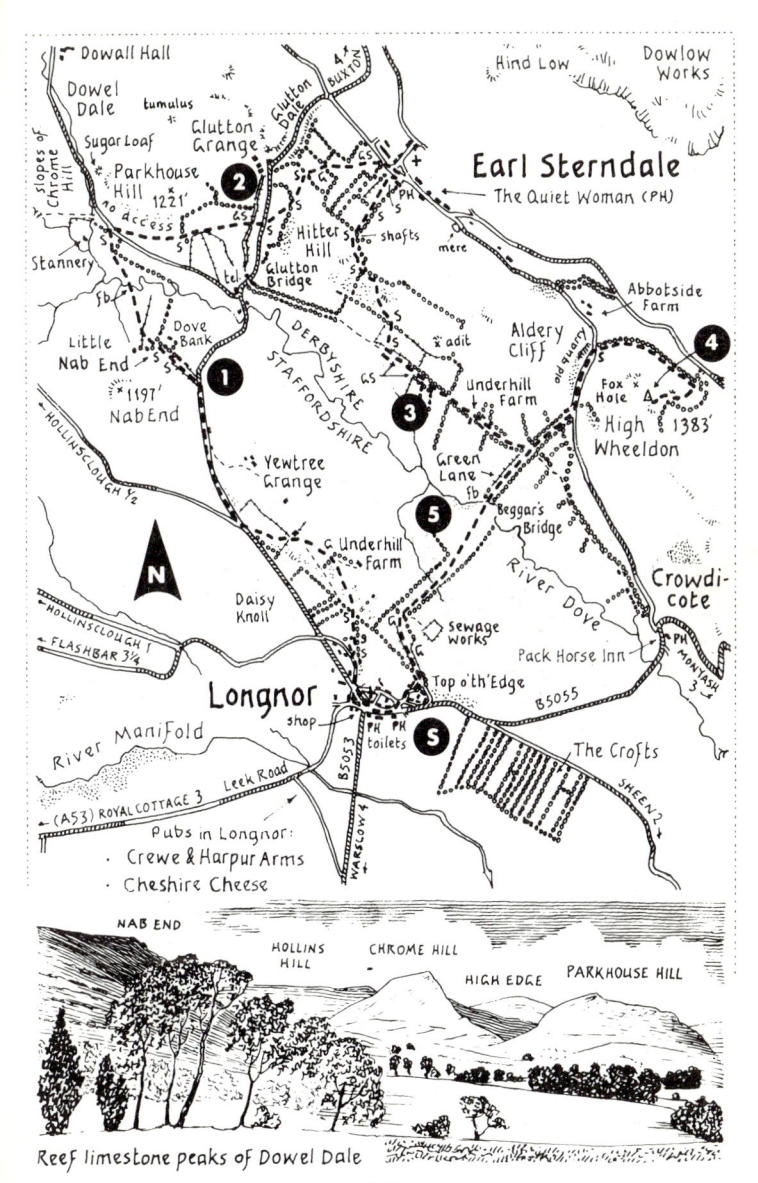

continued from page 120 ─────

the way a fine spot to relax. Upon the Quiet Woman signboard runs the true enough sentiment 'soft words turneth away wrath' but exactly how this is tallied with the poor headless wench is hard to tell. The oldest item in Earl Sterndale today is a C12th font in St Michael's church, quite a treasure. The church itself dates from 1829, with the chancel added in 1877, but it suffered war damage and had to be rebuilt and refurbished in 1950-52. The proximity of the Peakstone Ltd (Dowlow) quarrying conglomeration has had a tangible effect on the village, which must have grown up as a remote outpost of the Derbyshire limestone uplands, populated by flockmasters and herdsmen little trammelled by the outside world.

The route departs surreptitiously, going R of the pub, round the back of the premises by the shippon (footpath sign) to a stile. Advance up the pastureland to cross a stile in the corner (L of the gateway), progressing to the top where a stile gives access to the rougher ground along the spine of the ridge. Go L passing a notice giving advice to walkers unaware of the path diversion (as yet not shown on the Outdoor Leisure map), the footpath formerly running up the fields to this spot from the S side of the Quiet Woman. Following the wall round, with excellent views of the Dove valley and the summit of High Wheeldon overtopping Aldery Cliff, cross the stile unusually equipped with handrails. The path continues along the edge for 30 yards before diverting purposefully down the scrub bank (discernible path) to a stile. Complete the descent to reach the bridle track beside the beautifully refurbished dwelling. Go L to the gate/stile, keeping with the track via a further gate/stile and

3 continuing beyond Underhill Farm. Decision time. Consider your energies and determination, for Green Lane offers an early return to Longnor. You will, however, pay a high price of self-denial for this action, for arguably the finest accessible viewpoint in the upper Dove valley beckons L. Resolving upon the conical crest of High Wheeldon, follow the track onto the road, advancing up Sterndale to a stile R (N.T. sign).

Whilst the summit can be attained by a direct approach from this point, the prudent course of valour is to follow the path beside the wall to the point where the Wheeldon Trees track enters from the L. At this moment ascend the steep path R past the ruins of a lime kiln to the memorial O.S. trig. column.

continued on facing page ─────

122

continued from facing page —

Viewed from Earl Sterndale, High Wheeldon complies with the common perception of mountain form, and though the anticipated soaring summit proves, once atop, to be no more than the termination of a long broad ridge, the thrilling view (see the PANORAMA on pages 124-125) is more than adequate compensation.   Visitors may also like to satisfy a casual curiosity by locating the Fox Hole Cave, a short way down the NW ridge. Only an external inspection is possible of this short system of joints enlarged by solution and extending for about 180'. In the interests of archaeological conservation, the cave is kept locked, but it is interesting that official digs here (hence spoil) have discovered remains of Neolithic and Palaeolithic times, including many animal bones. The cave drops 8' into a passage leading to a chamber 20' long where there is a branch to the R leading to a third chamber and zigzag passages beyond (the finds are stored at Buxton Museum).

④ The meaning of the hill-name is not exactly clear: perhaps it refers obliquely to a nearby stone circle, now lost. Or is it a vague likeness to a prostrate wheel?   Retrace steps down the road, branching R to continue with Green Lane to Beggar's Bridge.

The footpath next traverses a **⑤** shallow ridge lined by traces of ridge and furrow cultivation. Rising to a gate beside a barn, trend L to climb the scarp with the track via a gate. The final view back across the Dove valley is dominated by High Wheeldon. At The Homestead ('Top o' th' Edge) notice the well discreetly concealed by a pentroof door R. Follow the road L, turning R down the lane by Two Rivers Studio keeping to the path via an alley into Longnor High Street. Go R past the Cheshire Cheese to the Market Place and that promised visit to 'Woodstringthistlefoss'

Fox Hole Cave

123

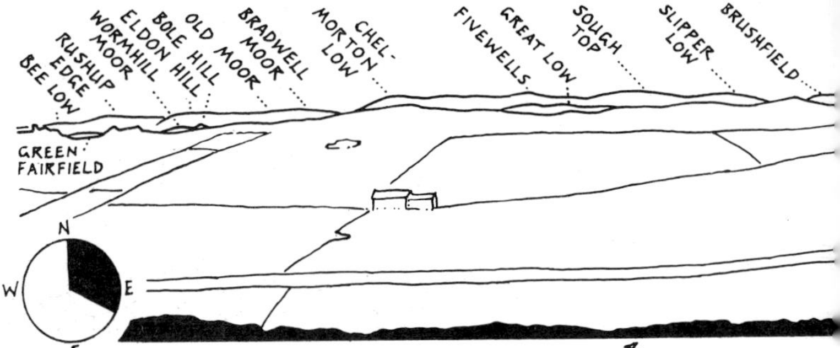
BEE LOW
RUSHUP EDGE
WORMHILL MOOR
ELDON HILL
BOLE HILL
OLD MOOR
BRADWELL MOOR
CHEL-MORTON LOW
FIVEWELLS
GREAT LOW
SOUGH TOP
SLIPPER LOW
BRUSHFIELD
GREEN FAIRFIELD
N
W
E
S

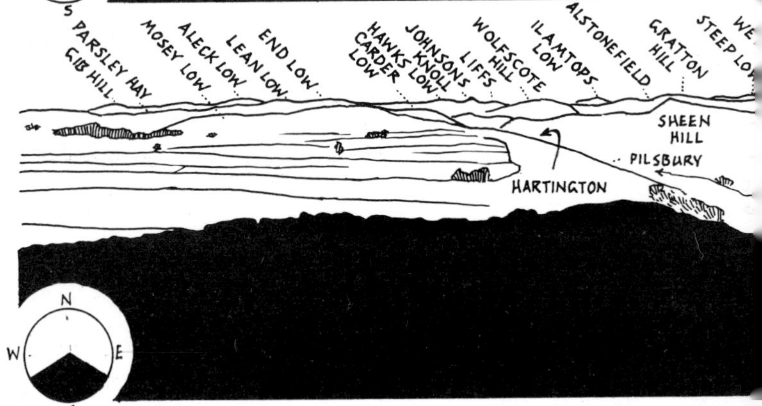
GIB HILL
PARSLEY HAY
MOSEY LOW
ALECK LOW
LEAN LOW
END LOW
CARDER LOW
HAWKS LOW
JOHNSONS KNOLL
LIFFS
WOLFSCOTE HILL
ILAMTOPS LOW
ALSTONEFIELD
GRATTON HILL
STEEP LOW
SHEEN HILL
PILSBURY
HARTINGTON
N
W
E
S

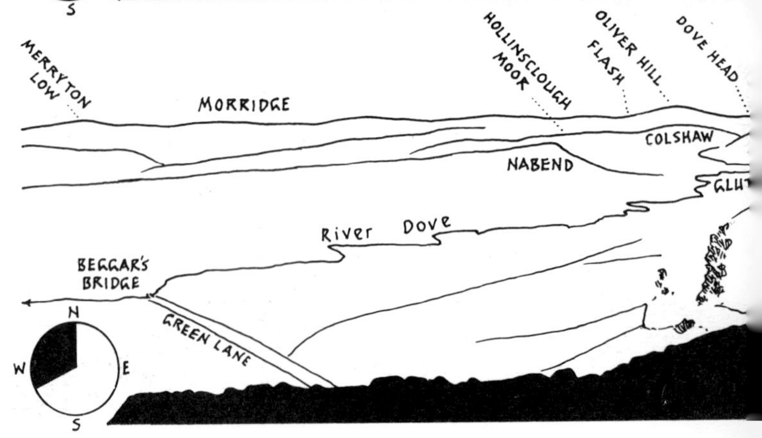
MERRYTON LOW
MORRIDGE
HOLLINSCLOUGH MOOR
FLASH
OLIVER HILL
DOVE HEAD
COLSHAW
NABEND
River Dove
BEGGAR'S BRIDGE
GREEN LANE
N
W
E
S

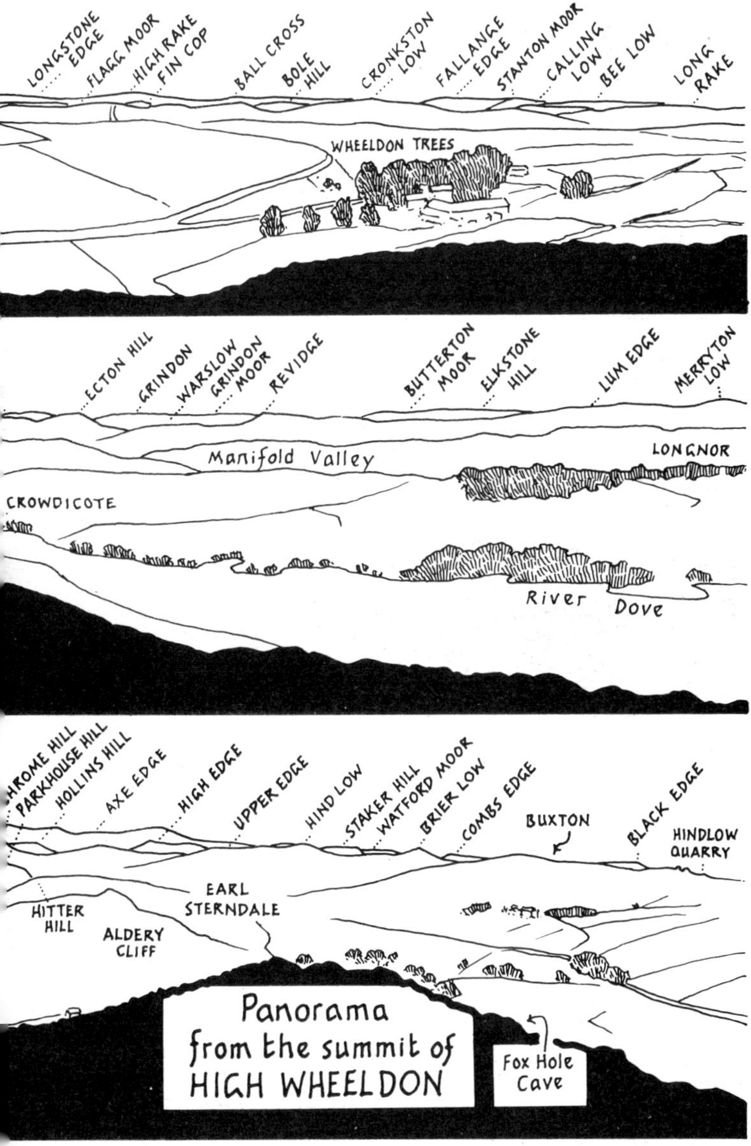

Panorama from the summit of HIGH WHEELDON

Pilsbury Castle looking NW to Axe Edge

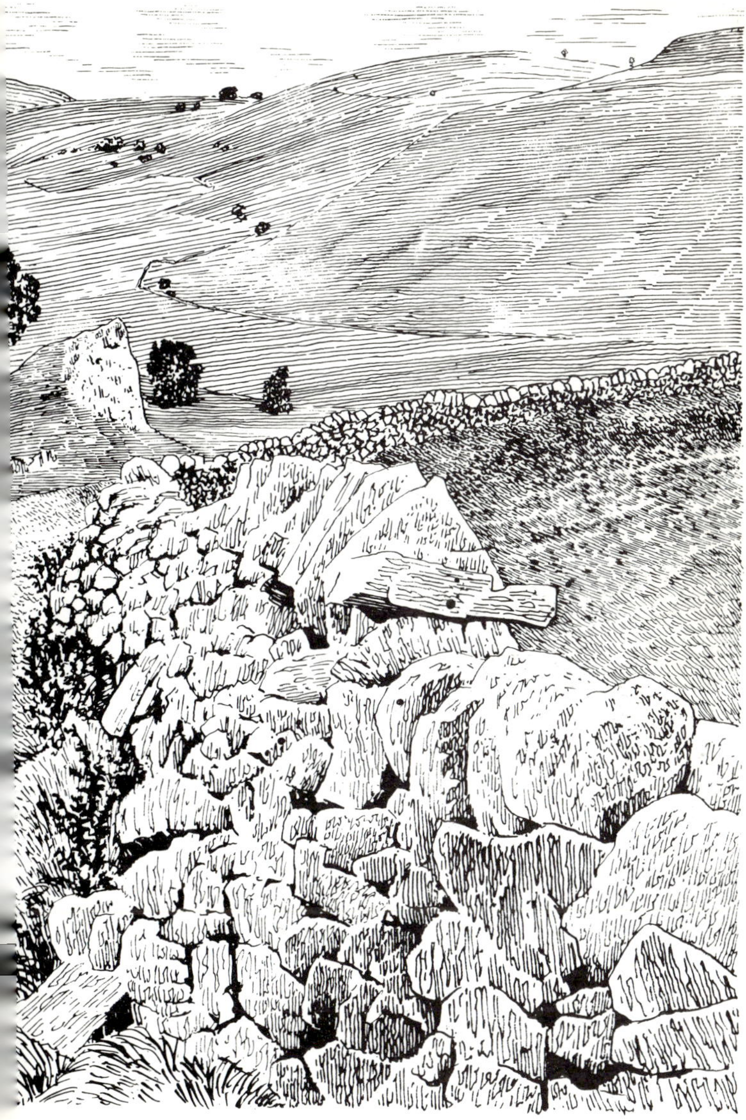

WALK 15   PILSBURY CASTLE

from Hartington   5½ miles

Escaping from the holiday throngs congregated upon Hartington market square can be an excuse for considering a country walk. While the majority of walkers may head for Beresford Dale, the wise few turn N and are well rewarded: here the Dove valley is considerably broader but no less distinguished. The views are truly fine to the gritstone summit of Sheen Hill and those tantalising limestone peaks beyond Longnor - visited on WALKS 13/14. The walk extends N to Pilsbury Castle, a complex of Norman motte and bailey earthworks in an impressive and romantically tranquil setting.   There are pubs at Crowdicote and Sheen.

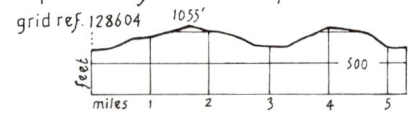

grid ref. 128604

S The walk begins from the centre of Hartington, an attractive village with excellent facilities including cafés, hotels, shops, banks and toilets, together with a most impressive Youth Hostel at Hartington Hall. Follow Dig Street N from the pond; directly after the road bends R, branch R up the green Wallpit Lane, rising to join Hide Lane, going L.

——— *continued on page* 130

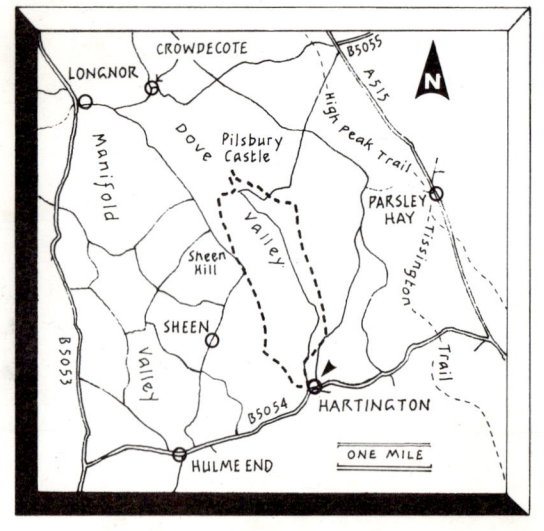

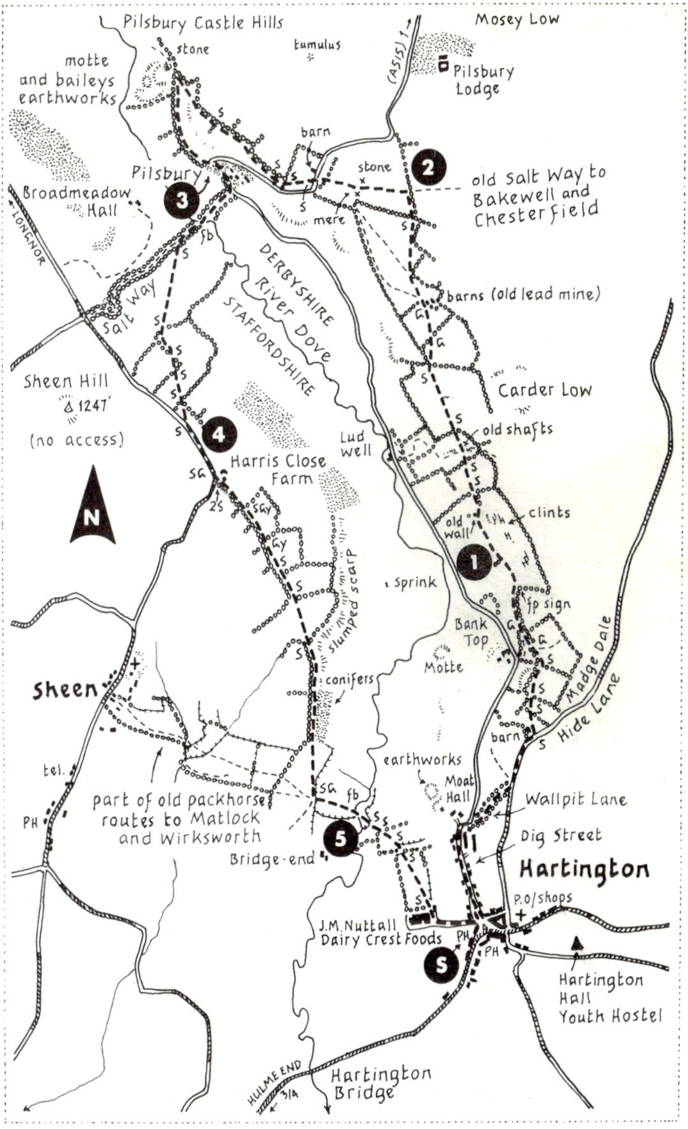
Pilsbury Castle Hills
Mosey Low
stone
tumulus
motte and baileys earthworks
(A515) 1
Pilsbury Lodge
barn
stone
2
old Salt Way to Bakewell and Chesterfield
Pilsbury
3
Broadmeadow Hall
LONGNOR
mere
fb
DERBYSHIRE
River Dove
STAFFORDSHIRE
barns (old lead mine)
Salt Way
Sheen Hill
1247'
(no access)
Carder Low
old shafts
4
Lud Well
Harris Close Farm
N
clints
old wall
1
Sprink
slumped scarp
fp sign
Bank Top
Motte
Madge Dale
Hide Lane
Sheen
conifers
barn
earthworks
tel.
Moat Hall
part of old packhorse routes to Matlock and Wirksworth
Wallpit Lane
PH
fb
5
Dig Street
Bridge-end
Hartington
P.O/shops
J.M.Nuttall Dairy Crest Foods
PH
PH
S
Hartington Hall Youth Hostel
HULME END
Hartington Bridge

continued from page 128

Whilst the valley road can be followed to Pilsbury (continuing with the bridleway to the Inn at Crowdecote for a pub lunch, before retracing steps), how much better to contour below Carder Low and enjoy the full splendour of the dale.

Where Hide Lane bends R, cross the stile to the R of the new barn and advance via three wall stiles onto the track from Bank Top. Go through the gate, descending to a gate at the hairpin bend. The footpath traverses below Carder Low ❶ with expansive views of the Dove valley. The limestone outcrops in the vicinity of mile one are a fragmented form of clints created by the dissolving effect of acid rain, leaving insoluble slabs or pavements of limestone exposed by a soil-denuding ice flow.

The paucity of areas of pavement in the White Peak, in stark contrast with the Yorkshire Dales must suggest that the crucial last scouring stage of the ice age was little evidenced this far S.

Cross the mineral rake, marked by old shaft spoil (take care!). Two stiles farther on, angle R to a field gate, thereafter gently ascend to a gate beside former lead mine buildings. Keep R following the walls to a stile then descend into the side valley. Turn L ❷ along the valley floor, passing a mere and a standing stone (?) - surely this is no menhir, more likely a simple, functional, cattle scratching-post, or a guide-stone on the old packhorse way to Chesterfield. Proceed through the gateway onto the unenclosed road; the right of way has recently been modified to exclude the cow pastures beyond the field barn. From the stile below the barn, bear L to cross the small field via two stiles. Follow the wall to the R, along the scarp edge, cross one more stile in a spur wall before drifting down to the Pilsbury track.

Sheen Hill from the 'menhir'

A White Peak rarity - clint pavements

130

continued from facing page

The Pilsbury motte and bailey earthworks do not conform to the convention of typical pure Norman invention. The supposition, borne out by the place-name (which is Saxon and refers to 'the fortified place associated with a man called Pil'), is that this remote site has deep historic roots, possibly stretching back to the Iron Age, and that the Normans only modified existing bank features circa 1100. Situated on a limestone spur with its own natural sentinel rock tower standing guard, the place is shrouded in mystery (never having been excavated); here walkers with a lively imagination may dream of fighting men doing battle and reflect on how serene it all looks today. The site can be visited by crossing the stile adjacent to the gate, scrambling to the top of the rock outcrop to survey the earthworks set amongst the meandering Dove and its herb-rich meadows.

As mentioned earlier, walkers welcoming a mid-walk break may continue directly N, on a well-marked valley path, to Crowdicote and the Packhorse Inn, preferably backtracking to continue.

The route switches S along the farm track to the road, proceeding down R through the hamlet of Pilsbury, abundant with evidence of a depressed farming economy ❸. Branch R along the strip pasture to the Dove footbridge, a pleasant spot from which to watch the bobbing, darting antics of dippers. A green lane (former Salt Way) begins the ascent of Sheen Moor, with Broadmeadow Hall, undergoing restoration, R. Take the stile L, opposite the Broadmeadow access gate, slant uphill via five stiles onto the minor road beneath the gritstone mock castle of Sheen Hill.
❹ Following the road L, depart L, at the R hand bend, entering Harris Close farmyard. Keep tight R behind the shed to two stiles. The well-marked footpath advances beside a banktop wall, a curious feature suggesting a boundary dyke. After three stiles and a gateway, the path declines to a smart new stile (1985). Follow alongside the wall, above the slumped scarp, threading through the top of a small conifer plantation before making a diagonal descent of the scrub-covered scarp to a gate/stile. The path, once part of a long overland packhorse route branching from the Leek/Bakewell Salt Way at Brund, crosses the meadow garlanded with buttercups in Summer months, to reach a footbridge.
❺ Bear R, negotiating a series of five stiles, into the forecourt of Nuttall's (Dairy Crest) famous Stilton cheese factory. Watchful of lorries, escape L along the access road into Hartington to finish.

Sheen (a name thought to derive ironically from the Old Norse skjaa meaning 'shed') deserves a visit if only in remembrance of Sir Nikolaus Pevsner, who made his final field notes for his monumental 'Buildings of England' survey at Butterfield's Rectory.

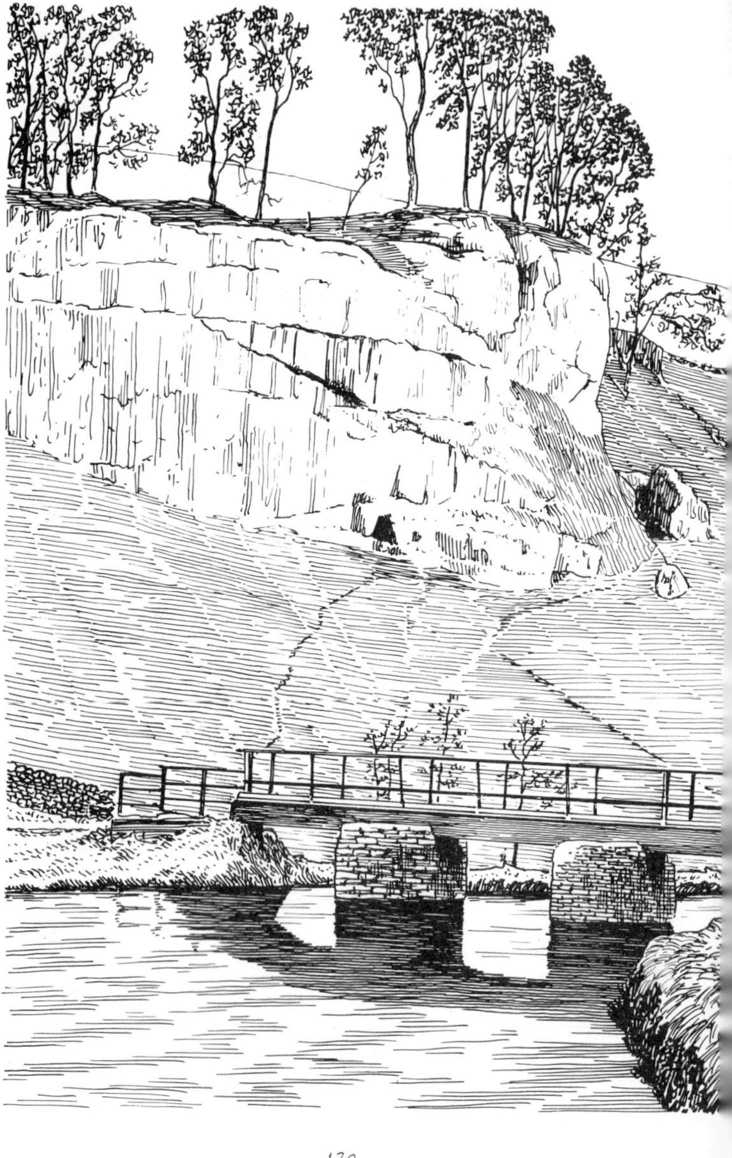

The entrance to Wolfscote Dale

WALK 16   WOLFSCOTE DALE
from Hartington   5¼ miles

Hartington is the gateway to the Dove gorge, the threshold of a pageant of happy delights. From here on, the river threads a deeply incised passage through the limestone plateau, in excess of six miles of renowned charm and often exquisite beauty, a truly memorable place to stroll.

The described walk falls into five distinct phases which express the quite differing aspects distinctive of the locality - an approach across valley pastures, the sylvan gorge of Beresford Dale (prone to be muddy), the open aspect of Wolfscote Dale beginning and ending with fine crags, the stony wilds of Biggin Dale, and finally (rising from that dry valley the limestone upland dominated by the ubiquitous grey-lichened walls.

grid ref. 128604

S From the centre of the village, follow the Warslow (B5054) road briefly, turning L between the pottery and public conveniences where a footpath sign directs into a field. Trend R, crossing a green lane by facing stone stiles then descend through the collapsed wall to reach the gate. Notice the strip lynchets on Pennilow telling of a time, possibly during the 13th century, when demand for tilled ground was at a premium to satisfy a swelling village population, either through healthy growth within the community or because of migratory settlement (and I don't mean Medieval holiday homes!).

Follow the rapidly diminishing wall to a stile giving access to an oft muddy passage into the wooded entrance to Beresford Dale. Directly below at this point, hidden from quizzical gaze in a loop of the river, is the Fishing Temple erected in 1674 by Charles Cotton of Beresford Hall (now demolished).

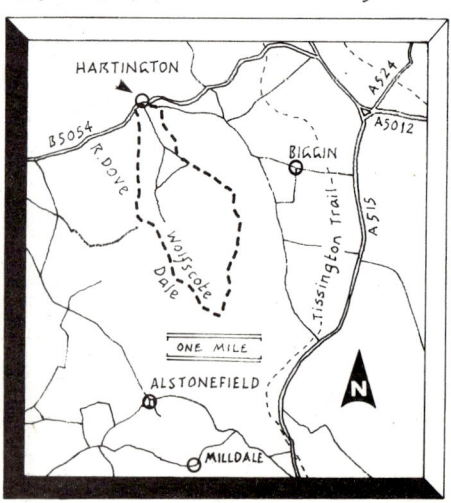

— continued on facing page

134

continued from facing page

Cotton's pavilion formed a fishing retreat often visited by his friend Izaak Walton, who wrote 'The Compleat Angler' in 1653. The fifth edition (1676) contained several chapters contributed by Cotton eulogising the virtues of the Dove as a trout stream.

The heart of Beresford Dale is a craggy embowered gorge overlooked by a gaunt Tudor-styled prospect tower, the only other remnant of Cotton's day. Crossing a footbridge, admire the rock stack from which the Pike Pool derives its name, walking on to a second footbridge beside the ford probably enshrined in the valley name ❶.

Pike Pool

The transition between Beresford and Wolfscote Dales is a joyous stroll through open meadowland to a squeeze stile. For a really special view of Wolfscote Dale, slip over the footbridge and scramble up the adjacent bluff, returning to continue. Up to the L are two large limestone outcrops, the nearest being Frank's Rock. At its foot is a small cave called Frank i'th' Rocks Cave. The chamber has a crawl on the R which leads through the cliff, emerging close to the entrance of a small rift passage. The main cave has been explored for 150' and has yielded archaeological remains of Roman and Anglo-Saxon burials: they are in the Buxton Museum.

The footpath beside the alder-lined Dove runs tight to the river. At times of high rainfall, the swollen flow can force walkers to seek higher ground at irregular intervals, often over scree — the deep 'V' shaped valley affords little additional scope this lends a gorgeously wild feel to this reach of the Dove. Unlike the Manifold, the Dove has no subterranean quirks; with weirs set into its bed thus supporting good fishing year round.

To have run this anomalous course through basically resistant rocks, the Dove must have exploited shale pockets and ancient weaknesses in the mountain limestone mass. The river has incised the gorge with deference to the isolated limestone reefs that outcrop at intervals, such as Drabber Tor and Peaseland Rocks, thus keeping to the inter-reef channel systems trending S.

continued on page 137

135

Two aspects of Wolfscote Dale

Peaseland Rocks

continued from page 135 ────

② Drabber Tor is an eye-catching severed buttress shortly succeeded by the impressive tiered craggy ribs of Peaseland Rocks which overlook the junction with Biggin Dale. Clearly in view at this point down the main valley to the L is Iron Tors Cave. This simple chamber has parallels with Dove Holes at the entrance to Dove Dale proper.

Turn L up Biggin Dale, a dry valley with a tremendous air of remoteness into which seasoned walkers will stride with immense relish. No matter how gregarious one is in normal life, the opportunity to wander alone up such a wild valley has great therapeutic value. The cave to the R is a trial level or adit: only 50 yards of gallery exist, apparently following a short thin lead vein and is quite safe to explore. The path goes up **③** beside the boulder-bedecked occasional stream to a gate into the Biggin Dale National Nature Reserve. The calcareous grassland supports precious and peculiar flora and fauna nurtured for posterity - so pick nothing but your steps carefully.

──── *continued on page 138*

Biggin Dale

continued from page 137 ─────────

　Where a side valley enters from the R, swing L, crossing the stile next to the mere. Advance along the main valley, veering L above the remains of a lime kiln, to a stile into a green lane. **④** The track passes a sturdy hipped-roof barn: notice the derelict well head and water pump in the yard. Continue straight ahead at the crossways. Leave the road at a stile R, by a clump of trees and mere. Trend half L across the broken wall to enter Leisure Lane, a modernised form of 'leasow', meaning 'the way to the meadow'.

⑤ The lane terminates opposite Hartington Hall, built in 1611 in early Jacobean style with slightly projecting wings and mullioned windows protected by hood moulds. Internally, there are oak panelled walls and some attractive plaster ceilings. It is claimed that Bonnie Prince Charlie spent a night here; indeed his tiny panelled room is part of the comfortable dormitory accommodation offered in this long-established Youth Hostel.　Go L down the minor road into Hartington, where refreshment may be had at a range of visitor-orientated facilities.

　Spare, if you can, a few minutes to inspect the parish church of St Giles. Built in paternal command over the township, it is distinguished by the presence of transepts, this plan dating back to the mid-13th century.

Hartington Hall Youth Hostel

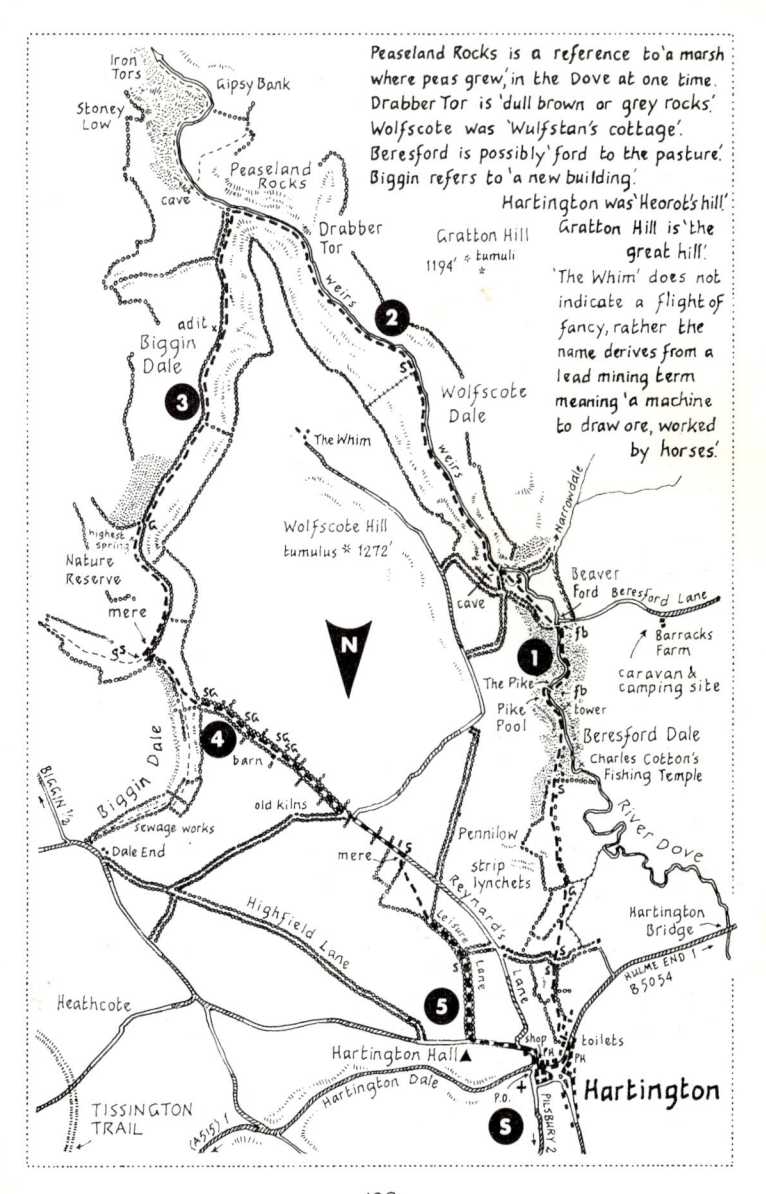

Peaseland Rocks is a reference to 'a marsh where peas grew', in the Dove at one time.
Drabber Tor is 'dull brown or grey rocks'.
Wolfscote was 'Wulfstan's cottage'.
Beresford is possibly 'ford to the pasture'.
Biggin refers to 'a new building'.
Hartington was 'Heorot's hill'.
Gratton Hill is 'the great hill'.
'The Whim' does not indicate a flight of fancy, rather the name derives from a lead mining term meaning 'a machine to draw ore, worked by horses'.

Drabber Tor

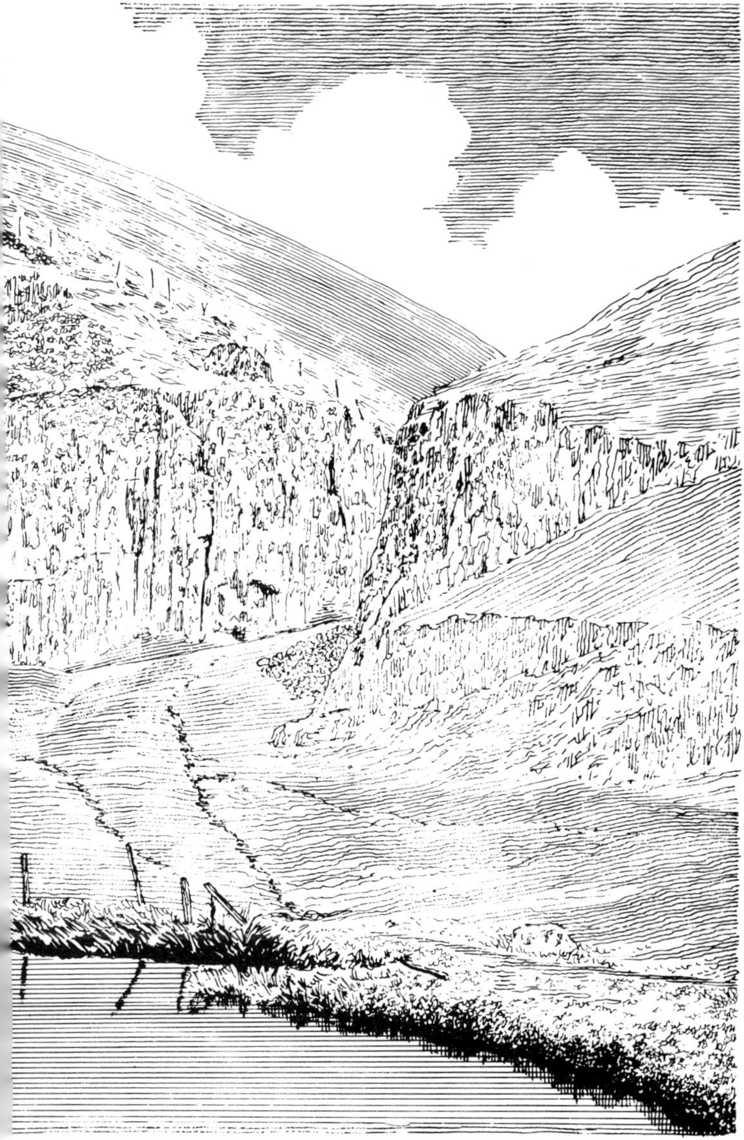

WALK 17 WOLFSCOTE DALE
from Alstonefield   7 miles

This is quite the best way to see Wolfscote Dale and provides the worthwhile bonus of lonely Narrowdale and attains the crest of Shining Tor for the impressive views of Mill Dale and Hopedale from Hanson Toot.

Alstonefield is recorded in the Domesday Book as Ænestanefelt, which meant 'Ælfstan's field or enclosure' and not as may be conjectured, 'all stony field'. The present village has a shop and National Park established car park, but of possibly more significance for the end of the day is the excellent pub 'The George'.

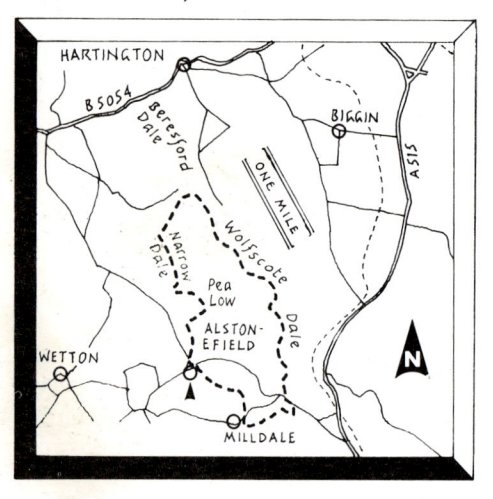

S From the car park, cross the road to a stile, almost at once negotiating a second stile. The footpath goes diagonally across the field beyond the farm buildings to a stile, rapidly succeeded by two more leading onto a track. Go R then L to a stile in the corner, following the wall via a stile/gate and two more stiles to emerge beside a ribbed mere. Go R uphill, passing through a gap, slightly hampered underfoot by the cow trod rising to Pea Low. grid ref. 131556
The burial mound is evident beneath the wall junction - the W side shows signs of excavation,

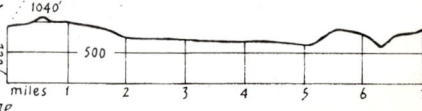

— continued on facing page

142

continued from facing page ─────

most probably by wall builders. The ridge is crossed at a stile; descending with the wall towards the barn and meres. Go L before they are reached, proceeding via two stiles above the head of Narrowdale to reach a gate into a lane. **❶** Turn R to a gate, descending beside a broken wall into the valley; unfortunately the two gates on the line of the bridleway are fixed, so respectfully treat them as stiles.

───── *continued on page 144*

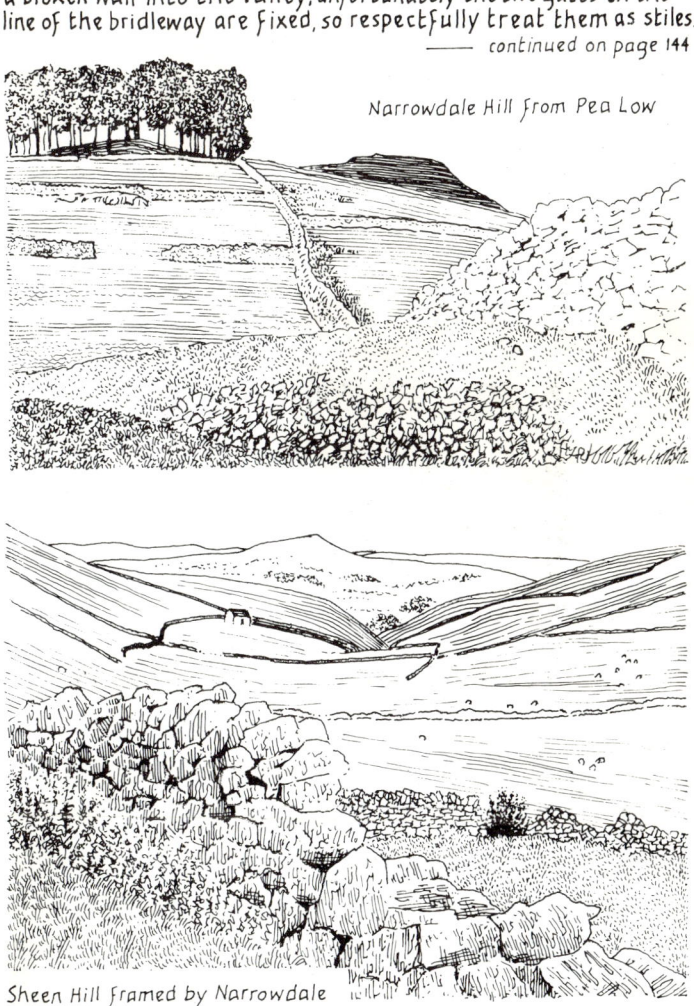

Narrowdale Hill from Pea Low

Sheen Hill framed by Narrowdale

continued from page 143

It is widely recognised that the principal beauties of the White Peak are shyly concealed in the dales, and whilst the Dove is clearly pre-eminent, solitary walkers will silently praise Narrowdale, which is an unsung scenic joy. Framed between the shapely scarp of Narrowdale Hill and Gratton Hill, the view concentrates upon Sheen and the distant Longnor Hills. Few casual travellers are aware of Narrowdale, an upland pastoral bowl which exits through a narrow passage, the abutments formed by a resilient reef limestone rockband. Entering the confines at the foot of the dale, pass the abandoned Lister water pump to reach a stile/gate, from where go R with the track (not up R), passing through three gates to reach ❷ a wicket gate R, off the track leading beside a wall in the woodland (prone to be muddy) to emerge close to the river Dove: go forward to the footbridge. Fine views abound, particularly from the outcrop R, of Beresford Dale's sylvan meadows, Frank's Rock and Wolfscote Dale distinguished by its simple 'v' shaped valley form. After crossing the footbridge, keep with the riverside path downstream. At times of flood, walkers are forced into taking evasive action scrambling up and down the scrub and scree bank.

❸ The river holds prime attention until the arrival of Drabber Tor, impressively flanking a minor re-entrant valley; thereafter the rock ribs of Peaseland Rocks and the bristly ridge at the confluence with Biggin Dale are notable features. There is a large resurgence at the foot of Biggin Dale, the dale being otherwise dry except in the depth of winter.

Crossing the causeway, the path goes beneath Iron Tors Cave, a small rock chamber and the

River Dove from Frank i'th' Rocks Cave

—— *continued on page 146*

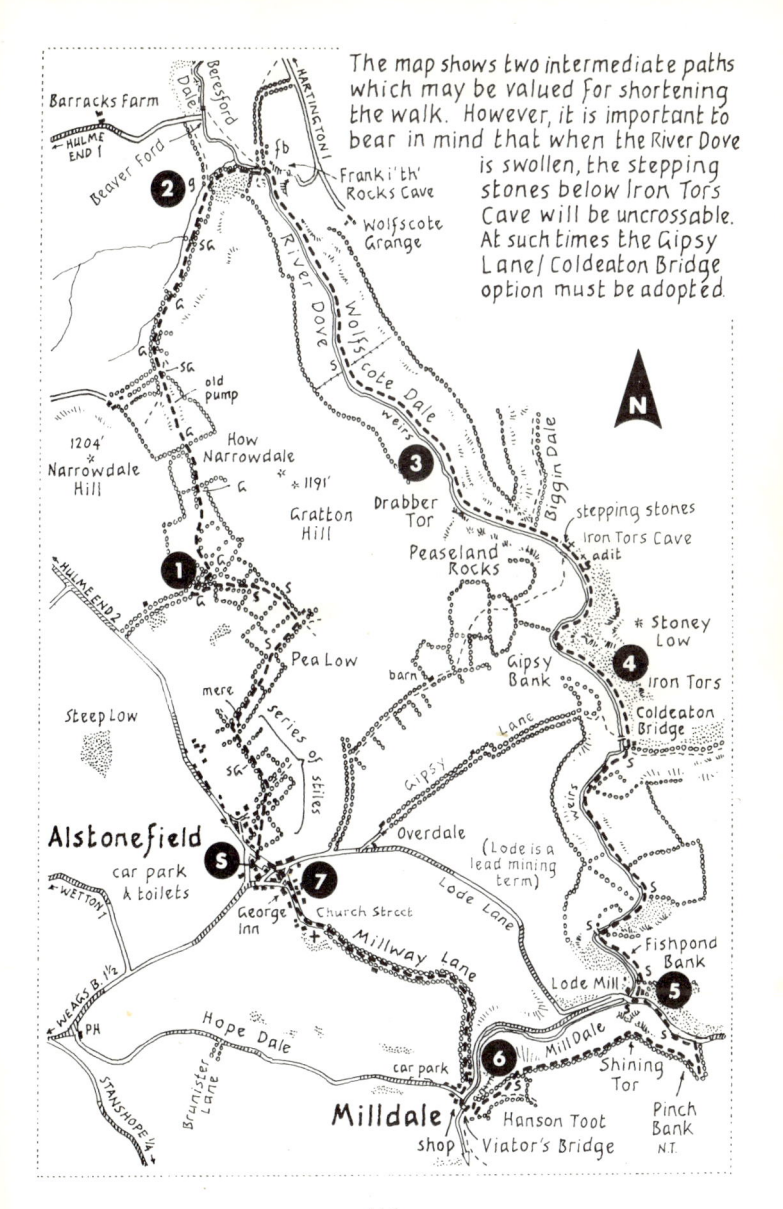

The map shows two intermediate paths which may be valued for shortening the walk. However, it is important to bear in mind that when the River Dove is swollen, the stepping stones below Iron Tors Cave will be uncrossable. At such times the Gipsy Lane/Coldeaton Bridge option must be adopted.

continued from page 144

remnant of some probably extensive cave system consumed by the downward cut of the river during an inter-glacial phase, to a stile. Notice the trial level at hand contemporary with the short gallery a little way up Biggin Dale; obviously an insufficient lode existed to warrant major development of the vein.   The riverside path next winds through light woodland beneath Iron Tors, ④ emerging at the Coldeaton footbridge where there is a Severn Trent Water Authority building and a stile. From here on the path treads the delightful meadow pastures via stiles passing a cottage overlooked by Shining Tor, to reach the minor road at Lode Mill. The crag-name Shining Tor is probably derived from a Saxon, or earlier, superstition or legend (now lost) relating to a mythical demon or spectre that may have haunted the cliff (shining is corrupted from the Old English scinna 'a spectre'). Turn L, ⑤ following the road uphill (or R for the easy road walk to Milldale). A steady climb leads to a stile R, ascending in a natural gully beside the wall. At the top, go R to the crest of Shining Tor, a simply superb viewpoint of the deeply incised meanderings of the Dove.   Being a devoted user of O.S. maps, I find I must comment on the sloppy register of the green dashes (footpaths) over this section (and I regret at certain other locations, like Coldeaton Dale WALK 23) such lack of care is out of character with their otherwise meticulous professionalism. Walkers who rely exclusively on a trusted O.S. map have every right to expect precision, especially on such a delicate issue affecting the relationship between landowners and map users, who may be given cause to doubt the path on the ground when the green dashes imply a variant course.

continued on facing page

Viator's Bridge

Lode Mill and Wolfscote Dale from Shining Tor

continued from facing page

The path provides delightful views into Milldale and upon Lode Mill, established as a lead smelt works, later a corn mill (mill wheel remains in situ) now redundant. Switching L over a stile **6** (just before the wall starts to decline) following the wall down to the Hanson Toot zigzags, 'toot' means 'lookout'. In the interests of path preservation, keep faithfully to the old way down, resisting any temptation to short-cut the carefully contrived way. At the bottom, cross Viator's Bridge (footbridge): the intriguing name derives from the Latin for 'traveller' and was given this name after a story related in 'The Compleat Angler' about a companion of Charles Cotton's who showed excessive caution in crossing the bridge (the parapets are a quite recent addition).

The hamlet of Milldale nestles serenely in the valley and is the natural focus of ramblers who congregate about the café. The final leg of the journey is in the company of Millway Lane **7**, a joyous traffic-free by-way rising directly into Alstonefield.

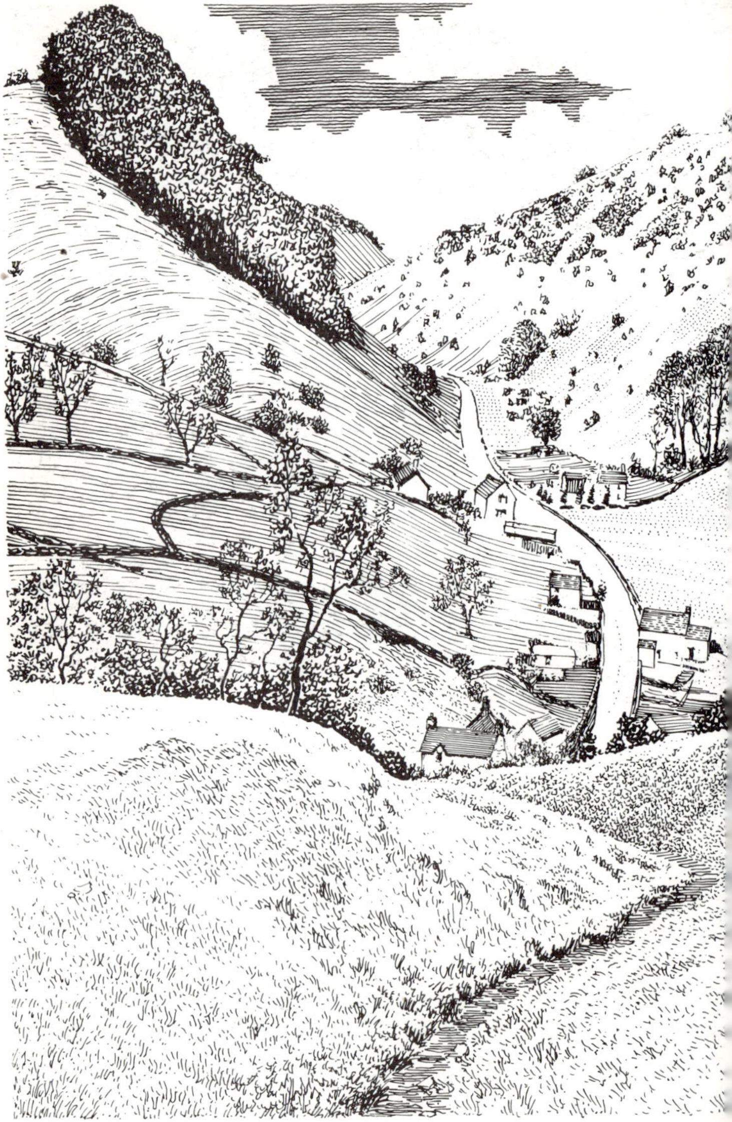

Hope Dale from Hanson Toot

WALK 18
from Alstonefield

MILLDALE
4¾ miles

Although the upper portion of Dove Dale may be better enjoyed from an Alstonefield base, quite the majority of walkers follow the Dove from the National Trust car park beneath Thorpe Cloud, arriving at Milldale to seek refreshment before retracing their steps. The little community of Milldale is understandably a popular resort, this being the only habitation before Hartington with café and loo facilities, so walkers naturally tend to congregate here, perhaps partaking of a cup of tea or ice cream ahead of a saunter back downdale.

This walk is therefore not a common undertaking, which for many devotees will be its greatest appeal. Crammed within small compass, the itinerary misses nothing of merit whilst seeming to walk against the grain of the main valley, yet the whole is surprisingly easily accomplished.

Hopedale, Hall Dale and Nabs Dale, each quite different in character, providing striking contrasts and intimate insights into the dramatic nooks of the parent valley. The valley paths between Viator's Bridge and the Ilam Rock footbridge are marked for the special benefit of visitors who wish only to saunter beside the Dove from the new (1986) car park in Hopedale. Few walkers relish retracing steps, so it is recommended that the downstream march is effected upon the initially undulating and infrequently used true R bank path, returning with the Royal road (path) on the opposite bank.

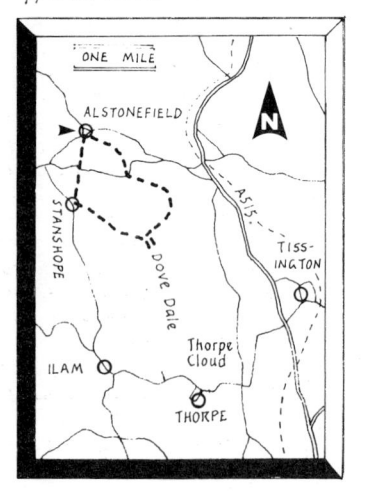

grid ref. 131556

S Leave Alstonefield on the Wetton road. At the junction, go W, take the lane L. Go through the gate opposite the R bend in the lane. Pass through another gate, descend more steeply to a simple wall stile onto the minor road in Hopedale. Cross the road and ascend Brunister Lane, lined with daffodils in springtime. Enter Stanshope, a hamlet of dairy farms, hence the almost permanent whiff of silage and slurry, though the advent of round bale bag silage has brought some degree of amelioration in the pungencies on many farms. **1**

—— continued on facing page

150

Hall Dale

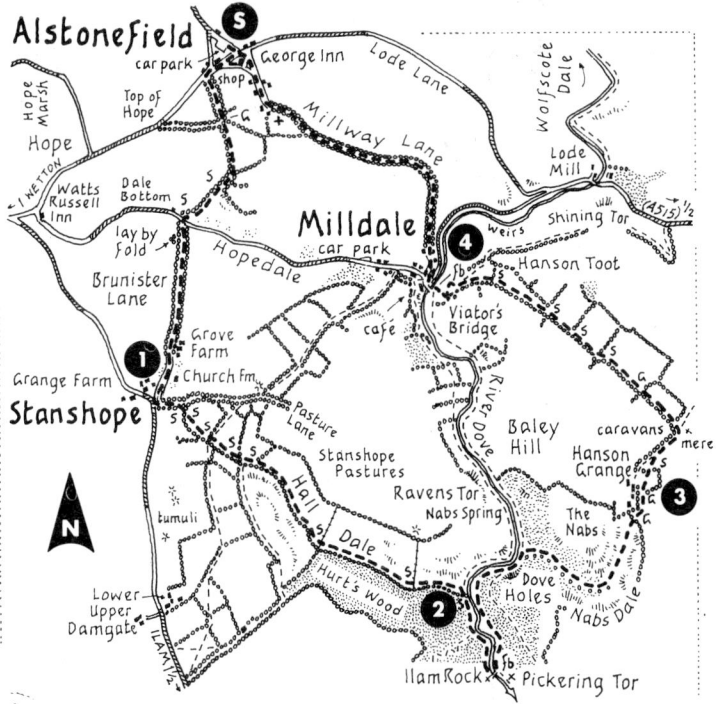

continued from facing page —
Upon meeting the road, proceed L along Pasture Lane, crossing a wall stile on the R after 100 yards. Descending into the shallow valley via a second stile, continue by a further three stiles to enter the rocky narrows of Hall Dale. As mentioned in WALK 6 this dramatic defile owes its name to the fact that it defined the N boundary of the Castern Hall estate while the Hurt family were in residence. evidently, its earlier name was Stanshope, meaning 'narrow sided rocky valley' (see L).

—— continued on page 152

continued from page 151

The dale twists, and with mounting anticipation falls through a defile beneath Hurt's Wood, crossing two fence stiles to arrive upon the Dove. ❷ Go R through the squeeze stile and just subsequent to the departure of the Ilam path (via Air Cottage) into a re-entrant, the fantastic twin pinnacles of Ilam Rock and Pickering Tor come into view. Ilam Rock, so named because it was a major landmark on the parish boundary, is a towering, slightly tilted flake, some 80' high and quite the most splendid example of its kind in the White Peak. Near its base is a small phreatic chamber cave of little merit, a more open version across the valley directly beneath Pickering Tor is easily reached up the bank from the footbridge. Pickering Tor, appears to be a late name, though it is tempting to suggest that it too was a boundary-name meaning 'rock of the people of the Peak'.

Ravens Tor

From the footbridge, go L, proceeding upstream past Dove Holes, two large phreatic caverns devoid of secret passages but grand shelters if you are caught unawares by a sudden shower. Branch R from the main valley path up into Nabs Dale, a short cragbound hollow rising to a gate. Advance to a gate ❸ keeping above the Hanson Grange farm buildings to a wall stile. The place-name Hanson has radically altered down the years since first recorded and it is suggested it comes from 'Hÿnci's hill'; Grange derives from the monastic landownings of Burton Abbey. Joining the farm access track, go R to the wall end, near the mere, then turn L, passing the occasionally parked caravans, via gates/stiles to Hanson Toot.

—— *continued on facing page*

continued from facing page

A toot was a 'lookout' and present-day travellers arriving at this location will surely take pleasure in the intimate view into Hopedale and upon the tiny community of Milldale. Descend the old zig-zagging way to Viator's Bridge. This unusual and attractive name originates from a companion of Charles Cotton, who is described in 'The Compleat Angler' as 'Viator'(from the Latin for 'traveller'). Cotton recounts an incident when riding beside the Dove: upon reaching the packhorse bridge his companion dismounted in horror at the prospect of negotiating such a precariously narrow structure. Eventually, following much discussion and complaint, Viator gingerly crossed on hands and knees. If you inspect the sides of the bridge it will be noticed that the parapet is a late addition, nonetheless Viator's caution seems a trifle excessive! The second arch spans a mill-race cut to power the almost lost mill; now the only grinding is of boots upon the cobbles.

The happy journey concludes very pleasurably in the company of Millway Lane, initially, passing the modern holiday conversion, a short row of traditional cottages where a cat may be seen basking itself in the afternoon sun, and the Methodist Chapel of 1835 with the thought-provoking notice 'Look around you, come in and give thanks.' ❹

Millway Lane nearing Alstonefield

153

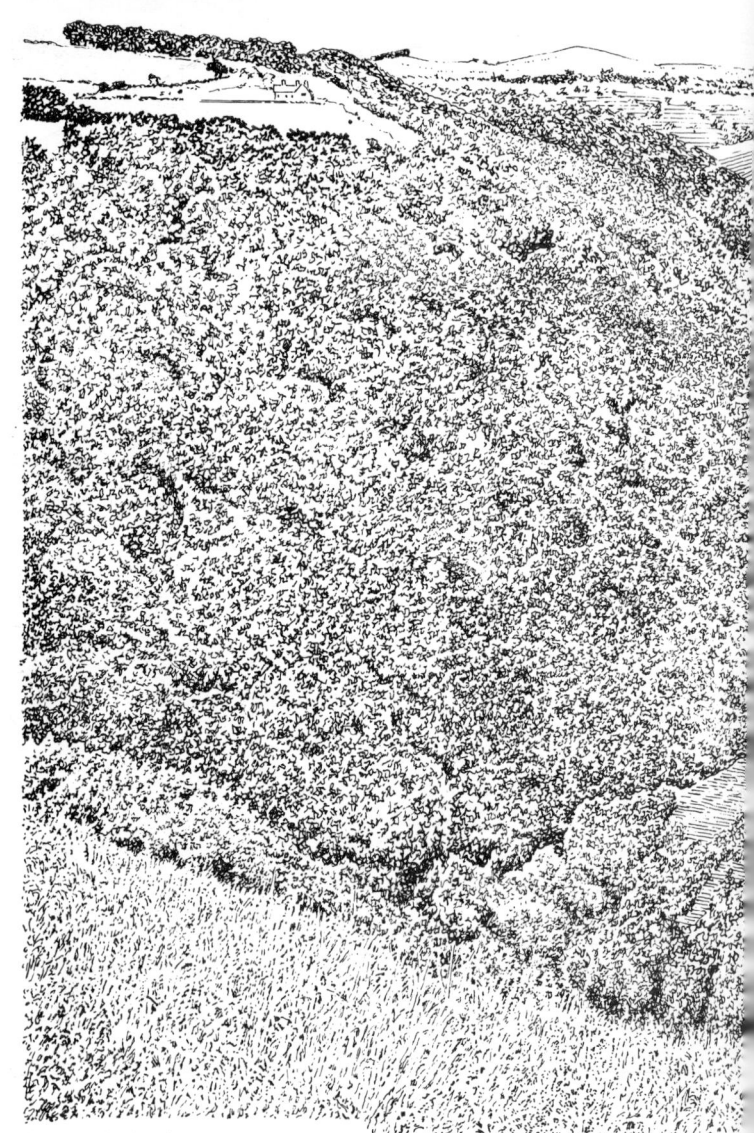

Dove Dale from Bunster Hill

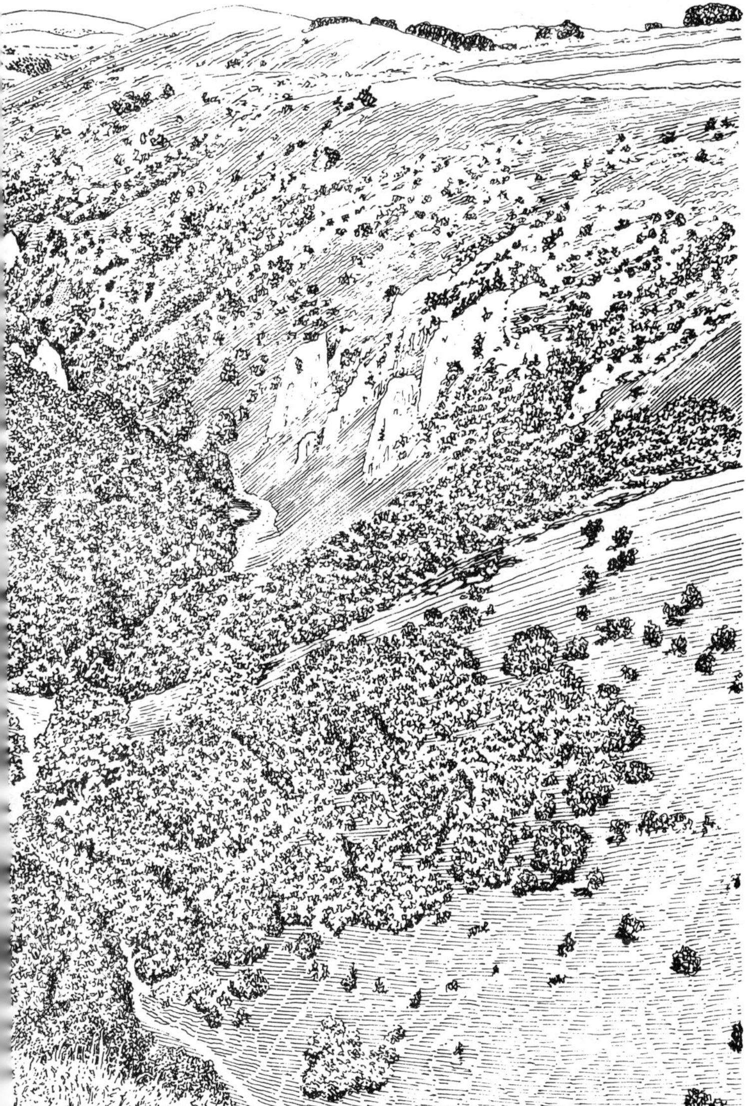

WALK 19   DOVE DALE
from the Dove Dale car park, near Thorpe

For sustained drama and sylvan beauty, there is no comparable reach of dale in the White Peak to rival Dove Dale. From its source, the Dove valley pulsates with scenic variety, the river acting both as a geological and county boundary. Downstream from Hartington the river intrudes into the great mass of reef, and associated, limestones as an almost continuous gorge. Yet it is not until the triumphal passage between Milldale and Thorpe Cloud that the valley proudly bares the particular name Dove Dale - a romantic crescendo of exciting rock formations amid ancient woodland. Come rain or shine, this compelling attraction ensures a steady flow of visitors patronising the Dove Dale car park, the prime rendezvous for explorations and gentle strolls alike. Walkers determined to see the very best of Dove Dale are encouraged not merely to stride N to Milldale and beyond upon the valley path, but to venture with respectful care onto the high ground on either flank. To assist recognition of the most favourable options (identified by letters) the environs of Dove Dale have been researched to give walkers the liberty to choose how they advance and return.

VALLEY PATH TO MILLDALE:
grid ref. 146508

2¾ miles

S   Leave the Dove Dale car park past the refreshment caravan* and Trent Water Authority flow meter. The sense of entering a totally new landscape is profound, the threshold where highland Britain confronts the gently rolling pasturelands, where hedgerows are replaced by drystone walls, and where the pulse races with anticipation of great things to come. The tame present-day stream was not responsible for creating this impressive gorge. It was produced by a raging torrent fed from glacial

——— continued on page 158

* not always in-situ.

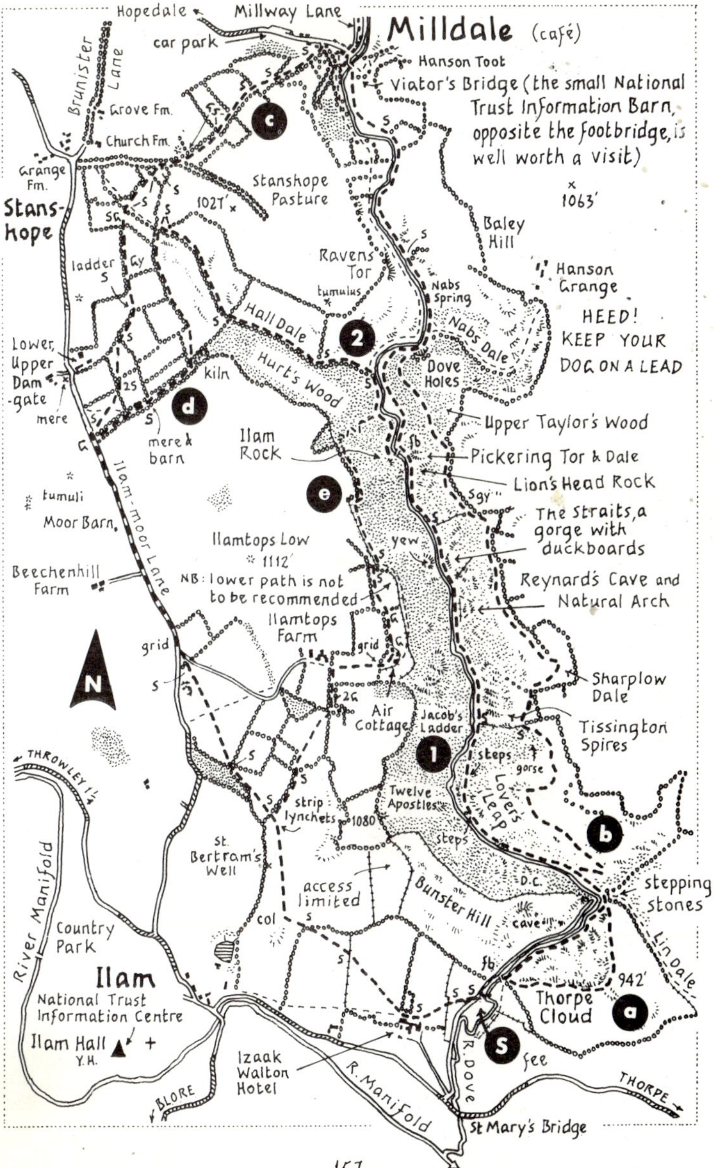
Milldale (café)
Hopedale
Millway Lane
car park
Hanson Toot
Viator's Bridge (the small National Trust Information Barn, opposite the footbridge, is well worth a visit)
Brunister Lane
Grove Fm.
Church Fm.
Grange Fm.
Stanshope
Stanshope Pasture
1027'
1063'
Baley Hill
Ravens Tor
tumulus
Hanson Grange
Nabs Spring
Nabs Dale
HEED! KEEP YOUR DOG ON A LEAD
Hall Dale
Hurt's Wood
Dove Holes
ladder
Lower, Upper Dam -gate
mere
kiln
mere & barn
Upper Taylor's Wood
Ilam Rock
Pickering Tor & Dale
Lion's Head Rock
tumuli
Moor Barn
Ilam-moor Lane
Ilamtops Low
1112'
The Straits, a gorge with duckboards
yew
Beechenhill Farm
NB: lower path is not to be recommended
Reynard's Cave and Natural Arch
Ilamtops Farm
grid
Sharplow Dale
N
Air Cottage
Jacob's Ladder
Tissington Spires
steps
gorse
THROWLEY 1¼
Lovers Leap
strip lynchets
1080
Twelve Apostles
St. Bertram's Well
access limited
Bunster Hill
stepping stones
col
cave
Lin Dale
River Manifold
Country Park
Ilam
National Trust Information Centre
Ilam Hall Y.H.
942'
Thorpe Cloud
Izaak Walton Hotel
R. Manifold
R. Dove
fee
BLORE
THORPE
St Mary's Bridge

continued from page 156 ─────────

meltwater sculpting a course through a hard, little yielding rock. If the river is running strongly then do not hesitate cross the footbridge R forthwith and proceed beneath Thorpe Cloud's steep W face. Should the river be in summer flow, then continue along the road beneath Bunster Hill to the famous stepping stones (a Victorian embellishment, as too are the fishing weirs which impound shallow sheets of water when, during periods of drought, the river is inclined to be reduced to a trickle).   The stepping stones have a common fascination; notice the cross-sections of brachiopod and crinoid fossils in the square cut stones. They pose no problems except when partially or wholly covered by water, or perhaps for participants in the Dovedale Dash!

A word of advice if the Bunster Hill ridge walk is likely to be considered later in the day during the return. You will notice that there is a rocky corner overlooking the stepping stones: this forms the final step off the ridge and whilst it can be descended with a spot of mild scrambling it is probably more sensible to keep R thereby completely avoiding such hazards.

The reef limestone wall of Bunster Hill forces a wedge into the valley causing the river to turn on the stepping stones from NE to NW. The valley path was radically 'improved' in 1984, some say damaging the aesthetic charm of the dale. However, with the sheer numbers of feet that regularly pound this way, effective action was necessary - time will mellow the presently obvious track.

───── *continued on facing page*

Dove Dale stepping stones from the summit of Thorpe Cloud

continued from facing page ―――

  Proceeding along the level valley path, lightly fenced to allow vegative recovery to the river bank, admire the first towering crags on the Staffordshire side, Dovedale Castle Rocks (D.C. on the map)-a subliminal presage. The gentle rise, upon rusticated steps, onto the Lover's Leap headland is accompanied by fine views of the Twelve Apostles, a cluster of rock towers amid the ash woods (partially cleared by the N.T.).

――― *continued on page 160*

Tissington Spires

continued from page 159

The Lover's Leap viewpoint affords the one and only raised prospect of the gorge from the otherwise purely valley bottom stroll. Foliage denies it a rating as a spectacle with only Tissington Spires, bedecked with yew shrubs, making a show above the ash thicket.

❶ Journeying on from the rocky knoll, a corresponding flight of steps leads down to the riverside once more. Soon Tissington Spires (so named because they are major landmarks upon this parish boundary as Ilam Rock is to Ilam and Pickering Tor to Newton Grange) claim attention R (see illustration L). This series of impressive reef limestone pinnacles and flakes, set slightly askew to the valley, have recently been made more visible by an expedient clearance of the invading ashwood by the National Trust.

On the Staffordshire W bank, the solitary Jacob's Ladder buttress stands guard; this tower is best viewed in silhouette looking S - it's alternative name is Dovedale Church.   Visitors of modern times see Dove Dale as a whole exquisite entity but historically, people have addressed the gorge differently, as a dividing line marking out a rigid demarcation of land ownership. Whilst it was once the practice to beat the parish bounds stopping at strategic points to read extracts from the bible which occasionally led to natural features gaining biblical names, the age of romantic travel writing from the late C18th is probably more likely to have been responsible for the several biblical references here. Writers especially prone to exaggeration found 'the good book' a powerful ally with which to impress early tourists of the awful splendour of Dove Dale.   The river-name Dove comes from dubo, one of only a handful of remnants from the archaic pre-Saxon language, meaning 'black'. Though the full length of the valley may once have borne the name Dove Dale, the retraction may well be due to the fact that it owes its origins to the dark, shadowy

———— continued on page 162

Air Cottage from Reynard's Cave

The Straits

Lion's Head Rock

continued from page 160

nature of its passage through this gorge. Farther on, the Natural Arch comes into view up the scree R. The more inquisitive are unlikely to resist the temptation of scrambling up to peer through to Reynard's Cave, itself easily reached up the gully. The name clearly derives from the former occupancy of foxes, now made impossible by the too frequent visits of humanoids! The view out of the shallow cave focusses upon Air Cottage on the skyline; seen as if looking over a gun barrel pointed at the river (Natural Arch), the sights being a notch above the Arch (see illustration on page 161).

The dale draws tight at The Straits with vertical crags overbearing to such an extent that the path has necessarily been set upon duckboards. The ravine is draped by a vigorous growth of yew. A resurgence, once used as a water supply, emits from a cave in an alcove at the end of the constricted passage (see above L). Beyond the second stile (after Lover's Leap), the path passes close under Lion's Head Rock (see above R), which bears uncanny likeness to that noble king of beasts. Perched precariously high above at this point is the Watchbox, the rocking stone of Dove Dale (better seen from a little farther N, looking back - see facing drawing).

Pickering Tor rears up to the R. and, whilst walkers may clamber up to the simple single chamber cave, their attention is more likely to be directed to Ilam Rock diagonally opposite. This tantalising tilted pike of reef limestone, of remarkably slender proportions, is arguably the supreme distillation of the dale's many natural wonders.

―――― *continued on page 164*

At the heart of Dove Dale - the Pickering Tor/Ilam Rock gorge

continued from page 162

② Keeping to the true L bank the path swings E to the Dove Holes. These two large water-worn caves come as quite a surprise, the first one looking like a giant yawning mouth. The small natural arch across the river must be a remnant of an associated phreatic system linked to Dove Holes. Again the valley switches N, with the ashwoods thinning out beyond the junction with Nabs Dale. Whilst strictly this more open section of the valley is not Dove Dale, the beauty does not diminish. Passing the Nabs Spring cressbeds, Raven's Tor commands attention. Walled enclosures make an appearance on the Staffordshire side, claiming sheltered pastureland on the rare easier slopes.

Milldale is reached following a delightful pastoral passage to cross Viator's Bridge (sometimes called Wheelbarrow Bridge), a former packhorse bridge across the Dove.

Pickering Tor

Dove Holes

Ilam Rock

TRAVERSE OF THORPE CLOUD:

½ mile grid ref. 148 510 942'
500' of ascent
—and descent!

(a) The village of Thorpe grew up from being an outlying farmstead linked with Mappleton, the steep banks of unenclosed Thorpe Pasture offering only sheep grazing on a grand scale. Thorpe Cloud may be of modest elevation but its endearing qualities are profuse and few with red blood in their veins would resist its challenge. This mountain in miniature is inextricably linked with the village, though most ascents begin conveniently from Dove Dale.

WEAR STOUT FOOTWEAR — Cross the footbridge and negotiate the initial rocky knot; thereafter the ascent is simple keeping reasonably near the predominantly grassy ridge. Climb at a steady rate and satisfy yourself that each subtle change in the view is noted, for the bare rock summit is all too soon underfoot. The hill's name Cloud is not a direct elemental reference yet, whilst it derives from the Old English clūd meaning 'rock', the later development to imply its susceptibility to mist is not an uncommon corruption. The summit is bereft of a cairn, as such would never survive the attentions of juvenile visitors. The view of Dove Dale is somewhat disappointing, though Air Cottage and Alstonefield church are prominent, the latter backed by Narrowdale Hill, the trees on Pea Low and Gratton Hill, with Baley Hill a little farther R. Descend the exciting N ridge to the stepping stones with the utmost care! Do not disturb stones or sheep.

Dove Dale from the summit of Thorpe Cloud

Thorpe Cloud from Bunster Hill

DOVE DALE'S EASTERN SKYLINE ROUTE :

grid ref. 152514   950'
1¾ miles

b This high level advance up the dale commands the attention of all discerning walkers who would welcome an opportunity to break from the gregarious gaggle beside the river. A whole new perspective is revealed with superb views and comparative peace is a cherished reward.

A narrow, yet distinct path strikes R from the level valley path shortly after the stone wall stile beyond the stepping stones. This kinks L, gradually gaining height onto the Sharplow ridge, where the path is lost in the turf. Crossing the ridge, it is a simple process to contour round the shallow re-entrant dry valley, keeping above the gorse scrub, to a stile at the end of the wall. Maintain height with views down on Tissington Spires, slanting R to the wall corner crossing the broken wall. Sharplow Dale makes a deep incursion into the main valley; again contour rising latterly to traverse adjacent to the wall, ① glancing occasionally down the fantastic edge. Descend into the third re-entrant valley to a stile in a narrow gateway. Keep near the wall till this rises R. Here, at the head of tiny Pickering Dale, follow the clear path slanting gently L down through Upper Taylor's Wood in tunnel fashion. With one notable glimpse into Hall Dale to relish, the old way declines to the Dove Holes.

ILAM MOOR ROUTE :
from Milldale

3 miles

grid ref. 139547   995'

c Milldale, nestling serenely in a deep fold of the limestone plateau has long served Alstonefield and the surrounding district as both a bridging point, enabling cross-valley communication and, obviously, as an important mill site. The demise of such milling operations may have deprived the hamlet of its former purpose, yet its dignity is secured within its present-day rôle in low-key service to a steady flow of appreciative ramblers and amblers who value the shy beauty of the place.

Probably the overwhelming majority of walkers arriving at Milldale from the Dove Dale car park will be content to turn about, retracing their steps downdale, rejoicing anew at the changing effects of light and shade within this magical pageant of nature's inspiration. Whilst this can be varied initially by following the true R bank path from behind the café to the Ilam Rock footbridge, though this seldom trodden

―――― continued on facing page

continued from facing page ————

way is inclined to be boggy in places, the emphasis will be on the well-made path. Fortunate walkers with their transport prior arranged continue N with the Dove delving through Wolfscote and Beresford Dales to finish at Hartington. Yet there is no small pleasure in rising over Ilam Moor as described below.

Walk along the Hopedale road, turning L up the narrow lane past a cottage (do not follow the branch lane L); keep within the upward dale, from the squeeze stile, to reach the stile at the top.

The footpath advances via a stile then three stiles/gates to join the Stanshope Pasture Lane (footpath sign), going R. Turn L beyond the dead Wych Elm (which might not be there when you pass!). Descend by a stile into the valley bottom (the head of Hall Dale), crossing directly over to a stile rising to stile/gate, thereafter following a wall by a gateway. Keep straight on where the wall ① curves R to a ladder stile. Again, follow the wall to a stile then slant L uphill to a stile in the field corner rising to a stile R, thereafter crossing the next field diagonally to a stile onto the Ilam-moor Road going L. Crossing the brow, admire the broad sweeping prospect across the Manifold valley and, too, the sympathetic conversion and garden tree plantings of Moor Barn.

Cross the cattle grid L with the unenclosed road to Ilam Tops and Air Cottage (B&B), branch R after the gateway contour the ② pasture keeping above the old quarry, and drop to a stile at the end of Moor Plantation (ash, sycamore and beech). The path traverses an area of strip lynchets, clear proof that the Ilam Vale was once

———— *continued on page 170*

Thorpe Cloud

continued from page 169 ─────

heavily cultivated (notice the ridge & furrow in the pastures below), the pressure of demand causing this S facing scarp bank to come under the plough. All these traces of cultivation pre-date the existing village which belongs exclusively to the Alpine fantasy of Jesse Watts-Russell in the 1830s. The path continues under the steep W flank of Bunster Hill to a col, thereafter descending to a stile. Cross the enclosure to a fence stile, beyond reach a stile at the rear of the Izaak Walton Hotel. Angle L to a stile near a gate (see illustration on page) concluding at a stile opposite the entrance to the National Trust car park ③.

HALL DALE ROUTE:

d Although Dove Holes mark a natural end of the Dove Dale gorge, Ilam Rock is the point of decision for walkers, for there are two good paths available for an interesting alternative return, via Hall Dale or Air Cottage.

1¼ miles   grid ref. 143 531   990'

Cross the footbridge, adhering to the sometimes muddy path to a wall stile at the foot of Hall Dale. Turn L up the dry valley, an attractive cragbound defile which derives its name from the fact that it defined the old N limit of the Castern Hall estate. Immediately after the third stile turn L, crossing a crude stile, and mount the very steep valley side path beside a wall. At the top, a ① detour offers the opportunity of a glimpse down into Hall Dale. Entering a green lane R, proceed via a ladder stile and an old barn to join the Ilam-moor road at a gate (here consult route **c**

AIR COTTAGE ROUTE:

e The footpath still shown on O.S. maps rising directly behind Ilam Rock has prudently been re-routed, so do not use that mud slide of a path. Instead, after crossing the Ilam Rock footbridge, follow the true R bank path curving R, L and at the next R bend of the river divert L up into Hurt's Wood (waymarked path). The new path is sensibly graded and stepped to minimise erosion problems up into the shallow re-entrant. New stock fencing erected by the National Trust helps define walkers limits too, so at the top, keep just inside the wood, threading through the trees, catching glimpses down upon the rocks about Pickering Dale, eventually reaching a ladder stile R, promptly followed by a second giving access to the farm track. The footpath shown on O.S. maps keeping dale side of the field

1½ miles   grid ref. 143 531   1010'

───── *continued on facing page*

continued from facing page ───────

boundary is no pleasure to walk. In any case, respecting the Trust's desire to keep certain areas of the old Dove Dale ash woods inviolate wilderness, please refrain from using this path or attempting to make a course inside the woods to Bunster Hill. The farm track leads via two gates through the farmyard and past Air Cottage, superbly perched upon the brink overlooking Dove Dale as if 'on air', especially so when the valley is filled with morning mist. Cross the cattle grid and follow the access road ① towards llamtops Farm, branching L before the road gate, along the track into a short lane to a barn. From the gate go R through a second gate, now descending the pasture to a stile, thereafter following the wall steeply down to join route ❻ at the strip lynchets under Bunster Hill.

Thorpe Cloud

The Dove Valley at Mappleton

featuring Okeover Hall, Bunster Hill and Thorpe Cloud

WALK 20   DOVE DALE APPROACH

from Mapleton Lane, Ashbourne   8 miles

The handsome little market town of Ashbourne stands strategically close to the interface of lowland and highland England. Traffic from the Midlands, drawn to the scenic excitements of the Peak District, is channelled through this charming town — which thereby undergoes a Jekyll and Hyde transformation on sunny Bank Holidays into a bottleneck to be avoided.

Bountiful returns may be had on time invested, prior to embarking on this walk, in exploring Ashbourne. a notable feature is the church of St.Oswald, standing impressively at the W end of Church Street beyond the old Grammar School, which too has considerable architectural merit. The main shopping area of St John Street and Market Street focus on the cobbled Market Square with its fine surround of buildings in brick and stone. The old town is built upon the steep southern slopes of a ridge above the Henmore Brook, over a mile E of the Dove at Hanging Bridge.

To reach the beginning of the walk, take the minor road for Mapleton. This crosses the Bellevue ridge out of Ashbourne, from where the entry into farmland is sudden and quite a joy. Despite the undoubted charms of dear old Ashbourne, the enticing prospect of the superb river scenery beside the Dove, combined with the easy walking along the Tissington Trail, make this a worthwhile venture in any season.

The Mapleton Lane car park and picnic area, by the blocked railway tunnel, is signposted R. The Peak Park run cycle hire facilities from this terminal point and, for many visitors, this proves to be the most satisfactory way to enjoy the Trail. Yet the real glories of this countryside are, as always, a gift to the walker, unshackled by gadgetry, breathing in the liberty of field paths and river meadows, free to diverge from the Trail where footpaths and fancy may together lead.

Locals have it that Mapleton is spelt with two p's, so in deference to their right to differ, I have given both forms.

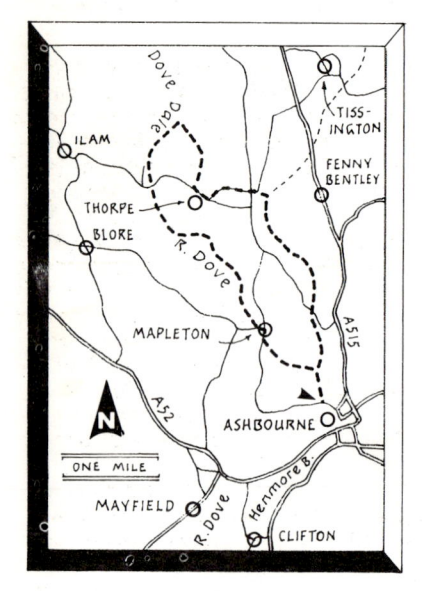

grid ref. 176 469   685'
                        500
feet
miles 1 2 3 4 5 6 7 8

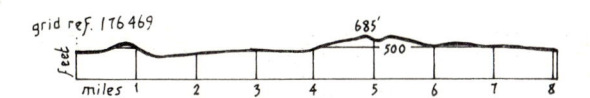

(S) Advance N along the Trail. The former railway bridge over Bentley Brook has been replaced by a low structure, therefore the track drops and rises (with gates at either end) at this point. Immediately a footpath from Ashbourne (which arises out of the Market Place via the steep ginnel called The Channel) crosses the track, and here our route branches L down steps: a stile gives access to the footpath to Map(p)leton. After the fourth stile, a fine view opens up to Okeover Hall and to Thorpe Cloud, the prime objective of this walk. Crossing the pasture to a stile, follow the hedge down to a wet gap; here turn R under the banked hedge. Looking SW, the extensive strip lynchet terracing at Upper Mayfield catches the eye, whilst at hand Map(p)leton is well seen. **(1)** Two stiles in quick succession lead to a hillside of ridge and furrow; slant L to a stile into a narrow passage onto the village street. To the L is the Post Office/shop, but we turn R to pass the Okeover Arms, taking the footpath L just before the parish church of St. Mary. This unusual church (circa 1750) was the product of James Gibbs, a pupil of Sir Christopher Wren.

Evidence that this locality has long been well endowed with trees is shown both by the name Mapleton 'farmstead amongst the maple trees' and Okeover 'bank abundant with oaks'. Proceed towards Okeover Bridge, crossing the road (not the bridge) by facing stiles. Henceforward, the route adopts the riverside path, upstream with the sylvan Dove. Two stiles and a gateway on the river kinks L, here cut across the meadow to a gateway, do not keep to the bank past the weir; otherwise orientation is governed by the vagaries of the river, facilitated by stiles **(2)**. Heed the notice approaching Dove Cottage, for the right of way steers away from the riverbank and through the farmyard. This cottage, dated 1867 above the door, has an arcadian air with free-range ducks, geese, poultry and goats (notice the goat weathervane). Keep dogs under firm control. The path advances to a gate, then up a track to Coldwall Bridge, a well buttressed structure. In Victorian days, the approach route to the awful splendours of Dove Dale for the gentry and fashionable travellers lay via this bridge. The imagination can quite easily be marshalled to consider the clatter of hooves and creaking coaches negotiating the cobbled way en route for Thorpe. N of the bridge, the narrow meadow is heavily used by bovine hooves, making pedestrian progress oft times less than swift. **(3)** The going improves

——— continued on page 176

continued from page 175

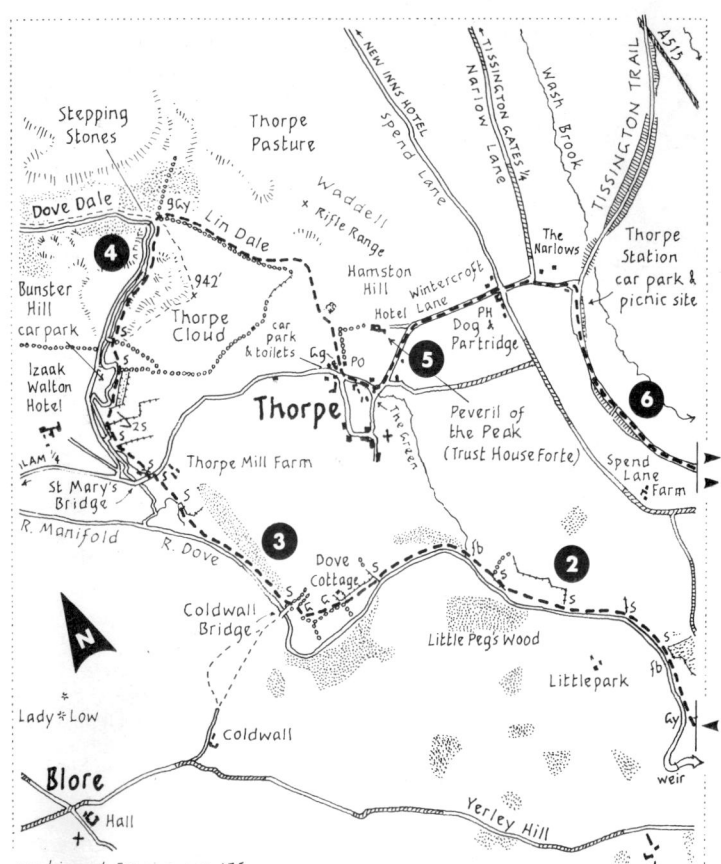

approaching Thorpe Mill Farm, with a stile then a gate leading across meadowland to the minor road between Ilam and Thorpe. Turn L, and R down the short lane to a barn, seeking a stile R. Go L to a stile, in the corner of the field next to the Dove. From the ensuing stile slant R from the river to a stile into a fenced passage between the Dove and a plantation strip. Across the river is the large and invariably well-patronised (privately run) car park, ideally landscaped into a loop of the Dove. The route keeps to the E bank, entering, at a stile, the Dove Dale gorge between Bunster Hill and Thorpe Cloud adjacent to the unsightly water flow monitoring station.

continued on facing page

176

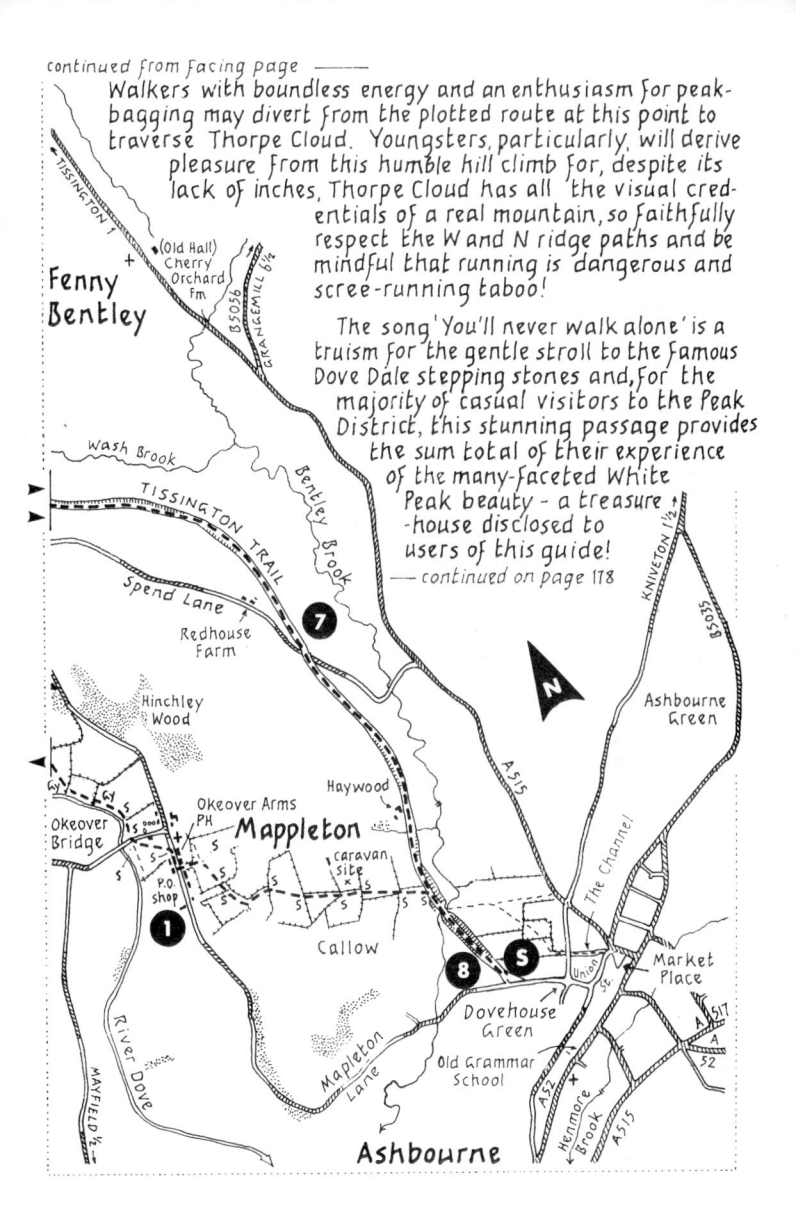

continued from facing page

Walkers with boundless energy and an enthusiasm for peak-bagging may divert from the plotted route at this point to traverse Thorpe Cloud. Youngsters, particularly, will derive pleasure from this humble hill climb for, despite its lack of inches, Thorpe Cloud has all the visual credentials of a real mountain, so faithfully respect the W and N ridge paths and be mindful that running is dangerous and scree-running taboo!

The song 'You'll never walk alone' is a truism for the gentle stroll to the famous Dove Dale stepping stones and, for the majority of casual visitors to the Peak District, this stunning passage provides the sum total of their experience of the many-faceted White Peak beauty - a treasure-house disclosed to users of this guide!

— *continued on page 178*

Hazelton Clump from Thorpe Cloud

continued from page 177 ————

4 Accessible cave systems in the Peakland limestones are not as prevalent as in the Yorkshire Dales. Many are shallow affairs, high and dry, formed aeons ago before the valleys were cut to the present depth by the ice age meltwaters. The cave spotted up to the L is a shallow rift feature, whilst farther up the dale, more impressive former caverns exist - Reynard's Cave and Dove Holes.

The route departs (regretfully prematurely) from the depths of Dove Dale via Lin Dale rising over the watershed under Hamston Hill. Red flags flying here warn of the rifle range over the brow in Waddell, which should be sufficient deterrent to anyone tempted to ramble over Thorpe Pastures! Passing the old quarry (dump), follow the track to a gate into the car park (short-term stay); upon reaching the road, go L. Alternatively, go forward for a preambulation around Thorpe village, visiting the parish church of St Leonard with its early Norman tower. The Saxon name Thorpe meant 'outlying farmstead' (of Mapleton), suggesting that, as a village, it developed late in Dark Age terms, but yet was substantial enough soon after the Norman Conquest to merit a stone-built church. The ubiquitous use of herbicides and artificial fertilizers in modern agriculture has made precious havens out of such sanctuaries as churchyards where a diversity of flora may dwell inviolate. Within Thorpe church porch is posted a list of 32 wild flowers that grow in this churchyard. In an age when the importance of conserving a wide-ranging stock of plants is being increasingly recognised, such records are of especial value and to be encouraged.

———— continued on facing page

Thorpe Church

Wild flowers of this churchyard:-

GROUND ELDER
WOOD GARLIC
COW PARSLEY
LORDS & LADIES
DAISY
HAIRY BITTER CRESS
MOUSE-EAR CHICKWEED
OX-EYE DAISY
PIGNUT
GOOSE GRASS
SHINING CRANESBILL
IVY
WHITE DEAD NETTLE
BUTTERBUR
PRIMROSE
LESSER CELANDINE
COMMON SORREL
ELDER
RAGWORT
GROUNDSEL
CHICKWEED
DANDELION
STINGING NETTLE

BUSH VETCH
ROUND-LEAVED SPEEDWELL
WALL RUE
WILD STRAWBERRY
HERB ROBERT
COW PARSNIP
WOOD FORGET-ME-NOT
RIBWORT PLANTAIN
GOLDILOCKS

Primrose

continued from facing page ─────

At The Green, go R with the plotted route along the road, **5** passing the Peveril of the Peak Hotel. Assisted by a pavement along Wintercroft Lane, reach the Dog & Partridge (public house) crossroads. Cross Spend Lane (Old English for 'fenced strip of land') the former main Ashbourne road, superseded by the present A515 via Tissington Gates and Fenny Bentley. Advance down the signposted lane to the former Thorpe Station yard, a car park/picnic site serving the Tissington Trail. Turn R, accompanying the Trail for the final 2¼ miles to Mapleton Lane car park. **678** The views from this stretch of old trackbed are not comparable with sections followed farther N, nonetheless it is nowhere unattractive and there is considerable scope for consolidating a steady relaxing pace.

Thorpe Cloud and Lin Dale

Newhaven Tunnel

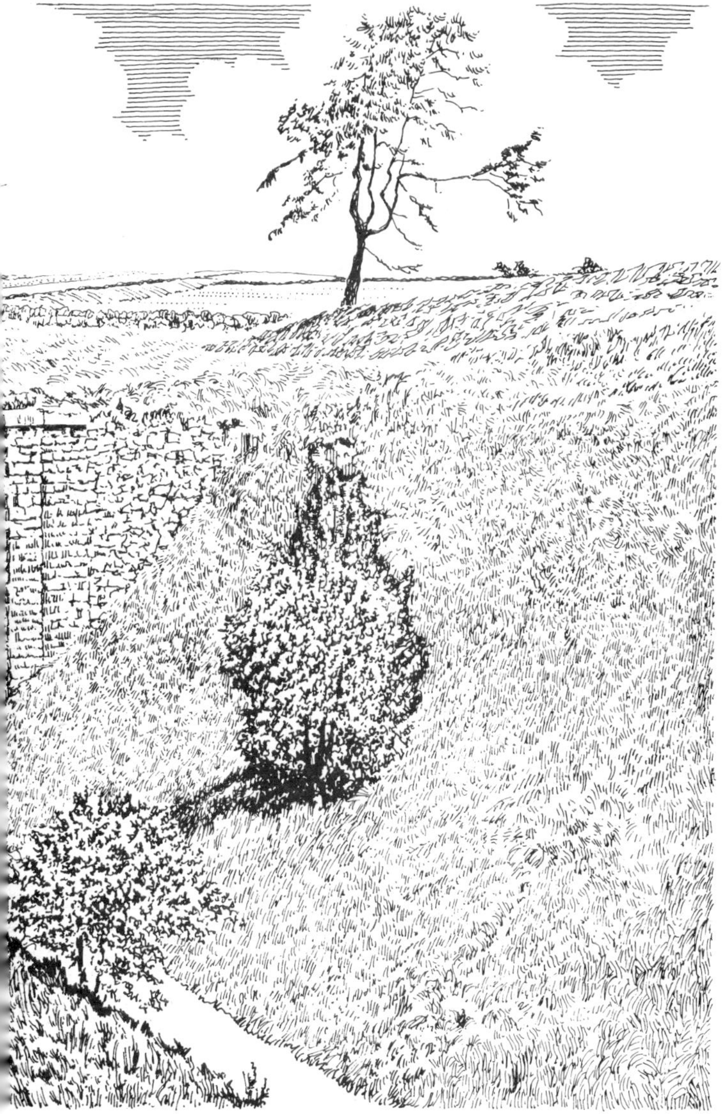

WALK 21   TRAIL WALKING
from Parsley Hay   3½ miles

Parsley Hay (enclosure where parsley grew) is the hub of casual visitor activity upon the high plateau S of Buxton. Here the National Park, slightly at variance with their non-profit-making brief, operates a very successful cycle-hire service, apparently meeting a growing need among non-walkers, particularly family groups. Trails lead off in three directions from this former junction: the High Peak Trail is founded upon the older railway created by canal engineers with tight corners and steep inclines, whereas the later southern branch line sweeps with gay abandon in gentle decline to Ashbourne and is known as the Tissington Trail.

S From the car park, walk S taking the R fork from the High Peak Trail, signposted Ashbourne and Hartington. Five forms of Carboniferous Limestone are encountered on this short outing. The initial Monsal Dale limestone of the Parsley Hay locality is replaced by almost level bedded Bee Low limestones within the deep cutting ahead. This is the sort of craggy cutting that elevates even the most docile uninterested walker into a rockhound in search of fossils. In this instance it may prove a temporary enthusiasm, for there turns out to be a dearth: never fear, there are better sites ahead to rekindle your interest. Beyond the cutting, Woo Dale limestones form the basis of the scenery, with views from the embankment down the aptly-named Long Dale.

1 After Hartington Moor Farm, a second, considerably more interesting cutting is entered with the junction of Woo Dale and Bee Low limestones well-defined by a ramp bedding plane. The last cutting before the Hand Dale viaduct is laden with fossils - brachiopods and crinoids in profusion.

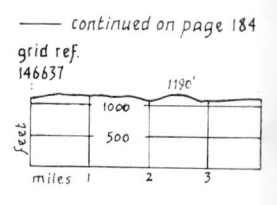

—— continued on page 184

grid ref. 146637

182

typical crinoidal limestone

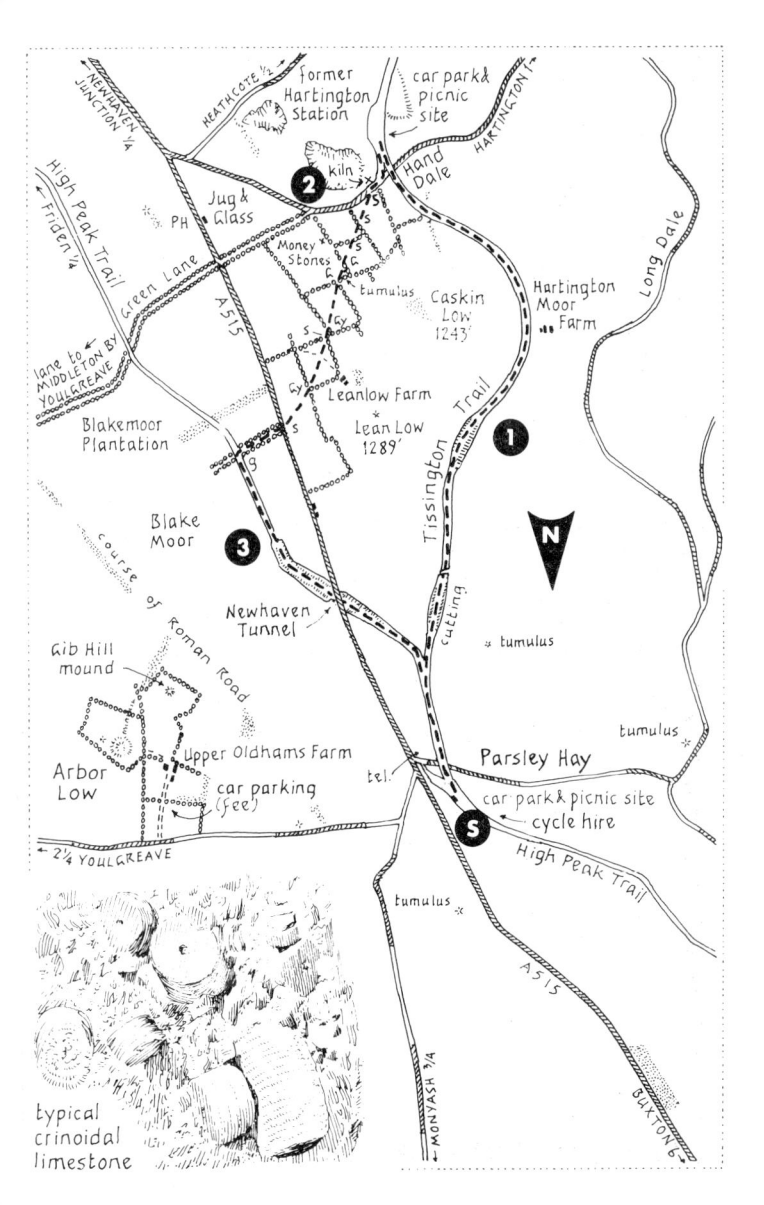

183

Old lime kiln

continued from page 182

Just beyond the Hand Dale viaduct, go L by the old Hartington Station signalbox (National Park information centre/toilets), descending with the access road to the B5054. Go R by the large old lime kiln, cross the road to a humble wall stile (footpath sign). Advance up the pasture diagonally to a stile, ❷ maintain course to a second stile, beyond which pass through a gate (notice the robbed, or at least crudely excavated, burial mound L, marked 'tumulus' on the map, known as Money (many) Stones). From the next gate, take a long diagonal to a gateway, then a stile at a wall corner (do not follow the track up to Leanlow Farm). A second long diagonal, crossing the Leanlow drive, reaches a gateway in the corner. Field boundaries have been removed in the subsequent field, yet the stile onto the A515 is easily located opposite the Blakemoor lane. With caution, cross this busy truck road into the lane to rejoin the High Peak Trail L at a gate.

❸ The walk enters a long cutting at a sharply-angled bend typical of the High Peak Trail, advancing to the Newhaven Tunnel (51 yards long). Notice the plaques positioned above the arches at each end. The first plaque shows a four-wheeled wagon and beneath it the Latin motto 'Divina Palladia Arte' (By the divine skill of Palle

continued on facing page

continued from facing page

or Minerva, the Greek goddess of engineering). Around it is a circular inscription: Cromford & Highpeak Railway Compy Incorporated 1825. Above is inscribed Jos^s Jessop Esqr Engineer and below Wm Brittlebank Esqr (he was solicitor to the railway company until 1855, and lived at Oddo House, Winster). At the N end is depicted a wagon surrounded by the words 'Cromford & Highpeak Railway 1825' and in the corners the letters 'PH & Co.' thought to be the initials of the constructors (which is odd because Porteous & Co are the only known contractors involved). The walk comes to its happy conclusion after re-uniting with the Tissington Trail.

<u>NB</u> The route map also serves to show how cyclists may complete a delightful short-circuit, using the Middleton lane E from Hand Dale, with the Jug & Glass a handy halfway house!

First cutting south of Parsley Hay on the Tissington Trail

Cycle hire centre at Parsley Hay Wharf

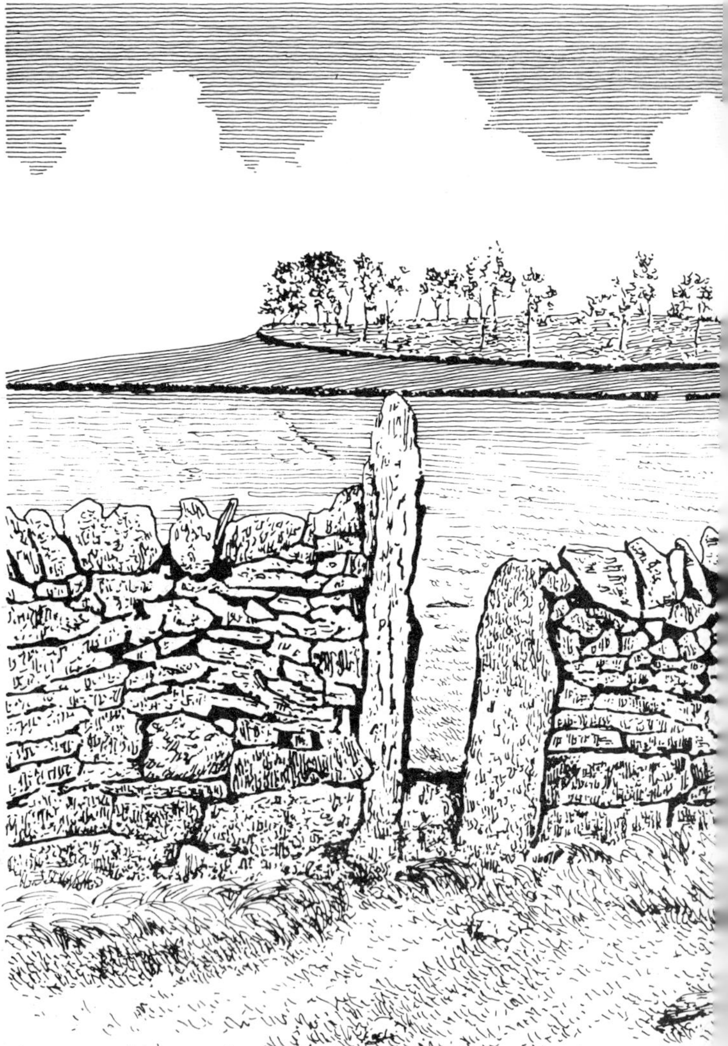

Aleck Low

WALK 22   TRAIL WALKING
from Hartington Old Station   5¾ miles

Newcomers to this limestone country prepared to entertain a three hour walk should certainly consider this particular circuit. Not that they should tackle it the way I did, in a November snow storm that all but halted traffic on the exposed A515. On that occasion, the Jug & Glass loomed out of the eye of the storm like some remote Highland bothy in a blizzard and I was grateful for the landlord's warm welcome.

The Trails are undemanding, being bereft of gradient whilst keeping well above the 1000 foot contour, so 'senior' walkers may set forth with some measure of confidence that their stamina will not be taxed too greatly. Cardlemere Lane and Green Lane offer easy options for the slightly more energetic crossing of Aleck Low, adding only ½ mile to the walk.

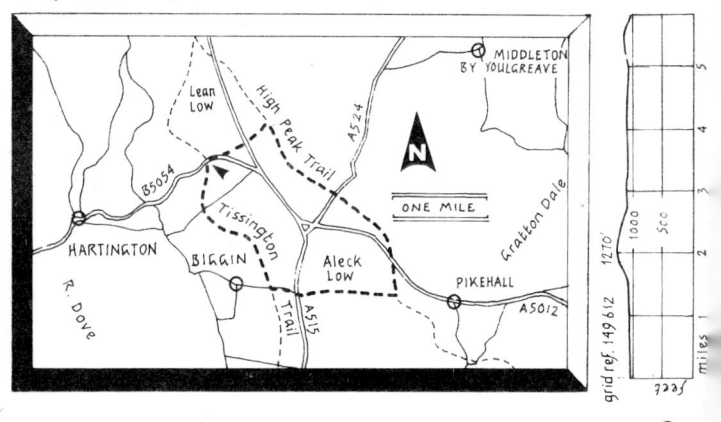

S Walk S from the car park, following the Tissington Trail **1** till, a few yards short of the Biggin road bridge, slant L down to a narrow gate onto the road (formerly, this road was part of an ancient packhorse route from Hartington continuing towards Wirksworth via Cobblersnook). Go L with this minor road to the A515. Cross over, passing Cardle View via stiles. The footpath keeps up L via two stiles, thereafter reaching a gate L of a mere. A series of four **2** stiles direct to a large cultivated field, where drop to a track beside a truncated length of wall. Go L, joining the High Peak Trail at a gate: go L **3** by way of Newhaven crossing, Friden picnic site **4** and brickworks. Beyond Brundcliffe, **5** branch L off the Trail, following a lane across the A515 to conclude with the B5054 to the old station.

188

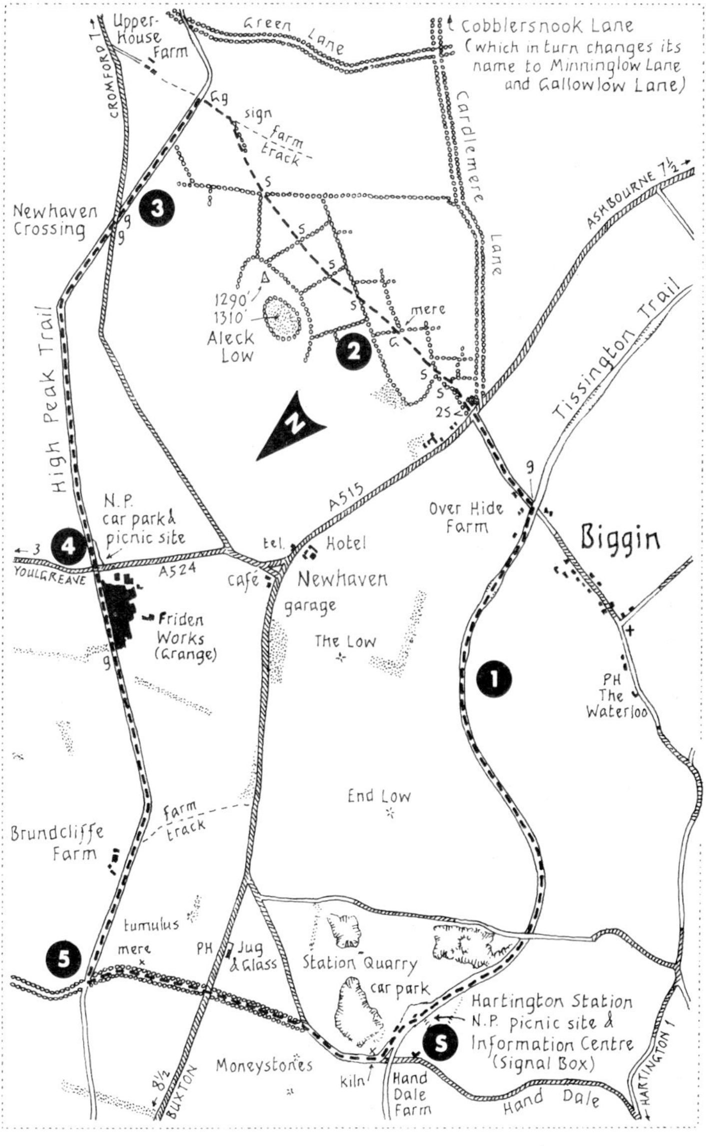
Upper-House Farm
Green Lane
Cobblersnook Lane (which in turn changes its name to Minninglow Lane and Gallowlow Lane)
CROMFORD 7
sign
farm track
Cardlemere Lane
Newhaven Crossing
ASHBOURNE 7½
Tissington Trail
1290'
1310'
Aleck Low
mere
High Peak Trail
N
25
A515
Over Hide Farm
N.P. car park & picnic site
3
YOULGREAVE
A524
tel.
Hotel
Biggin
café
Newhaven
garage
Friden Works (Grange)
The Low
PH The Waterloo
End Low
farm track
Brundcliffe Farm
tumulus
mere
PH
Jug & Glass
Station Quarry
car park
Hartington Station N.P. picnic site & Information Centre (Signal Box)
HARTINGTON 1
Moneystones
kiln
Hand Dale Farm
Hand Dale
8½
BUXTON

The heart of Biggin Dale

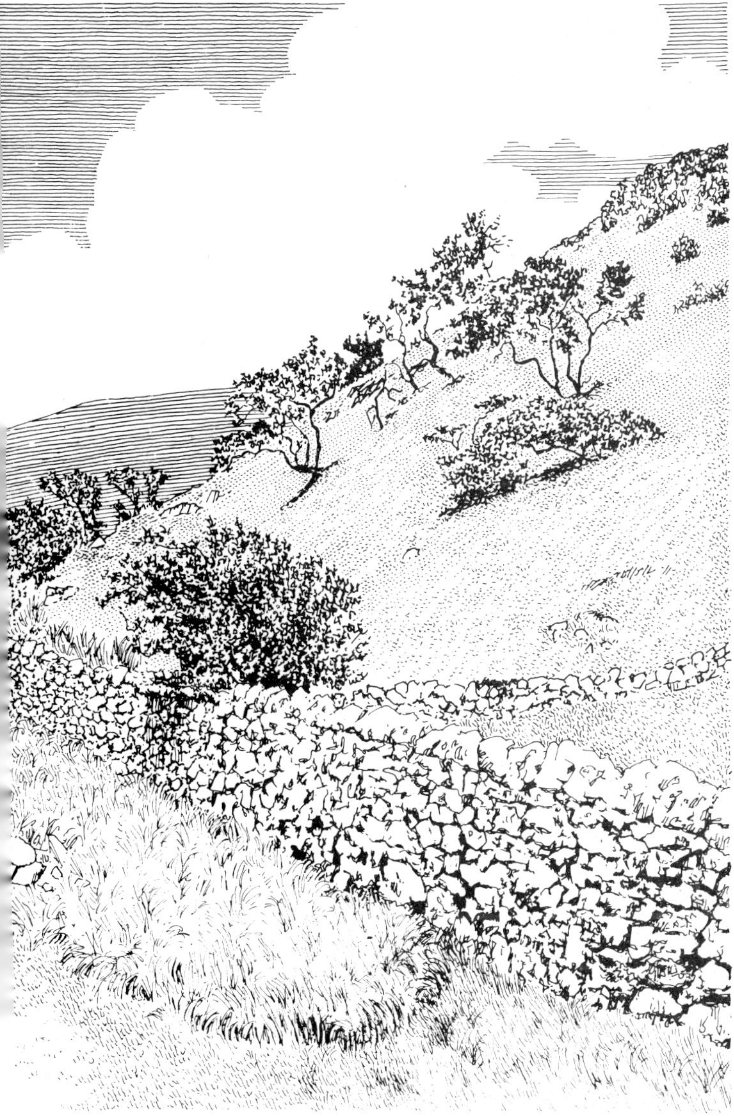

WALK 23   BIGGIN DALE

from the Tissington Trail, Alsop Moor   6¼ miles

This walk pays due attention to the limestone upland E of the Dove, so well seen from the Tissington Trail, and includes two quiet dales. These dry tributaries each of completely different character to the Dove, with the long, sinuous Biggin Dale a beautiful sanctuary, recognised, in large part, as a National Nature Reserve for the quality of its calcareous grassland habitat. Despite the popularity of the Trail, this too holds considerable interest in both scenic and (whilst confined within Coldeaton Cutting) geological terms.   Walking this way one day in November, the whole neighbourhood seemed to be gathered on Biggin for the annual grand autumn sheep sale. Held in the field opposite 'The Waterloo', it gives farmers the chance of filling the pub to overflowing, with earnest talk on the sheep trade paramount.

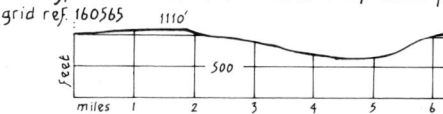

grid ref. 160565   1110'

S   Two lay-bys near the Biggin turn off the A515 on Alsop Moor serve as the springboard for this pleasurable outing. The S access from the larger lay-by is the simpler.   However, the Biggin bridge poses no real difficulty, being equipped with a wicket gate on the W side.

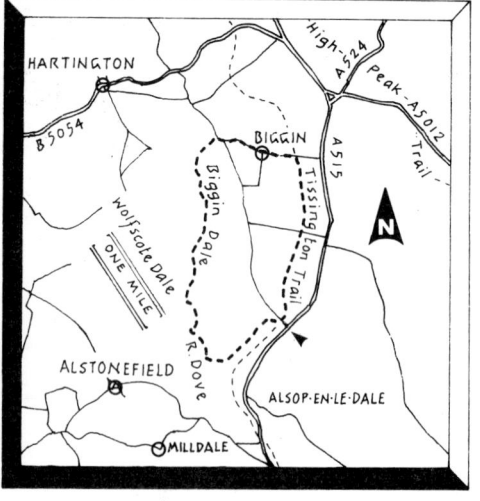

Follow the Trail along the curving embankment, entering the half mile long Coldeaton Cutting. The curious side lane on the R was created to give the farmer an E-W link to his fields.

Because of the gentle N dip in the bedding plane, two distinct types of limestone can be seen: the Bee Low Limestones, succeeded

— *continued on page 194*

Biggin

Bradbury's Bank

continued from page 192

by the Monsal Dale Limestones which are characterised by the abundance of brachiopods and corals. These features are clearly evident at the bridge which, for some unknown reason, is built of coarse sandstone and cherty limestone rather than from the material excavated from the cutting. Photographers, blessed with a suitable sky, may consider this high arched bridge a fine frame in which to set a view of the Tissington Trail.

The Trail emerges from the cutting to reveal most satisfying views to the W. ❶ Crossing Back Lane and an embankment over a shallow side valley at the head of Biggin Dale, the Trail passes through a short cutting rich in brachiopod fossils. The next embankment heralds the departure from the Trail down to a stile R at the Biggin road bridge. Pass under the bridge, following the road into Biggin - a name that has its roots in the Scandinavian word byggia 'house' and was in quite common usage in England during early Medieval (Middle English) times. ❷ The route passes the church (St. Thomas' built in 1844-8) and 'The Waterloo' (a welcome refreshment halt); largely hidden behind is Biggin Hall dated 1642. Continue along the road into the dale. Just after a road junction, enter Biggin Dale, signposted L at a stile/gate. Whilst passing the innocuous sewage plant, note the strip lynchets on the bank ahead. Proceed through the wall gap to the valley which curves L with, of course, no hint of surface water! ❸ Immediately after the stile, notice the

continued on page 196

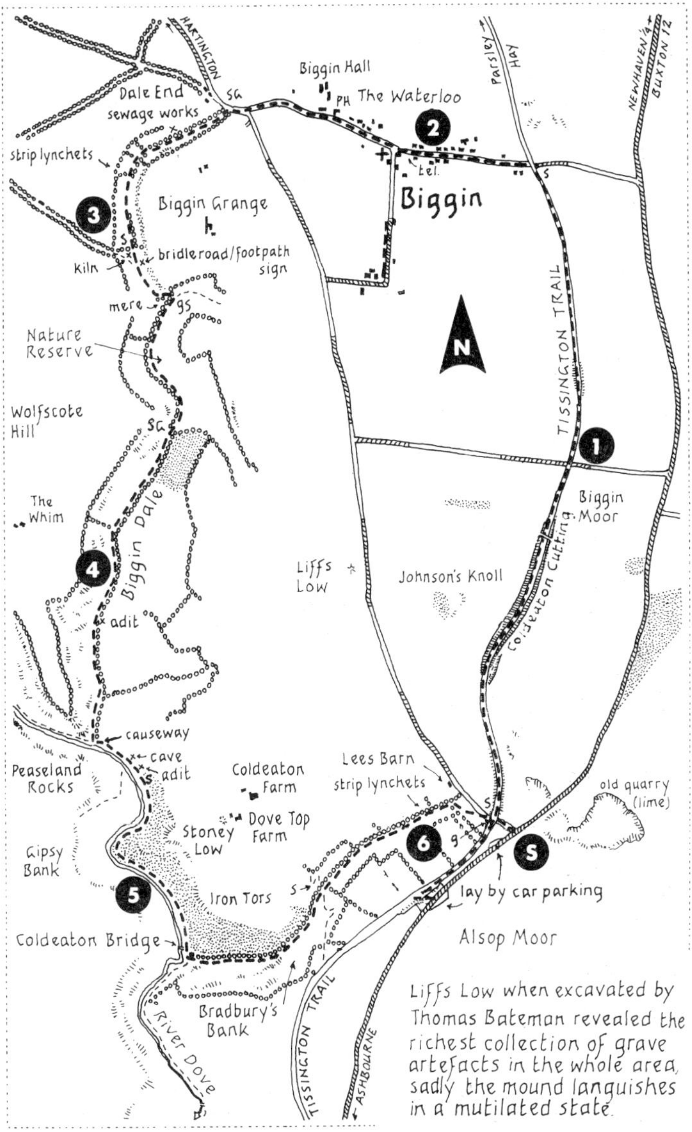
HARTINGTON
Parsley Hay
NEWHAVEN 4 BUXTON 12
Biggin Hall
PH The Waterloo
SG
Dale End
sewage works
strip lynchets
Biggin
tel.
Biggin Grange
S
bridleroad/footpath sign
Kiln
mere
gs
Nature Reserve
N
TISSINGTON TRAIL
Wolfscote Hill
SG
The Whim
Biggin Dale
Biggin Moor
Coldeaton Cutting
Liffs Low
Johnson's Knoll
adit
causeway
cave
adit
Peaseland Rocks
Coldeaton Farm
Lees Barn
strip lynchets
old quarry (lime)
Dove Top Farm
Stoney Low
Gipsy Bank
Iron Tors
lay by car parking
Alsop Moor
Coldeaton Bridge
Bradbury's Bank
River Dove
TISSINGTON TRAIL
ASHBOURNE
1
2
3
4
5
6
S
Liffs Low when excavated by Thomas Bateman revealed the richest collection of grave artefacts in the whole area, sadly the mound languishes in a mutilated state.

continued from page 194 ──────

ruinous limekiln opposite the signpost. At the dale junction, the path swings L to a wicket gate/stile beside a mere to enter the Biggin Dale Nature Reserve. Go R' downdale.

To untrained eyes, the valley sides seem quite bare and devoid of interest. Whilst it is true the grazing is poor in terms of modern, high stocking rate grazing régimes, these unimproved banks harbour a variety of delicate species of lime-tolerant plants and associated insect life fully deserving protection. So refrain from straying off the valley floor path and most certainly pick nothing but your steps!

Biggin Dale Nature Reserve

Proceed via a stile/gate with scree boulders littering the valley floor, indicating both the steepness of the valley sides and the thickness of the bedding planes. **4** Pass a short mine adit (trial level), which is safe to enter with a torch. Presumably, this was a speculative and abortive attempt to discover new lead ore veins. During the 'wet' season the dale below the adit carries surface water; at other times the water issues forth at the junction with the River Dove.

────── *continued on facing page*

continued from facing page ───────

At the foot of Biggin Dale, go L in popular procession beside the Dove (as per WALK 17), passing through the light woodland beneath Iron Tors. ❺ At Coldeaton Bridge, turn away L from the merry chattering Dove, rising up the narrow side valley.   Soon the dale becomes hemmed in by rocky ribs of dark, thinly-bedded, Milldale Limestones containing nodules of a very finely grained silica, similar to flint, known as chert.   The grassy Bradbury's Bank is less imposing and, at a stile, the National Trust land is left. Higher up, notice the strip lynchets just before Lees Barn. ❻ Go through a wall gap, then slant R to a stile onto the Biggin road next to the Tissington Trail bridge.

The Dove valley from the ridge above the junction of Wolfscote Dale with Biggin Dale, looking SE

197

Johnson's Knoll from the Tissington Trail at the Biggin road

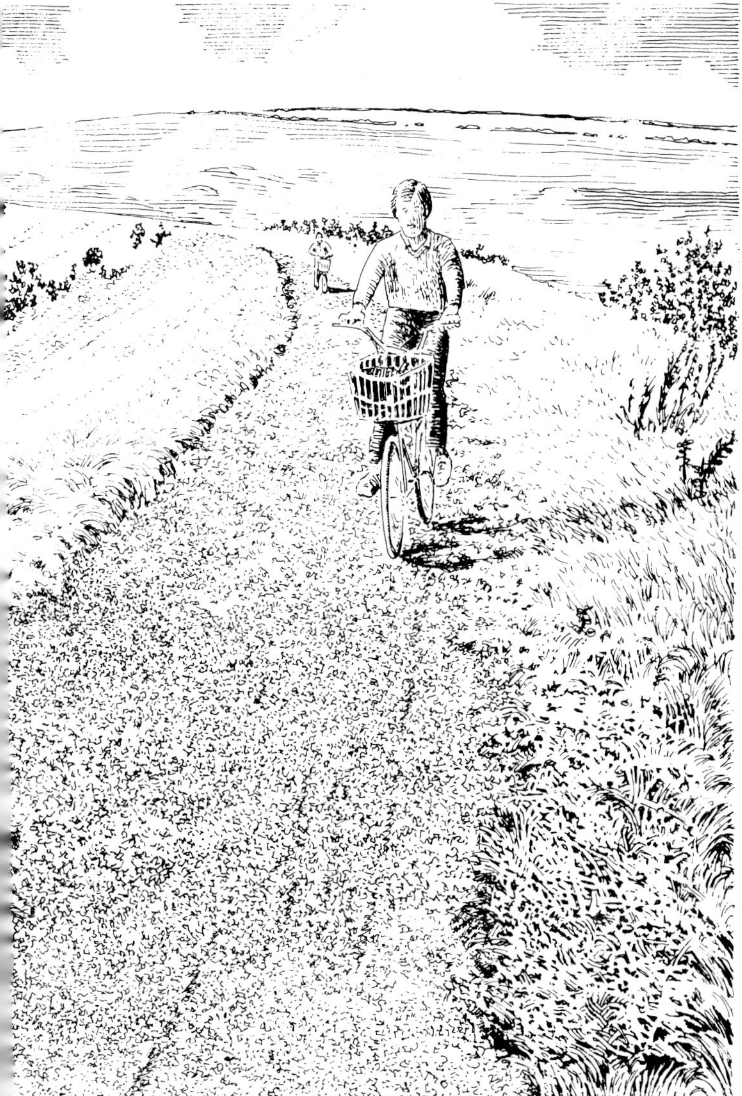

WALK 24 TISSINGTON'S TRAIL

from Tissington Old Station   8½ miles

With over four miles of level Trail to develop your pace and wipe away the cobwebs, this is a walk to invigorate jaded joints. Turning your back on the high Trail, the route heads E into the hinterland, descending via secretive Eaton Dale to Parwich, nestling snugly in a tuck of the hills. Then, as if to confirm your regained vitality, the walk slips over a low ridge and across the long trough of the Bletch Brook valley, rising for a last time to enter Tissington.   Whether approached this way or by the park gates off the A515 along the lime tree avenue, Tissington is seen as an estate village of considerable charm. Unlike Ilam, the

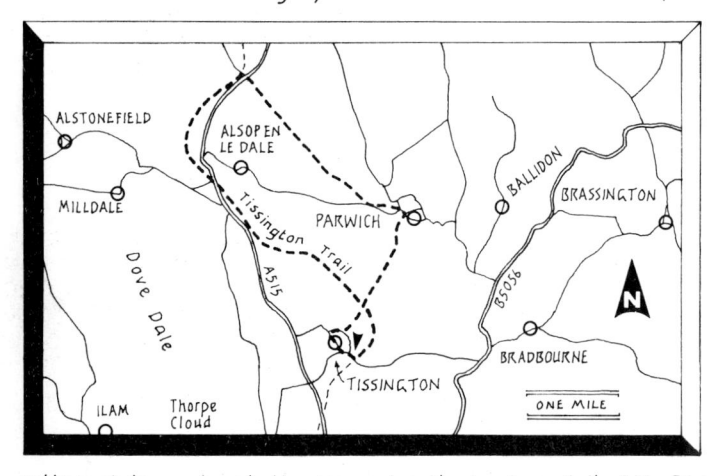

cottage styles are true to the vernacular; the Jacobean Hall of the Fitzherbert's and the parish church of St Mary laden with their memorials, together quietly impose a solid air of sobriety. This conscious formality is relieved by the ducks on the pond, the green spaces and the passage of tractors and stock-confirmation that this is a village that refuses to discard its rural identity.

In the minds of Derbyshire folk, Tissington is synonymous with, and therefore made special by, its long-established tradition of well-dressing. From here the unique custom has spread, adopted by many White Peak villages for whom the uncertainty of summer drought has long been an important concern, due to the underlying limestone's notorious unwillingness to release spring water at such critical times.

On Ascension Day and for the subsequent week, Tissington plays host to an unfailing flood of visitors in annual pilgrimage to witness and admire the year's themes. The five wellheads are adorned with superb motifs; scenes taken principally from the Bible, executed with all the loving care and justifiable pride befitting a church-cum-folk festival. The fleeting brilliance of the designs is determined by the use of materials gleaned from nature's perishable parlour. Apart from the puddled clay base to the panels and certain stable items like stones, cones, mosses and lichen, the predominant colourful effect is provided from delicate flower petals overlapped like roof tiles to allow rain water to run off.

Historians sense the practice of floral dressing and blessing of well water must, like so many present-day Christian customs, have its roots in pagan rites. Whilst religious suppression may have extinguished its earlier form, its Christian rekindling confirms the fundamental importance of water in sustaining any community, whatever its beliefs.

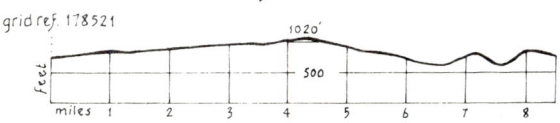

grid ref. 178521

S From the old Tissington Station yard, go N along the trackbed.

1 Beyond the second farm bridge at Crakelow (crow's mound) Farm the view improves across the Bletch Brook valley. The Tissington Trail shortly sweeps W, slicing through a ridge to expose a fine rock cutting, and over a dry valley embankment. The beech clumps around Alsop-en-le-Dale are a particularly pleasing complement to the scene.

2 Having become attuned to the natural sounds harmonious with Trail walking, the close proximity of the A515 comes as something of a rude imposition. Yet there can be few walkers who will be disappointed with the open views which seem to improve with every step. [I passed this way one damp early November morning and was tempted by the 'coffee' notice on the Trail at the New Inns Hotel. The halt proved a good move(!), for the twenty minutes spent in the annexe sipping the warming drink allowed the sun a chance to break through] The route goes beyond the National Park picnic site and under the long road bridge; notice the skew brick alignments to accommodate the arches at either end.

3 The views W feature Alstonefield church set against a backdrop of shapely hills. At Nettly Knowe, there is a brief glimpse into Coldeaton Dale. Soon the Trail passes the remnants of a former quarry sidings: directly ahead, on either side of the A515, are two huge derelict quarries, in gaunt witness to the railway's productive years, well and truly lost.

——— continued on page 202

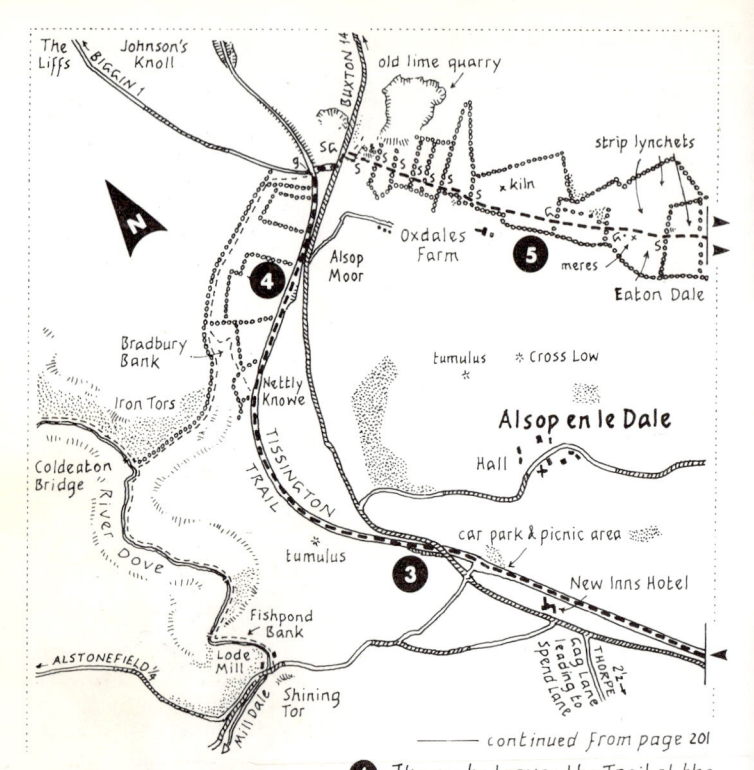

— continued from page 201

④ The route leaves the Trail at the Biggin road bridge, descending L to a wicket gate. Pass under the bridge to the road junction, advancing L with the A515 for 100 yards. Turn R at the old quarry entrance gate (adorned with the weathered notice 'Mond Division Lime Group'); from the adjacent stile proceed to a fence stile then down the clinker spoil bank to the first of a series of aligned squeezer stiles. The fifth of these is the most awkward to negotiate; thereafter, with little deviation from a general SE direction, pass a copse to a wall corner stile. By following a wall past Oxdales Farm, **⑤** cross the watershed to enter Eaton Dale at a gate. Continue via a further gate beside Eatondale Wood, into the broad sheltered (from prevailing W weather) combe of Eaton Dale, where strip lynchets tell of medieval or earlier cultivation, presumably linked to the now lost Eaton farmstead. At the foot of the combe, a wall stile gives access to a narrowing of the valley, again with traces of S slope strip lynchets (i.e. on the L handside). Do not

— continued on facing page

Map annotations (clockwise / by area):

- (A515) 2
- PIKEHALL 2½
- Parwich Hill
- Parwich
- PIKEHALL 2¾
- strip lynchets
- mere
- Middlehill — 6
- Eaton Dale
- series of 5 stiles
- shop
- PH
- Pever Brook
- ruin & gap
- Sycamore Inn — 7
- Peakway
- cave
- fp sign
- Flaxdale Holding
- Parwich is pronounced par-witch
- ALSOP EN LE DALE ½
- Bletch Brook
- fb
- fp sign
- Shaw's Farm
- N (compass)
- exits from Trail
- 1
- fp sign
- Crakelow Farm
- S/cattle grid exit from Trail
- Crake Low
- 2 — TISSINGTON TRAIL
- old hollow way
- Hunger Hill
- High Flats
- 8
- NEW INNS HOTEL ½
- Newton Grange
- tumulus
- Tissington
- Stand Low
- 'x' marks the five wells
- [see page 206]
- tel.
- siegework
- LEA ford
- A515
- Hall (private)
- old school — teas
- mere
- car park picnic site
- 5
- Tissington Gates
- lime avenue
- Thorpe car park ¼
- THORPE 1
- Wash Brook
- ASHBOURNE ¼

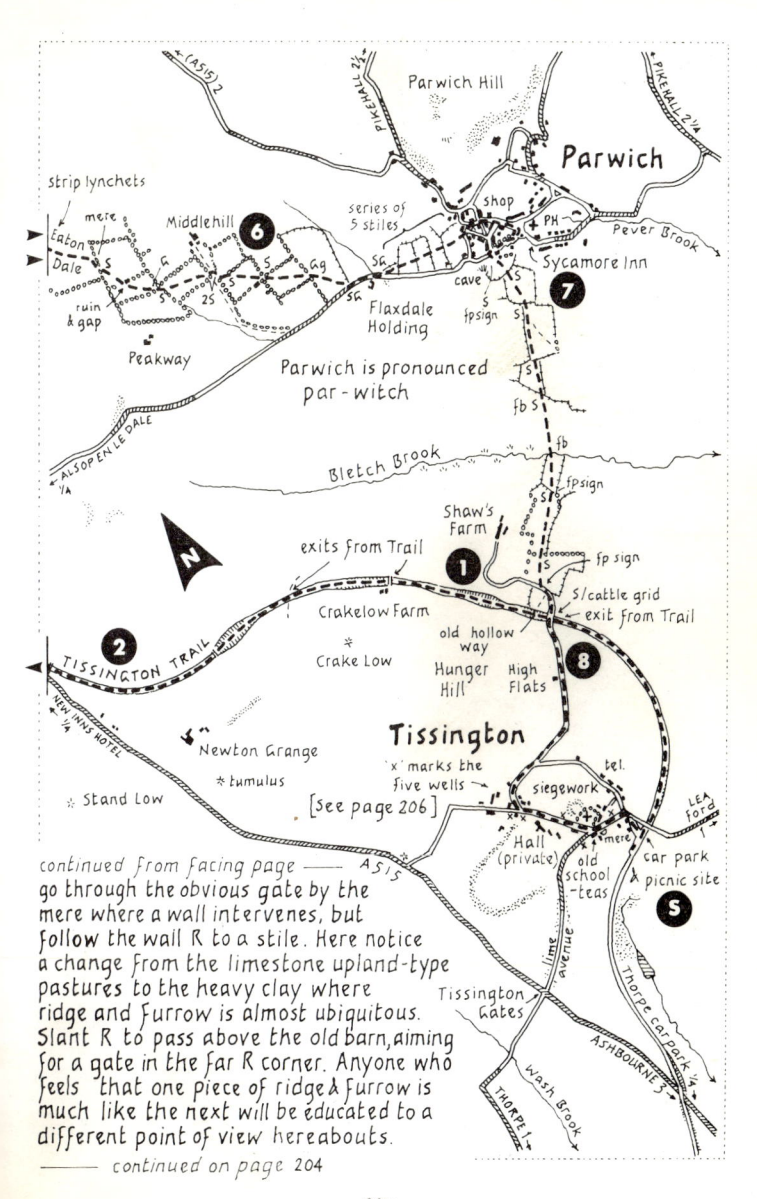

continued from facing page — go through the obvious gate by the mere where a wall intervenes, but follow the wall R to a stile. Here notice a change from the limestone upland-type pastures to the heavy clay where ridge and furrow is almost ubiquitous. Slant R to pass above the old barn, aiming for a gate in the far R corner. Anyone who feels that one piece of ridge & furrow is much like the next will be educated to a different point of view hereabouts.

——— *continued on page 204*

203

continued from page 203 ─────

In two successive fields, the ridges are surprisingly large whalebacks suggesting it was developed by a larger than usual plough team, say six oxen or a two-furrowed plough. These fields have, over recent decades, served only as cow pasture. Clearly, however, there was a period of sustained cultivation practised here, demanding that every sunny bank succumb to the plough to meet the needs of an evidently substantial population around Parwich.

From the aforementioned gate, go forward to the nearby stile and traverse the second 'whaleback' ridge & furrow pasture down to a wall stile L of the far R corner. Cross Middlehill Farm access drive hop over the ditch, seeking a stile to the R of a small rock outcrop. Proceed round the nettle-bank, keeping to the R to discover a somewhat secretive stile. Again cross the next field diagonally to a stile in the corner next to Middlehill Barn. ❻ Maintain course to the next field corner, where a narrow gate is fixed to a squeezer stile adjacent to a field gate. Descend the bank to reach the Parwich road via stile/gate. Go L, passing Flaxdale Holding evidence that flax was once grown in this valley, linseed fibres being spun and woven to make rope and material (linen); might Lin Dale beneath Thorpe Cloud owe its name to the fact that flax was cultivated there during pre-Conquest times?

Having perhaps briefly spoken to the pony at Flaxdale, branch L at the stile/gate (signposted 'Lenscliff'), proceeding by a series of five stiles, easily located to bring the walker into the lane by Parwich Primary School, an attractive Victorian building.

─────────── *continued on facing page*

Cottage at Parwich

continued from facing page

Parwich, a name derived from Pever wic, 'outlying farm on the Pever stream', is an old settlement despite its remote name. Indeed, though 'wic' approximates to 'thorpe' the latter is of Scandinavian origin and therefore reflects late Dark Age colonisation. The village has attracted modern infill housing, fortunately without losing its intrinsic character: the numerous attractive cottages are dominated by Parwich Hall, built in 1747 consciously in red brick to stand out in a predominently grey stone built community.

Passing the village shop, go R down the street to the Green overlooked by St Peter's church (largely the product of late Victorian styling). Of much less visual appeal is the red brick Sycamore Inn, though it is redeemed by its internal character and friendly landlord who welcomed the author, standing reticent at the front door with muddy attire, with the comment 'treat us like you would your own home!'

Depart along the lane by the village pond and along the confined path beside Pever Brook, going W to emerge onto the minor road at a stile. Go L at a signposted stile: notice the small crag up to the R with a cave. Ascend the bank to a hedge stile, rising higher to a stile, **7** thereafter accompany a hedge in a ridge and furrow, ridge top pasture to a stile. Maintain direction to a stile/footbridge amongst a holly hedge, descending over slumped ground to the Bletch Brook footbridge. Upstream, marshland implies a silted lake. The name Bletch probably comes from a Saxon personal name like Blecca (presumably a landowner), the stream defining the boundary of his land: it remains a parish boundary to this day.

The footpath mounts the pastures directly via two stiles to join the Shaw's farm access drive (footpath sign). Notice the old hollow way ahead which will have provided access to the farm before the railway was cut, necessitating a bridge.

Cross the bridge, taking the opportunity to glance down upon the Tissington Trail (see drawing L) and follow the lane by **8** High Flats onto the minor road into Tissington to finish.

Town Well

Tissington's famous wells

1 : HAND WELL
2 : TOWN WELL
3 : HALL WELL
4 : YEW TREE WELL
5 : COFFIN WELL

Hall Well

Dale below Roystone Grange

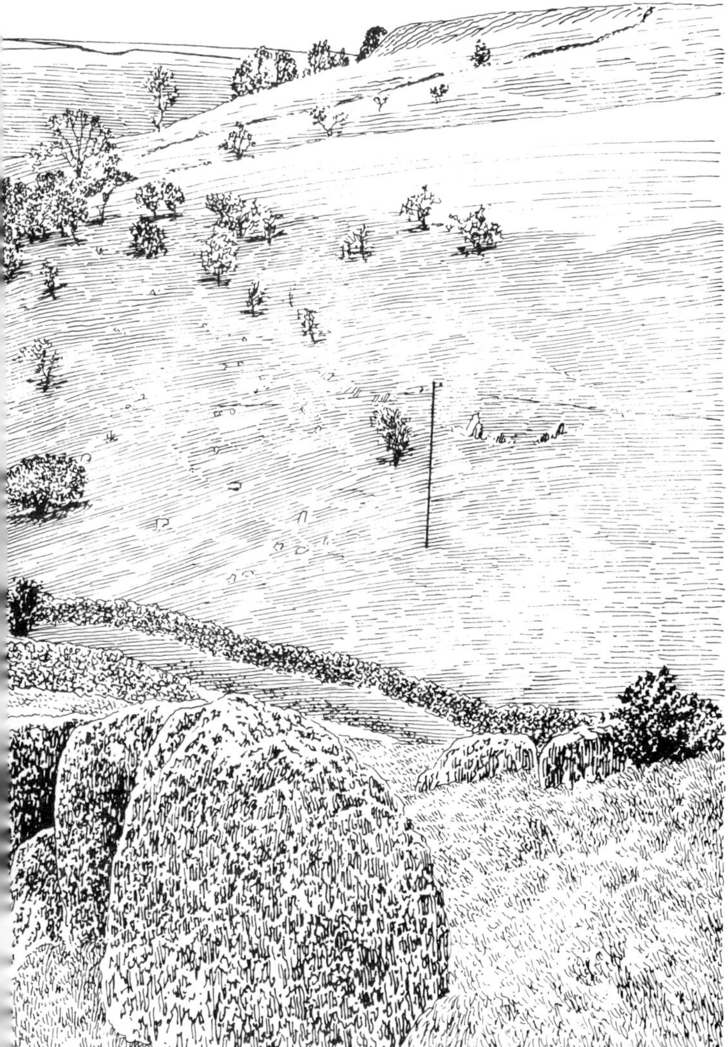

WALK 25   MINNINGLOW

from Minninglow picnic site   5½ miles

It seems the eternal fate, that desire of each generation to banish the old in favour of the new. Whether previous values are respected or not makes no difference: the modification process comes from external pressures compounded upon the search for individual or group identity. Static societies fall prey to radical influx and so it is that priorities change.

Tenuous evidence of these historic overlays, largely absent in the lowland countryside, cling precariously in the higher valley heads of Peakland where settlement reached its limits in times past.

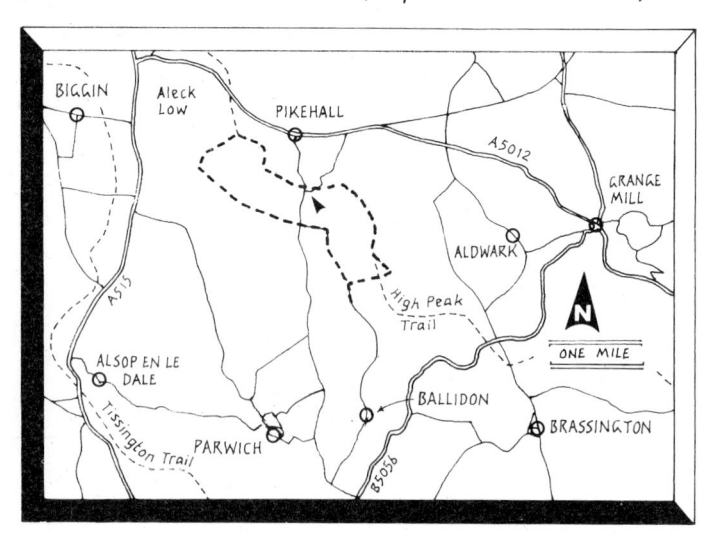

One such classic location is the Roystone Grange valley above Ballidon. With the enthusiastic support of the farmer, the research project run by Richard Hodges of Sheffield University and Martin Wildgoose of Closes Farm, Kniveton has been able to examine in considerable detail, not merely medieval, but Romano-British estate characteristics. Existence must always have been hard at Roystone, sodden by showers, buffeted by winds, held in the grip of frost and snow for long months: an unforgiving climate, a cruel retreat. So the humble people who braved this spot did so with good reason, imposed by circumstance. Much as when, in the Second World War, farmers were dictated to bring under plough old pastures to feed and sustain the nation under the threat of naval blockade, then, perhaps the Roman authority placed demands on all social orders, at critical times, to provide more of their own food and staple commodities. Evidently the latter phase of Romano-British settlement suggests a taxing economic environment, for the steep hillside down the dale and above Ballidon fossilises fourth century cultivation terraces probably never since tilled.

The walk, based upon the most attractive passage of the High Peak Trail, incorporates the Roystone Grange Archaeological Trail (for which there is a fascinating guide published jointly by Sheffield University and the Peak Park Authority). The expedition is a history lesson of the best kind, embodying elements from the full breadth of man's influence on the Peakland landscape. Minninglow, the principal landmark visible from the High Peak Trail, is distinguished by a wind-tormented clump sheltering a burial mound of the New Stone Age (no access). Roman orthostat walls (large single stones standing in a line) lurk beneath medieval, 17th century and subsequent field boundaries. Old ways contained between walls, like the prehistoric Gallowlow Lane which, with several changes of name, crosses the limestone plateau from Hartington to Wirksworth. A short detour down the valley is recommended to glance at Ballidon, which has medieval village traces in the pasture next to the isolated church, though the intervening quarry (due for even greater expansion) is a rude shock, made all the more unwelcome by the growing body of tangible, historically valuable evidence emerging from research close by. The most convenient pub for this walk is the Sycamore Inn at Parwich - though it is necessary to resort to the charabanc (car) to reach it before or after the outing!

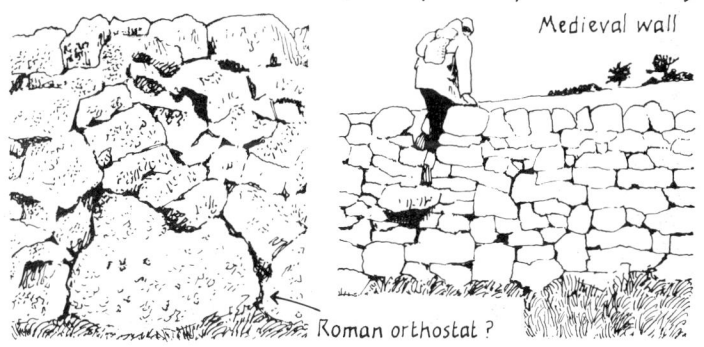

Medieval wall

Roman orthostat?

grid ref. 195582

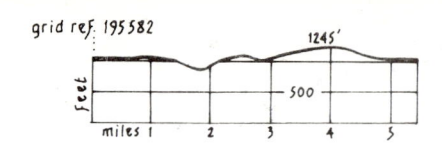

S From the car park, walk E across the minor road, advancing with the High Peak Trail. Crossing the impressive walled embankment, the Trail curves from NE to SW, with attention focussed upon Minninglow. Following the quarried cutting, it switches S, then crosses a second substantial walled embankment. To the L can be seen a collapsed lime kiln, whilst a little farther on, at the point where Minninglow Lane meets the Trail, notice the remains of the 19th century brick kiln. Constructed in the 1860s exploiting the nearby deposits of silica sands to create high firing bricks for the steel industry (furnace lining), this was the first such site along the former Cromford & Highpeak Railway, the process being continued and expanded later at Friden Grange and Harborough (Hopton Works).

Minninglow from the brick kiln site

1 Leave the Trail via gates L entering, the broad Gallowlow Lane (guided by the yellow waymark arrows specifically marked 'R' for the Roystone Archaeological Trail). The lane dips and, as it begins rising, cross the stile R, turning your back on Minninglow. This S flanking wall of Gallowlow Lane contains the odd orthostat stone, implying that it may well have defined an outer boundary of the Roystone Roman farm (other large wall base stones may be detected on the descent into the Roystone Grange valley). Passing a mere, go beneath the Trail by a gate/squeezer stile.

——— *continued on page 214*

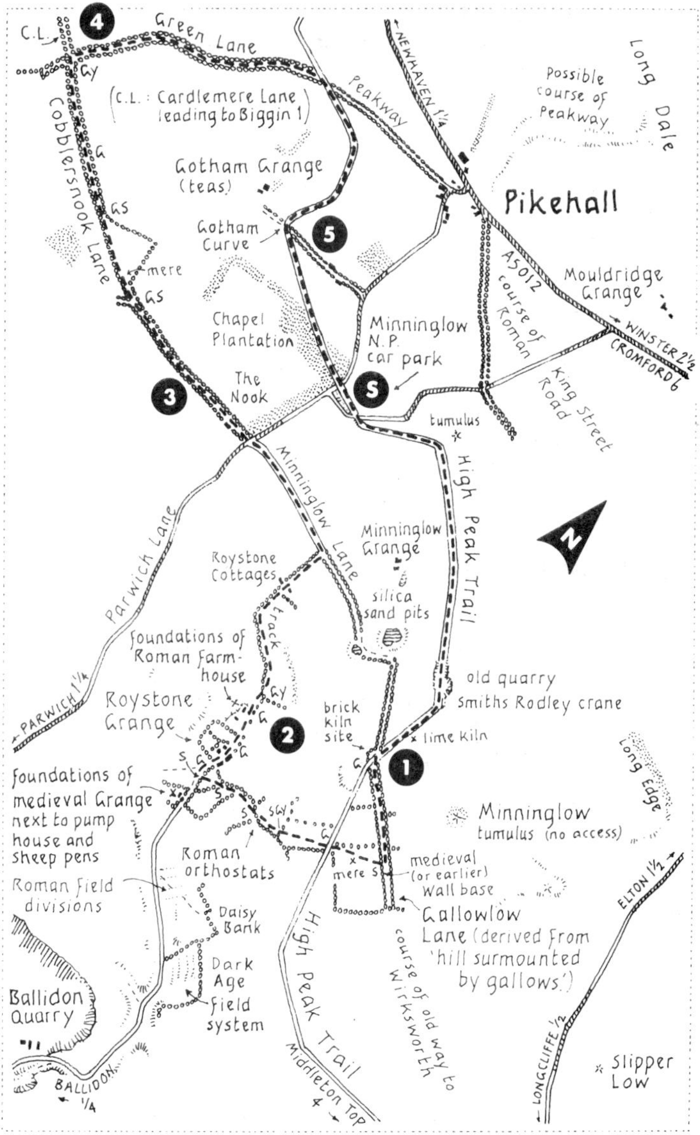

4
C.L.
Green Lane
Gy
(C.L.: Cardlemere Lane leading to Biggin 1)
Cobblersnook Lane
G
GS
mere
GS
Gotham Grange (teas)
Gotham Curve
5
Peakway
NEWHAVEN 1¼
Possible course of Peakway
Long Dale
Pikehall
A5012
course of Roman
Mouldridge Grange
WINSTER 2½
CROMFORD 6
King Street Road
Chapel Plantation
Minninglow N.P. car park
S
The Nook
3
tumulus
High Peak Trail
Minninglow Lane
Parwick Lane
Minninglow Grange
Roystone Cottages
silica sand pits
track
foundations of Roman farm-house
old quarry
Smiths Rodley crane
Roystone Grange
Gy
G
2
brick kiln site
lime kiln
1
Long Edge
PARWICH 1¼
foundations of medieval Grange next to pump house and sheep pens
S
SGY
Minninglow tumulus (no access)
Roman orthostats
mere
medieval (or earlier) wall base
Roman field divisions
Daisy Bank
Gallowlow Lane (derived from 'hill surmounted by gallows.')
ELTON 1½
course of old way to Wirksworth
Dark Age field system
Ballidon Quarry
High Peak Trail
Middleton Top 4
BALLIDON ¼
LONGCLIFFE ½
Slipper Low

continued from page 212

Notice how it has been necessary to reinforce the walled embankment with ballast cages, creating the impression of passing through a castle gatehouse. Continue downhill via a stile/gateway, watchful for the stile L leading off the tractor track (before the second gateway). Advance with the descending wall through another gateway to a stile R, angle L through the paddock to reach a stile set into a high medieval structured wall (see drawing on page 211).

Although the plotted route turns immediately R at this point, a detour downdale is recommended. Follow the track L, entering the enclosure R of the track (waymarked as per Roystone Trail) through a gate. The chapel-like building ahead contained an engine which sent air up to primitive pneumatic drills used in the quarries either side of the High Peak Trail. An interpretive board upon the pumphouse end wall describes the locality, particularly in respect of the early 'Cistercian grange' farm on this site. Exposed R are the foundations of the dairy annexe (still undergoing excavation in 1986). In the 12th century, Adam de Herthill gave Revestone (Roystone) to Garendon Abbey in Leicestershire, such gifts of the poorer grazing land being common to enable monks to develop sheep ranches for the prized wool crop. This site appears to have been vacated circa 1400 in favour of a drier site to the N (traces of this later community are delectable in the paddock most recently passed through to join the Roystone track). Follow also the minor road down the attractive winding dale from the sheep pens to examine both the Saxon strip lynchets, and most fascinating of all in the vicinity of the Daisy Bank track, the faint baulks running up the hillside of Roman field divisions. In certain lights the vague impressions of lazy beds (spade cultivation) show up contouring the steep slope. Backtrack to continue.

continued on facing page

Strip lynchets on Daisy Bank

continued from facing page

Pass, via farmyard gates, though the present Roystone Grange, dating from the 18th century. No doubt the sturdy construction embodies masonry from earlier stone-built dwellings. The range of farm buildings is in itself interesting, but visitors should not pry. Instead, advance ❷ to the final building on the L, an old brick cowshed (with interpretive board), above which, set upon a small terrace are the foundations of the principal Roman farmhouse. This house site, and others nearby, appear to have been occupied between the 2nd and 4th centuries, when the valley was cultivated and stock-rearing was undertaken within ring enclosures (composed of orthostat walls) which embraced the valley surrounds in irregular alignments.

Following the improving road up the valley, pass Roystone Cottages to the junction with Minninglow Lane: go L. At the meeting with Parwich Lane, a R turn can bring a swift end to the walk beside Cobblersnook Plantation. However, the stroll along the facing Cobblersnook Lane and down Green Lane onto the Trail is scenically most rewarding and fully justifies extending the itinerary. Passing Nook Cottage, ❸ ascend Upper Moor. In just under ½ mile the lane forks, keep R to a gate/stile. Negotiate the final rise along the boundary of an open field with clear views back to Minninglow. Re-entering the lane at a gate/stile, proceed via a gate and then a gateway to the lane junction. Turn R with Green Lane: ❹ unusually for this locality, the fields to the L are regularly cropped with barley. Upon meeting the High Peak Trail go R, enjoying the views over Pikehall. Gotham Curve, in its day the tightest curve on any British line, turns through 80 degrees. As a result, only short wheel-based locomotives and wagons were able to use the line S of Friden and round the bend itself had to observe a 5 m.p.h. speed limit. The walk concludes pleasantly with the Trail. ❺

Sharp curves and steep embankment walls characterise the High Peak Trail

215

Robin Hood's Stride from the Portway

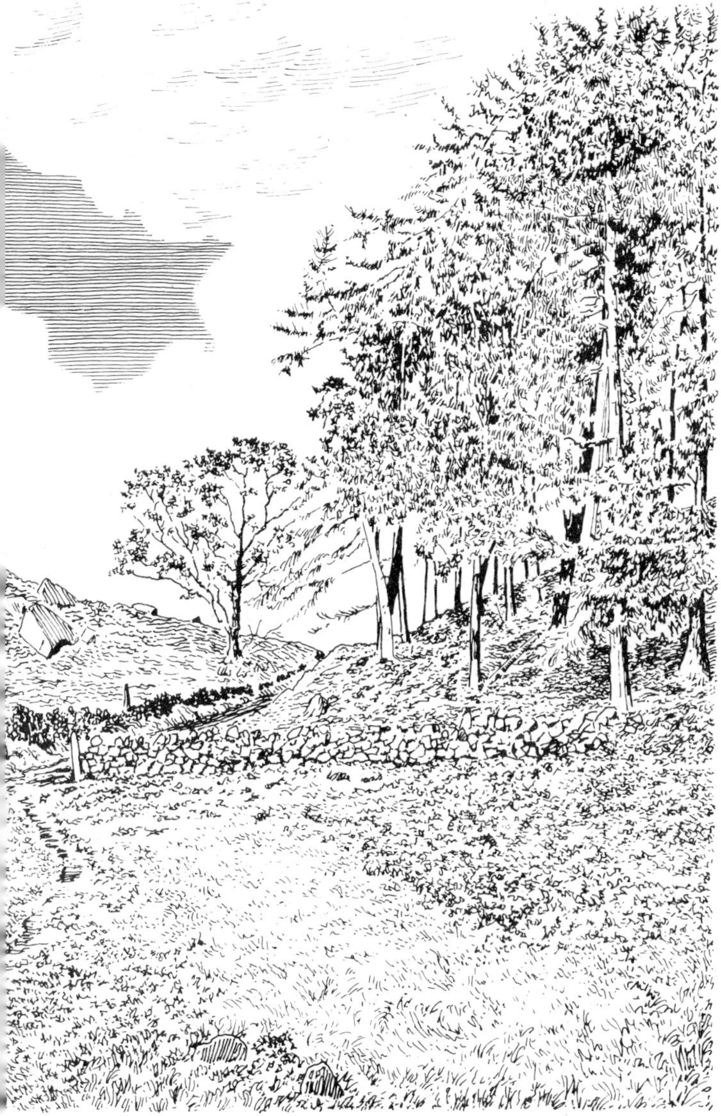

WALK 26   HARTHILL MOOR

from Elton   3½ miles

First impressions of Elton are deceptive. True, the basically one-street, springline community harbours few really exceptional buildings despite the age of some like the Youth Hostel, which bears the date 1668. The bleak N facing aspect is no elixir for imaginative growth; nonetheless, a settlement appears to have existed here since early Saxon times. At least since Roman times, lead has been valued for its moulding, water-carrying or protective qualities and the environs of Elton, notably the Common above the village, have been worked for many centuries to win from lead ore deposits.

The rock features of Harthill Moor are the principal objective of the walk they stand aloof from the mundane, day-by-day concerns of Elton. However, considerable evidence exists linking Dudwood Lane and its continuing track leading onto the Moor with the ancient Port Way. It would appear that this access route across the Peak, has served as a means of plying trade over several millenia, materialising from the prehistoric network of trackways as the prime artery. Present day travellers on foot whose only mission is introspective, therefor the sheer joy of walking free, may sense the ghosts of folk from long ago who passed this way; a procession made visible within the veil of subconscious perception. The antiquarian stone and earth bank relics upon the Moor are crucial documents to the importance of this high ground astride the old way prior to the coming of the Romans.

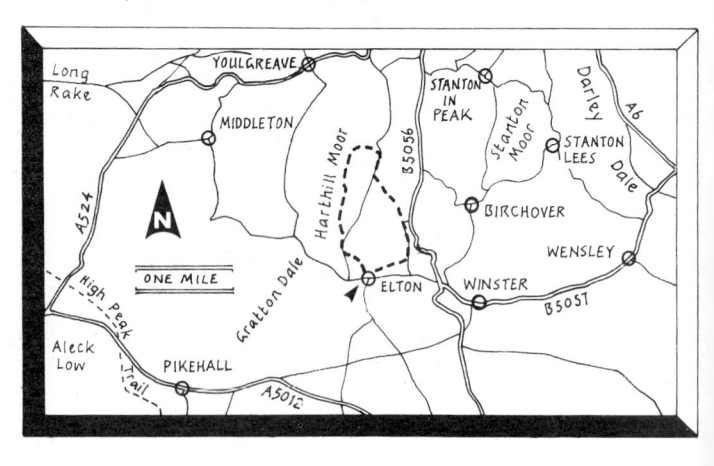

Weasel Pinnacle **Innaccessible Pinnacle**

Robin Hood's Stride or Mock Beggars' Hall

Nine Stones circle, thought to have been constructed in the Bronze Age, has since gaining its present name dwindled to four stones. The blocked-in gateway in the foreground would appear to have been the recipient of one ancient stone; others will no doubt have found their way into various structures over the years, though they are now lost.

Cratcliffe Rocks

HERMITAGE CAVE

S Parking in Elton is difficult, so use your discretion. Well Street provides, one option (beside the church); otherwise, there is space for two cars on the verge at the foot of Dudwood Lane.

Follow the footpath signposted through All Saints churchyard to a stile, cross the lane to a second stile descending, into pastureland. Cross to a stile/footpath sign, aim for the stile (part-hidden by the hedge) in the R corner of the field. Initially, the footpath runs along the top of the scarp bank: it then angles down to a fence stile, continuing to a stile/footpath sign (Limestone Way) into Dudwood Lane. Go L downhill, at the bottom negotiating the stile then follow the track uphill. About half way up, **1** the Old Port Way becomes visible as a hollow way on the L. It converges with the track farther on, where the surface becomes bedrock and rough paving. This line of ascent onto Harthill Moor provides grand views of both Cratcliffe Rocks, and, after the gateway, Robin Hood's Stride (sometimes referred to as 'Mock Beggar's Hall'. Notice too the change in flora from lime-tolerant species to acid tolerant plants such as bilberry, bracken and heather higher up.

—— *continued on page 222*

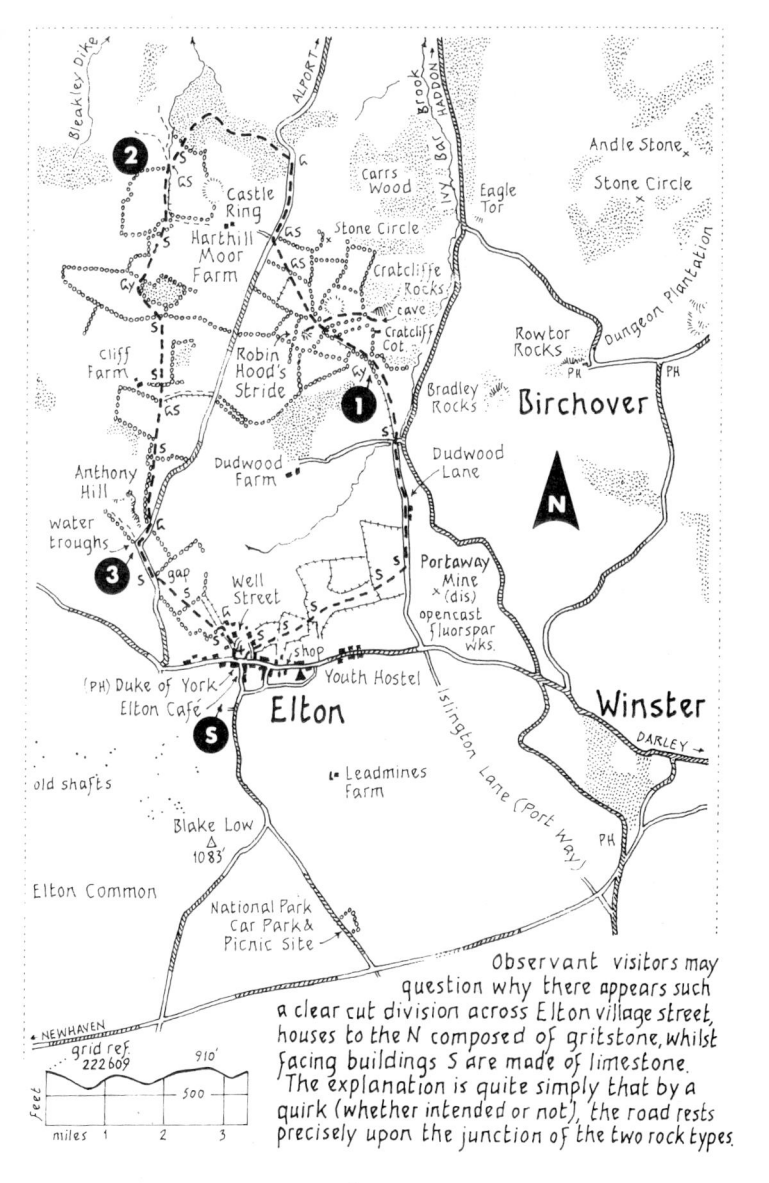

Observant visitors may question why there appears such a clear cut division across Elton village street, houses to the N composed of gritstone, whilst facing buildings S are made of limestone. The explanation is quite simply that by a quirk (whether intended or not), the road rests precisely upon the junction of the two rock types.

continued from page 220 ———

Upon reaching the brow, walkers may be undecided which natural landmark to visit first. For Cratcliffe Rocks, branch R across a ring earthwork (of unknown date and function, it may have served as a corral for some British settlement. The crag, a popular venue for rock-climbers, may have been used as shelter to guardians of the Old Port Way through many centuries. 'The Hermitage', the prime attraction, can be visited by keeping down R through the large boulders at the E end of the crag. This simple rock shelter, concealed by two mature yew trees and protected by a wall and metal fence, has within a sculpted crucifix about 4' high. At the side is a niche, probably for a lamp, overhead can be seen a drip course, and nearby slots for beams of a lean-to. During the Middle Ages it was common practice for hermits, who were respected as holy men, to reside at lonely points along important thoroughfares, such as this, to give sanctuary to weary travellers.

Retracing steps, eyes should be diverted R across two fields to Nine Stones (well, four actually!) stone circle. Cross over the old way in the depression, picking your way onto the giant weathered gritstone outcrop of Robin Hood's Stride. The two blunt pinnacles that lend special distinction to this crest will have acted as important landmarks down the ages: it can be no coincidence that the Old Port Way slips by so closely much in the spirit of a 'ley route'. That the 'legendary' outlaw of Loxley' ever stood here one cannot say (certainly he could not have strode the pinnacles), but he just might have had cause to operate in the vicinity of this important trackway. The romantic place-name suggests, however, that whoever this Robin Hood figure was, his many deeds must have impressed the local imagination sufficiently to attribute feats of superhuman proportions as adequate memorial!

There are several short rock climbs (little more than boulder problems by comparison with Cratcliffe) on this fragmented outcrop. Attempts at immortality by rock etchers is both unsightly and regrettable: visitors to this summit should curb the temptation to further mutilate the rocks with initials - it is a sick joke! This is a fine viewpoint, notably N to the wooded hills above Haddon Hall and Chatsworth House. Engulfed in the bracken of the facing hillside (SW) is an area of hut circles of probably prehistoric date (no acces

Rejoin the Port Way once again, going L via gates/stiles to Cliff Lane opposite the entrance to Harthill Moor Farm. Go R, accompanying the Limestone Way. The road begins its descent for Alport: at a gate, go L upon the track through the conifer plantation. Our brief sojourn with the Old Port Way is deflected

——— *continued on facing page*

continued from facing page

here to a similar final fleeting passage with the route of modern invention. The Limestone Way, of course here upon gritstone(!), runs (nay, walks!) from Matlock to Castleton - though why it was felt necessary to create a route of this nature at all with such a superabundance of well-maintained paths at walkers' disposal is beyond my ken.

The intimacy of the woodland path is a pleasant contrast to the earlier phase of the walk. Contouring upon the Castle Ring spur, the path emerges at a stile, now cross the pasture to a gate/stile; then cross the streambed. At this point the Limestone Way (originally it was to have been known as the Rotary Way, which would have avoided any confusion with the Limey Way) departs R bound for Bradford Dale.

❷ Follow the track rising L. The near skyline L shows the edge of the Castle Ring rampart, one of only seven Iron Age hill forts in the White Peak region. The footpath proceeds almost due S, bound for Elton, and as it is extremely well waymarked, it poses few navigational problems. After the farm track diverges L, advance to a stile from which a notice advises walkers to follow the telegraph poles, via the gateway, curving round Tomlinson Wood to a stile near the L corner of the field. The path rises beyond to a stile, then crosses Cliff Farm access track by stile/gate through a fence: aim for the wall corner upon the crest of the hill continuing with the wall on the R to a stile. The easy descent beside the enclosure wall of Anthony Hill Quarry lays open excellent views across the valley to Elton, set high on the shadowy side of the hill below Elton Common.

At the foot of the inclining path, pass through the gate, going R with the minor road. ❸ At the bend, a line of stone water troughs remain from the days when draught horses drew the heavy wagons of dressed gritstone from the adjacent quarry (see below).

Continue to the signposted footpath L; at a stile immediately cross the wall gap then mount the pasture to a wall stile, thereafter completing the ascent to the top of the hedgeline. Cross the stile, via a gate (muddy) into a lane leading into Well Street (footpath sign) to finish.

Gratton Dale's upper sanctuary (minus pylons!)

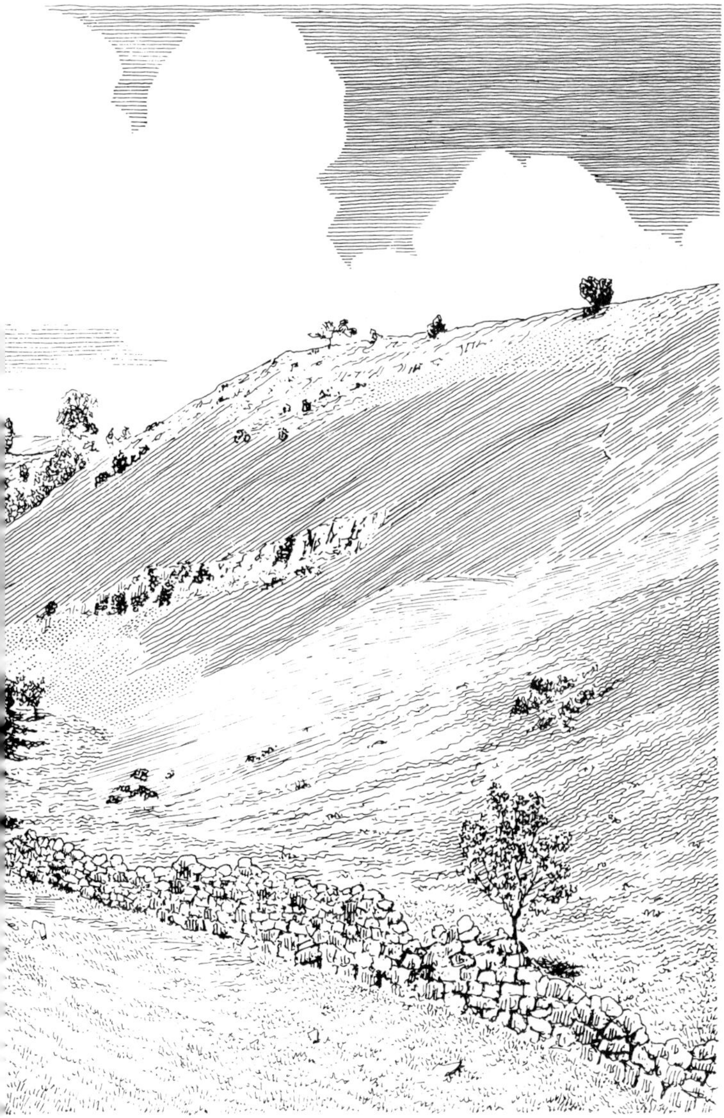

WALK 27   GRATTON DALE

from Youlgreave   8 miles

Youlgreave may be admired for its imposing and internally beautiful church, and for its proximity to the deeply entrenched Bradford Dale, a sequestered wooded valley containing a string of lovely fish ponds. Walkers may elect a stroll exclusively within this dell, or else they may gain Rusden along Weaddow and Stinking Lanes, thereby sampling the delights of Middleton-by-Youlgreave.

However, it is the prime intention of this narrative to encourage walkers to stride out along the mediaeval Peakway to visit the lonely reaches of Long Dale and the remotely beautiful wilds of Gratton Dale. All refreshment has to be carried for only at Youlgreave are there pubs and a café (unless a detour is made to Elton).

Long Dale and Gratton Dale are a joy to explore, each quite different in character. True, they are both largely dry valleys, but at an abrupt right angle, the soft and sinuous countenance of Long Dale (higher up Friden Dale) is transfigured into the craggy features, efflorescent with thorn scrub, of Gratton Dale. It has been suggested that the two dales have different origins, Long Dale belonging to an older valley-forming period. By contrast, the deeply-incised structure of Gratton Dale has been fashioned by a later stream, strong and surface-flowing, which quickly cut back to capture the transverse dale: the lowering of the water table has subsequently caused this process to cease.

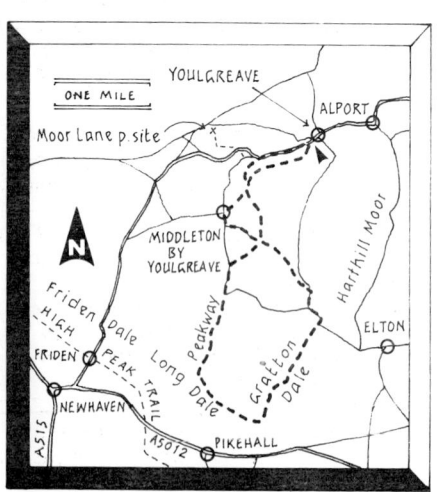

Subsequently, rain has percolated into the cracks and fissures of the subsurface to leave the union high and dry. Gratton Dale's one spring rising can be temperamental, seeming to flow on a whim, though winter months can see a formidable flow racing down the track from the gate to the old kiln.

Bradford Dale

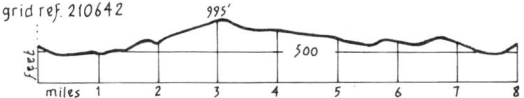

grid ref. 210642

(S) Youlgreave is not profusely endowed with car parking facilities, therefore, in the absence of convenient parking at the head of Holywell Lane, walkers are advised to use the Moor Lane picnic site at grid reference 194 645 (where follow the Limestone Way waymarks down past Lomberdale Hall into Bradford Dale) or contemplate a different starting point on the route.

The walk begins by descending Holywell Lane via Meadow Cottage into the Bradford valley. Cross the footbridge and, from the wicket gate, go R beside the crystal clear waters of the diminutive river. Passing four progressively larger fish ponds as the gorgeously wooded valley turns beneath Moatlow Knob (which means 'assembly hill or mound'). From the gate, continue with the track by three further redundant fish ponds, **(1)** the last reached after the old sheep wash pens where the path switches to the far side of the valley. Notice the tremendous resurgence crossed by a slab. Where the crags diminish, the footpath is forced over a footbridge and up steps going R, descending to cross the clapper bridge across the infant river Bradford. The path advances across the pasture to a wall stile and continues via three further stiles to enter the metalled lane. Walkers can follow this lane R to enter Middleton if only a casual perambulation of the environs of the Bradford is sought.

——— continued on page 228

continued from page 227 ─────

Proceed directly across the lane, following the stream into the dell. At this point, our walk within Bradford Dale encounters a third change of mood, as broad meadows yield to attractive limestone cliffs, and our attendant watercourse now bears the title of Rowlow Brook ('Rowlow' meaning 'rough mound') as it winds on. The walk slips R, over a resurgence adjacent to the unusual water-worn concave cliffs at the foot of the re-entrant dry valley. Rising L to a wall stile, proceed R, parallel and above the cragbound wooded Rusden (meaning 'rushy valley') to a modified wall stile, then descend the bank to join Weaddow Lane at a stile beside an occasional spring. Again an abridgement of the walk is possible R - but weaken not your resolve!

Go L along Weaddow Lane. This unusual name probably meant 'the sheltered way' ❷ - indeed, there is strong evidence that this is the ancient Peakway mentioned in a thirteenth century land grant. Where the road bends sharp L, our route continues ahead into the lane which has been worn down to the bedrock, becoming a holloway. Presumably the location of the medieval Smerrill Grange was influenced by the course of this old trackway across the Peak, for it will have provided a dry flock droveway corridor, perhaps forking from the Port Way at Alport and running S via Pikehall, Green Lane, Hawk Low and Peakway Farm W of Parwich. Evidence on the ground for this route (if indeed it constitutes one complete way at all) is at best patchy, but it is surely more rewarding to contemplate surmised Smerrill ways than modern Merrill ways!

───── *continued on page 231*

Weaddow Lane

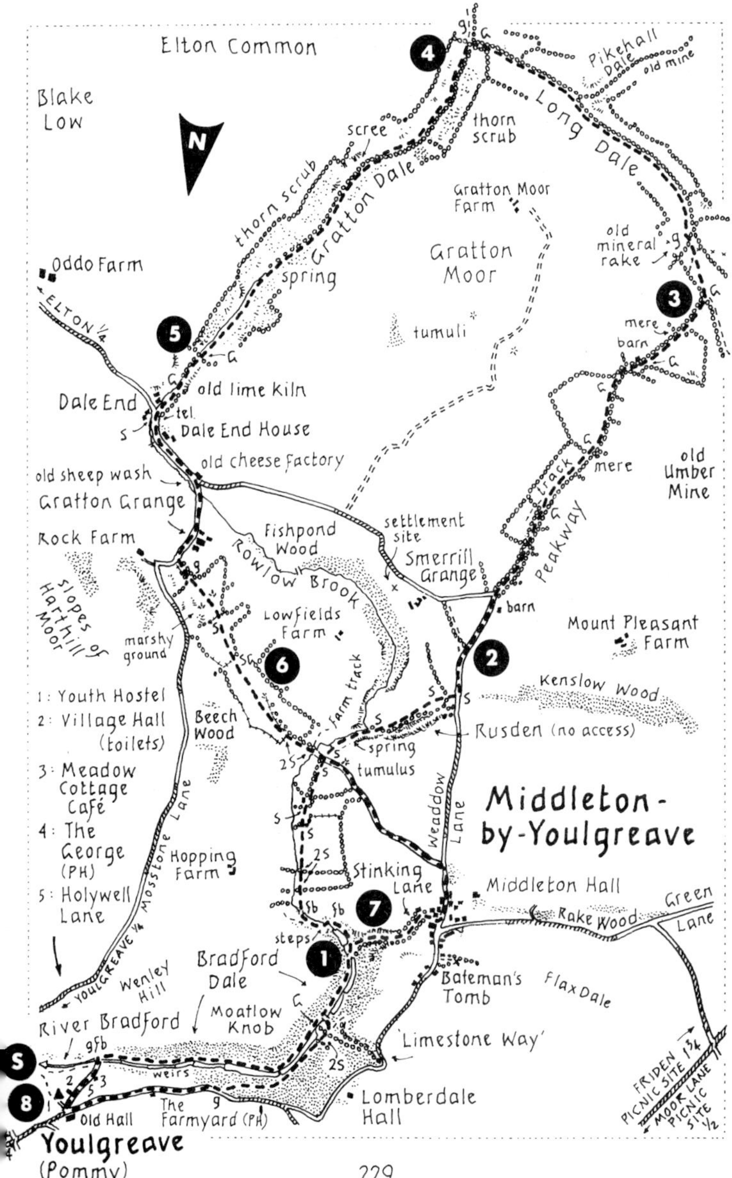
Elton Common
Blake Low
N
Oddo Farm
ELTON 1/4
thorn scrub
scree
Gratton Dale
spring
thorn scrub
Pikehall Dale
old mine
Long Dale
Gratton Moor Farm
Gratton Moor
tumuli
old mineral rake
mere
barn
old lime kiln
Dale End
tel
Dale End House
old cheese factory
old sheep wash
Gratton Grange
Rock Farm
slopes of Harthill Moor
Fishpond Wood
Rowlow Brook
settlement site
Smerrill Grange
track
mere
old Umber Mine
Peakway
barn
Mount Pleasant Farm
marshy ground
Lowfields Farm
farm track
Kenslow Wood
Rusden (no access)
Beech Wood
spring
tumulus
1: Youth Hostel
2: Village Hall (toilets)
3: Meadow Cottage Café
4: The George (PH)
5: Holywell Lane
Mosstone Lane
Hopping Farm
Weaddow Lane
Middleton-by-Youlgreave
Stinking Lane
Middleton Hall
Rake Wood
Green Lane
steps
Bradford Dale
Bateman's Tomb
Flax Dale
YOULGREAVE 1/4
Wenley Hill
River Bradford
Moatlow Knob
'Limestone Way'
weirs
Lomberdale Hall
FRIDEN PICNIC SITE 1 3/4
MOOR LANE PICNIC SITE 1/2
Old Hall
The Farmyard (PH)
Youlgreave (Pommy)

Long Dale

upper Gratton Dale

continued from page 228

The sunken Weaddow Lane terminates at a gate, with the Peakway clearly continuing as a holloway, though it rapidly peters out. Joining the farm track up to the L, advance by a gate next to a mere, and passing beneath 11,000 volt power lines enter a short lane at a gate. Proceed past the wooden cattle crush into a kite-shaped gathering enclosure. On my visit the pole barn contained a Claas combine, here ensconced ready for early autumn action upon the broad acres of Gratton Moor which were then under plough for spring barley.

Notice the sudden alteration in the walls in this vicinity, to a coarse khaki brown rubble composition analogous with the orthostats of Roystone — though it would be stretching credulity to suggest that they are anything like so old.

The clue to the rock change lies in the nearby defunct Umber Mine. The limestone in the immediate area contains hydrated oxides of iron (ochre) and manganese (wad), a source of 'burnt umber' pigment. The question nevertheless remains — why does such an apparently crude construction exist?

Dating the local limestone drystone walls is a science currently being pioneered by Martin Wildgoose of Kniveton. It is to be hoped that his award-winning research, currently centred on Roystone Grange, will lead him onto Smerrill Moor, thereby aiding the resolution of this particular conundrum.

Beyond the mere, the regular grey limestone returns in the wall flanking the Peakway, though a smaller than usual size of stone. At a gate, where the walker's eyes are drawn to the distinctive clump to the SSE on Minninglow, his feet are drawn into Long Dale. ❸ The old way slants L, descending the gorse-clad bank to cross the tell-tale pitted alignment of a lead rake, striking askew across the narrow dale. The bridleway arrives at a bridle gate, but lo- it is impossible to open! Naturally, failing all endeavours to prise it free, walkers resort to climbing o'er. A plea — can someone restore an efficient catch before irretrievable damage is done to the bars? Precisely how horse riders deal with the obstacle is not known, for it cannot be jumped.

continued on page 232

continued from page 231

The walk advances beside the rugged dale bottom wall which here defines the boundary between the parishes of Gratton (which has no nucleating village) and Hartington Nether Quarter (with its focus at Biggin). The second southern re-entrant valley, Pikehall Dale, marks the probable departure of the Peakway. The bridleway is clearly defined on the ground: indeed the triple connecting dales, Friden, Long and Gratton must have been prime landmark features for travellers down the centuries providing sheltered passage. However, in the days when wildboar, wolves and bands of thieves lurked in these lonely districts, the advantages of a sheltered way had to be balanced with the possibility of falling foul of ravage or ambush.

Once a rash of nettles has been circumvented a gate is reached, smartly followed by a wicket gate L at the junction with the Mouldridge bridleway. Gratton Dale cuts into a thick band of dolomitic limestone, hence the variably toned and striated rock strewn and outcropping down the dale ahead. Dolomitisation was caused by the percolation of magnesium-rich brine from overlaying sea-bed Permian limestones, long eroded away, from which came a molecular marriage of calcite and magnesia:

$$CaCO_3 + MgCO_3 \longrightarrow CaMg(CO_3)_2$$

continued on facing page

upper Long Dale towards Friden Dale

lower Gratton Dale

continued from facing page ———

Upon the Elton Common plateau, archaeologists, taking advantage of the ploughing since the 1960s, have discovered crude evidence of late Neolithic settlement. This comes in the form of flint scrapers and sickles, together with Langdale axes, spread over a hundred-acre site. Four other known sites within three miles of Elton Common confirm that this limestone upland harboured a stable populus 2000 BC, Bronze Age infiltration only consolidating on existing settlement and assuming stewardship of monuments (of importance to this day) such as Arbor Low and Minninglow.

——— *continued on page 234*

continued from page 233

4 The initial section of the path down Gratton Dale weaves through boulders and mature elder scrub. The thorn-smothered bank beyond the wall is infested with rabbits, badgers too have found safe haven; in fact the whole valley is renown as a wildlife sanctuary of some importance. Beyond the small conifer plantation, look to switch through the deteriorating wall, the prominent scree slope finally arresting progress on the R flank. Thorn scrub crowds in upon the occasionally muddy path, but not oppressively. The principal resurgence is encountered bubbling up with some gusto and accumulating either side of the broken wall before concentrating on fulfilling its destiny of speeding on down to the Wye via secretive Fishpool and Bradford Dales. Near the lane gate, a large limestone slab all but forms a natural bridge over the brook, which impetuously gurgles beneath this fallen rock.

5 In winter, the brook flows under the gate and fully occupies the track: walkers, though, are little inconvenienced. Directly after the next gate, a fine example of a lime kiln may be inspected. It was found that, by firing the quarried stone, a water-soluble calcine lime was produced: this powder was ideally suited for periodic spreading onto acidic pastures, thereby improving their productivity. An ash tree has taken hold of this structure, threatening the sturdy masonry and, with the flue open, at the top it is necessary to regard the (w)hole with circumspection! Cross the horse paddock to a squeeze stile onto the road at Dale End, a welcoming party of two steeds casting approval on your progress! Dale End is all that exists in strict community terms within the parish of Gratton (which means 'great farm').

continued on facing page

Old cheese factory, Gratton

continued from facing page

The distinctive gritstone quarried from Anthony Hill is much in evidence in the walls of the houses hereabouts, special merit being accorded to Dale End House for stone and sensitively tended garden alike. Facing the road junction is a large square warehouse of a building: built in 1884 as a cheese factory, it looks down upon a sheepwash.

Take the lane rising R. At Gratton Grange, glance in at the gate to admire not only the Friesian calves, but also the simple beauty of the cartshed with tooled lintels and round pillars bearing the date 1853 and the initials $^W_I{}^P_T{}^T$. What sense of aesthetic priorities accords to Man the utilitarian portal building above, while saluting his mute inglorious vehicles with this transport of delight?

Continuing with the road seek the short confined lane L. Only a few yards more the road reaches the Rock Farm corner where a row of water troughs may be seen. They lie upon the old Derby Road and may have served to refresh packhorse teams (another set beyond Anthony Hill Quarry along the same trackway is seen on WALK 26).

Re-aligning our minds to the present walk, follow the lane to a gate, thereafter adopting for the most part the line of the power lines. Cross an area of marshy ground to reach a stile; beyond the next fence stile **6**, keep R of the holloway (stone dump at its top). Descend via two fence stiles and cross Rowlow Brook (Gratton's stream and Bradford Dale's river) to follow the lane ahead up to Middleton.

— *continued on page 237*

The Square House

Rusden

All Saints, Youlgreave

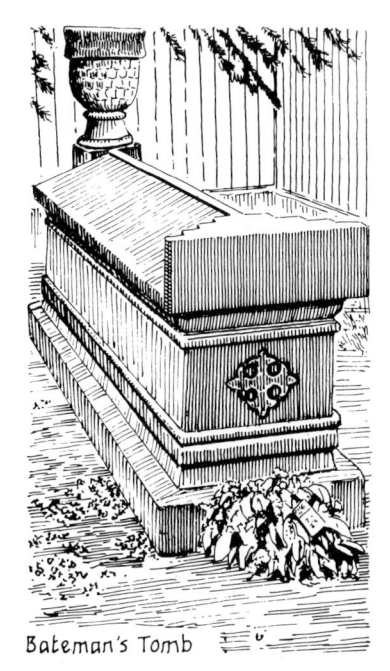

continued from page 235

Turn R along Weaddow Lane into the village, glimpsing the stately Hall through the screen of trees L and St. Michael's church R. This is every inch an estate village: apart from the foundations of Fullwood Hall, nothing visible pre-dates the C19th. The spacious road before Square House (former village inn) is in stark contrast with the cramped thoroughfare in 'Pommy.' Here there is trim order, a pleasure to behold.

Visitors should seek out the former United Reform Chapel, to the L up the Youlgreave road, for, tucked behind, reached via a path, is Bateman's Tomb (see L). Thomas Bateman of Lomberdale Hall took advantage of his wealth to indulge in an obsessive quest to explore the tumuli of the surrounding limestone plateau. Sadly, however, his eagerness to excavate would leave much to be desired

Bateman's Tomb

from present-day archaeologists. His amazing collections and beautifully penned personal notes are now housed for the most part in Weston Park Museum in Sheffield. The tomb of 1861 is crowned with a stone replica of a Bronze Age cinerary urn. The walk continues down Stinking Lane (thankfully no longer living up to its name) ❼, a dramatic gorge-like return to the sylvan depths of Bradford Dale. At the bottom, notice the foundations of a pump house which once supplied Middleton with water.

Go L downdale, branching L over the bridge as directed by the Limestone Way footpath sign. However, instead of rising with the obvious track, go R to the wall stile, soon succeeded by another. The footpath beside the pond begins to mount as the valley turns, rising on an easy gradient to join the road. Conclude the walk by going R past the public house with the quaintly rustic name of 'The Farmyard' ❽. In local conversation, Youlgreave (the yellow grove) is affectionately known as 'Pommy'. If asked why, villagers will offer up a 'cock and bull' story about a rather special pig upon a wall vocalising 'tiddley pom pom pom' as it watches a brass band march along the street! So you find this beyond belief, then look in at The George where the 'Gents' are 'By Royal Appointment'!!

Nine Ladies stone circle, Stanton Moor

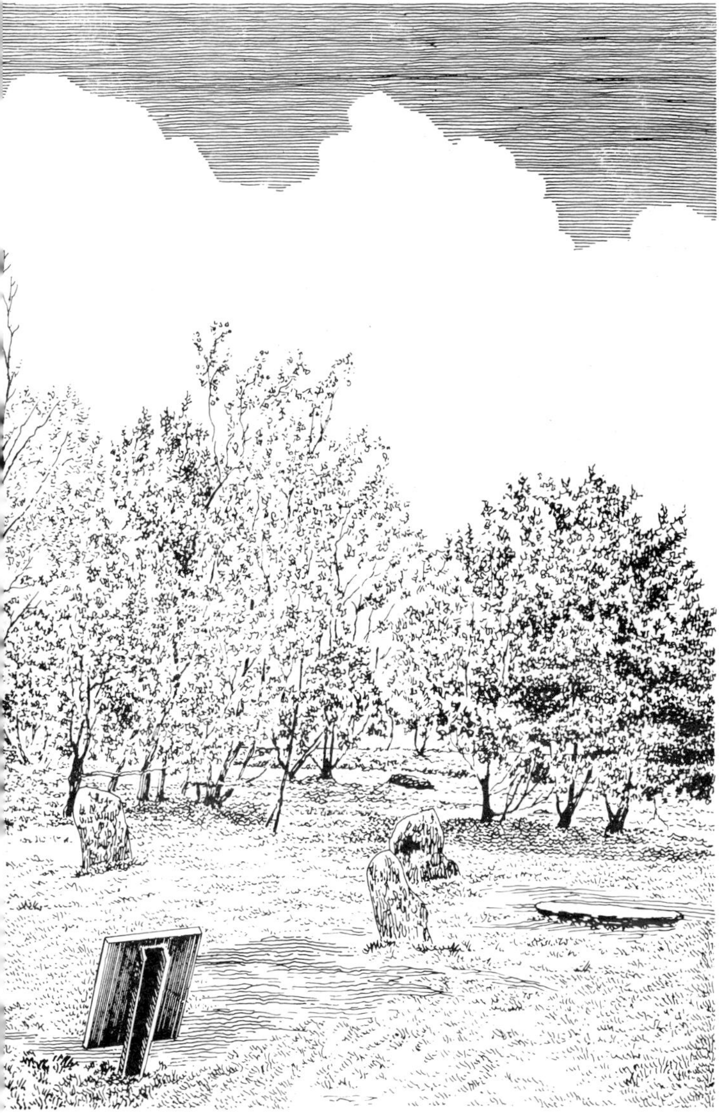

WALK 28
from Winster

STANTON MOOR
6½ miles

Stanton Moor has been likened to an island, an isolated gritstone landmass, strangely aloof from the hubbub of Darley Dale and tangibly different from the limestone country to its W. So it is no wonder that people have long been drawn to investigate its antiquarian secrets, see the old wind-weathered stones, the Nine Ladies stone circle, Rowtor Rocks and parade along the E scarp. For such enticing fare, Winster, a village of fine architecture and endearing nooks, serves well as a start point. From this approach, the mysterious 'lost world' of Stanton Moor is little suspected and comes as a joyous surprise. The walk sustains interest once off the Moor too, with prospects of Robin Hood's Stride and Cratcliffe Rocks, together with the limestone country along the old Portway. The concluding passage down the steep winding street to the fine old Market Hall at the heart of Winster sets the seal on a good day out. Birchover and Winster are both well served with pubs and shops for refreshment.

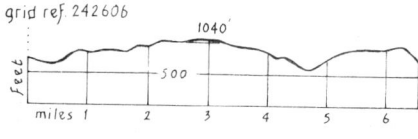

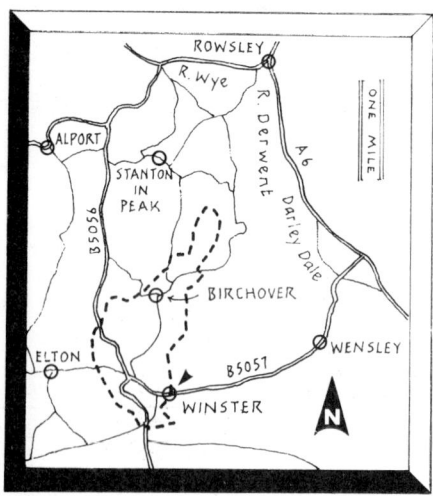

grid ref. 242606

S Beginning from the Market Hall (N.T. shop/information centre), follow the lane N signposted 'Birchover'. This lane descends ominously towards a waste dump. However, fear not: from the gate, keep to the wall L to the stile, continuing downhill, partially upon paving slabs, to a stile.

The path crosses the potentially marshy depression of Millclose Brook. Rising over a shallow ridge and passing through old hedge gaps, the path leads to a stile before slipping across a second depression, with evidence again of paving slabs.

The route now rises, though, due to the poaching effect of cattle, the path

continued on page 242

241

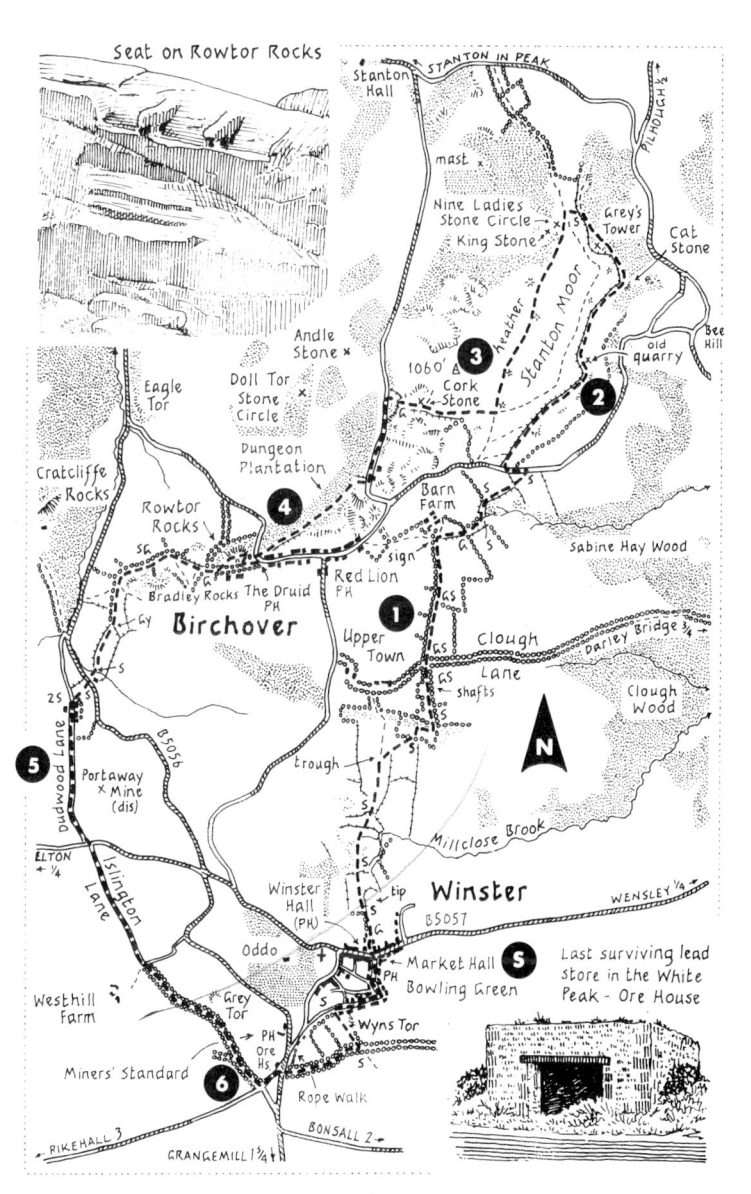

continued from page 240 ———

is less definite through the tussocky pasture (currently marked on O.S. maps as woodland, which appears to have been cleared long ago!). On reaching a circular cattle water-trough, slant up R to a wall stile. Ascend the slope to join an old path cut into the hillside. At the top of the scarp, cross the stile and follow the wall N, passing an old spoil heap associated with the Yatestoop lead vein. Ahead, a large mound with a shaft capping is located above the Cowley Sough (400' below). The sough drained lead mines at Elton, Placket (below Winster church) and Portaway into the Derwent near the famous Millclose Mine.

Cross Clough Lane by facing stiles/gates, rising to a further stile/gate combination. ❶ The footpath advances towards Barn Farm; at the signpost, do not follow the S side of the fence R, keep to the muddier N side. Pass through a muddy gateway, keep to drier ground beyond before going L to a fence stile. Follow the fence beside a young plantation to a second fence stile. Continue round the edge overlooking Sabine Hay Wood, then through a hedge gap to a stile/signpost onto the minor road, where go L

Follow a track R, beside a fence backed by dense bracken, onto Stanton Moor. This popular way rises past an old sunken quarry and gritstone outcrop (viewpoint). The well-defined path lies a few yards back from the edge. ❷ ——— *continued on facing page*

My oft companion Rod Busby on the Cat Stone

continued from facing page ────────

Just beyond the next prominent spur, there is a second perilously deep quarry concealed to the R of the path. This is an unusual type of quarry requiring stone to have been winched directly out to avoid cutting awkward tracks on the scarp face. Within, several trees have found safe harbour, including oak, ash and a fine fir. [NB children must be kept under control in this vicinity: romping through the heather is not an advisable antic].

With the open heatherscape of Stanton Moor to the L, dotted with over seventy recorded antiquarian sites associated with the Bronze Age, the view R down to Stanton Lees and Darley Dale Churchtown strikes a colourful contrast. The Derwent valley rings to the sound of thunderous lorries and regrettably, the air may be charged with the unmistakable scent of industry too! If you consider the smells less than pleasant, then it may well be you are inhaling the poisonous fumes belching from the tall chimney at the former Millclose Mine (lead-smelting blast-furnace owned by Enthovens). Millclose was the largest lead mine in Britain; around the site are tips of lead slag and tailings from the washing plant now being worked for fluorspar.

At the next headland, take the spur path R to visit the Cat Stone, one of three similar hard rock features on the moor that have curiously resisted erosion. This great block of gritstone with its overhang and chiselled steps bears numerous etchings, most prominent of which is "E IN 1831". There are rock basins in the top created by the action of rainwater.

The main edges path is rejoined, proceeding through light birch and oak wood, soon to pass beneath the Reform Tower, erected by the Thornhill family of Stanton Hall in tribute to Earl Grey who carried the Reform Bill through Parliament in 1832.

Shortly a fence stile is crossed; here leaving the scarptop, the footpath comes to a trackway turn L. This well used path passes the Nine Ladies stone circle on the R.

Reform Tower

(Rapunzel's tower!)

──── *continued on page 244*

243

continued from page 243 ———

Since the removal of the enclosing wall in 1985, the stone circle has regained that precious quality of mystique vital for the proper respect of prehistoric monuments. Measuring 35' in diameter, the circle is in truth all that remains of a burial mound from the Bronze Age (c.1500 B.C.). One hundred yards SW of the clearing stands a tilted standing stone, known as the King's Stone: this stunted megalith bears the cryptic 'Billstumps' and '+0' beneath, etched in the C19th, by some latter-day Druid!

Returning to the main path through the light woodland of Stanton Moor Plantation onto the open heather moor, numerous ring enclosures and tumuli are encountered. All were excavated systematically between 1927 and 1953 by J. and J.P. Heathcote (father and son) who established a private museum of their finds in Birchover.

The first of these disc barrows passed on the R is the largest, 80' across with two well-built entrances. A small barrow in the centre had a glazed faience bead with its interment, supposed by archaeologists to have been made in Egypt.

Continuing S some 100 yards, there is a large barrow on the L, mutilated by poor excavation methods (sadly a common state for the funerary monuments of this too accessible plateau). Another 300 yards brings the visitor to a second circular bank feature 60' across with at least one entrance. On the inside of the bank are seven small stones (formerly standing). In the centre is a small disturbed mound. 100 yards on, at the path intersection, is the largest of the 36 cairns that have been excavated. **❸** Two bushes surmount the spoil mound, at the centre of which may be seen a small stone burial chamber: this contained the cremated remains of a boy, a broken urn and fragments of a bronze pin. There are two concentric rings of large stones, not upright. The mound contained

——— *continued on facing page*

244

continued from facing page

over a dozen other interments, some with urns, one with a food vessel and one with an incense cup. Nearly all had flint scrapers or knives with them. Turn R. After a further 100 yards, the small barrow on the L of the track contained the interment of a woman buried with a stone battle axe.   Adjacent to an old quarry is the Cork Stone, a close cousin to the Cat Stone. It has elaborate hand and foot holds inserted (presumably in the C19th); though taller than the latter, there is no top to stand on - can you resist grappling with it?

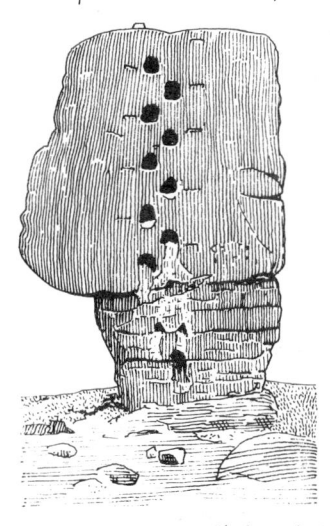

The track declines off the moor to a stile/gate reaching the Stanton/Birchover road (a popular scenic drive). Across the field to the R is the Andle Stone (anvil); unfortunately there is no access to it. Turn L following the road beside the old Stanton Park Quarry: much of the W side of Stanton Moor has been extensively quarried for building stone as well as grindstones. The only active site is Birchover Quarry, the entrance to which is shortly passed. The sign proclaims 'Natural Birchover Gritstone - Ann Twyford, member of the Rio Tinto Group.'

Branch R off the road just beyond the quarry entrance (quarry car park), follow a path down between the old Barton Hill Quarries and Dungeon Plantation. ❹ After the quarry spoil, the path treads the narrow ridge overlooking Birchover (birch covered bank) becoming a hollow way which emerges onto the minor road opposite the Druid Inn (how convenient!). A walled lane advances W down to a gate.

However, walkers should be aware of the unique hidden gritstone delights of Rowtor Rocks (rough rocks) in the trees up to the R. Whilst there is no right of way, there is no local objection to respectful visitors inspecting the caves and carvings (attributed to the active imagination of a Victorian vicar). Care is definitely required as the N side falls away precipitously. See the steps, shelter and seat all neatly cut into this coarse rock; notice also the obelisk (of cryptic purpose). Either backtrack to the steps or descend, with caution, from the SW end to enter the lane over the broken wall.   Follow the track from the gate, continuing, at its hairpin, forward to a gate. Contour above the wall, ignoring the track mounting to Rocking

continued on page 248

The Andle Stone or Tupenny Loaf

Birchover Quarry

Dragon devil carved in gritstone above the entrance to Rowtor Chapel

Rowtor Rocks

continued from page 245

Stone Farm L coming to a stile/gateway beyond a scrubby area. The view is dominated by Cratcliffe Rocks and Robin Hood's Stride (Mock Beggars Castle), with Eagle Torr down the valley to the R. To link this rock feature with actual eagles may be no more than a flight of fancy, the probable derivation, in common with the Eagle Stone on Baslow Edge, is from the superhuman stone lifting feats of the early Saxon god Aigle.

Descend the pasture to a stile (and rudimentary footbridge), rising to a stile/footpath sign onto the B5056 road. Go directly over the road to a stile, slanting up L to two stiles/footpath sign beside a cottage garden wall, here joining Dudwood Lane going L. **5** This lane is part of the principal Iron Age N-S route through the Peak, later adopted by the Saxons, hence they referred to it as the 'Old Portway'. The 'market way' survives in place-names such as Alport in the Woodlands valley, Alport near Youlgreave, and Alport Hill S of Wirksworth. The old CIT* lead mine on the L higher up Dudwood Lane was known as the Portaway Mine.

At the top of the hill, cross the B5057 into Islington Lane (again on the line of the Portway). 'Islington' refers to a 'lost' village. Beyond a farm access, the lane becomes no more than a quiet footpath passing the craggy mass of Grey Tor (drawing above). **6** Reaching the next road, turn L, then R where roads converge to enter a farm lane that rises above Winster. Take the waymarked footpath L over the stile, descend past Wyns Tor. Do not confuse this name with that of the village: this limestone outcrop, though a prominent feature above the village is a later hybrid form. Winster is considered to mean 'Wine's thorn' after a Saxon landowner, not a plonk!

Cross a stile at the foot of the slope, and follow the byway R wending down to finish the walk at the Market Hall, the first property acquired by the National Trust in Derbyshire (1906).

Being a native 'Cotsaller,' I am aware of the similarity between the Cotswold 'wool' towns (e.g. Chipping Campden) and 'woollen mill' villages (e.g. Painswick) with the Peakland lead mining industry exemplified by Winster. Both limestone areas reflected a desire to adopt urban architectural vogues among the homes of the ruling classes. For Winster it was the mine/sough owners and ore dealers who raised the houses of prevailing fashion along the main street, backed by the cottage styles of the miners and craftsmen upon West Bank. To contemporary eyes, the product is a cohesive and pleasing whole, a classic conservation area - so before you depart, take advantage of a stroll around.

The Market Hall, which palpably takes centre stage, is supported on arches thought to be 500 years old: the upper stone and brick portion was rebuilt in 1905. It is likely that this was originally half-timbered (unfortunately the arches were bricked-in to give support to the building). Elsewhere, there are fine C17th and C18th houses, the most notable being Winster Hall (public house), standing squarely back in all its early Georgian pomp - to my eyes a misfit. The Bowling Green and Miner's Standard, a name derived from the dish used as the standard unit of measurment for lead ore, are both C17th pubs serving the community. The church has an C18th tower; the remainder is Victorian with innovative internal form.

Winster Hall

Winster Market Hall — National Trust Information Centre

Harborough Rocks, upper tier

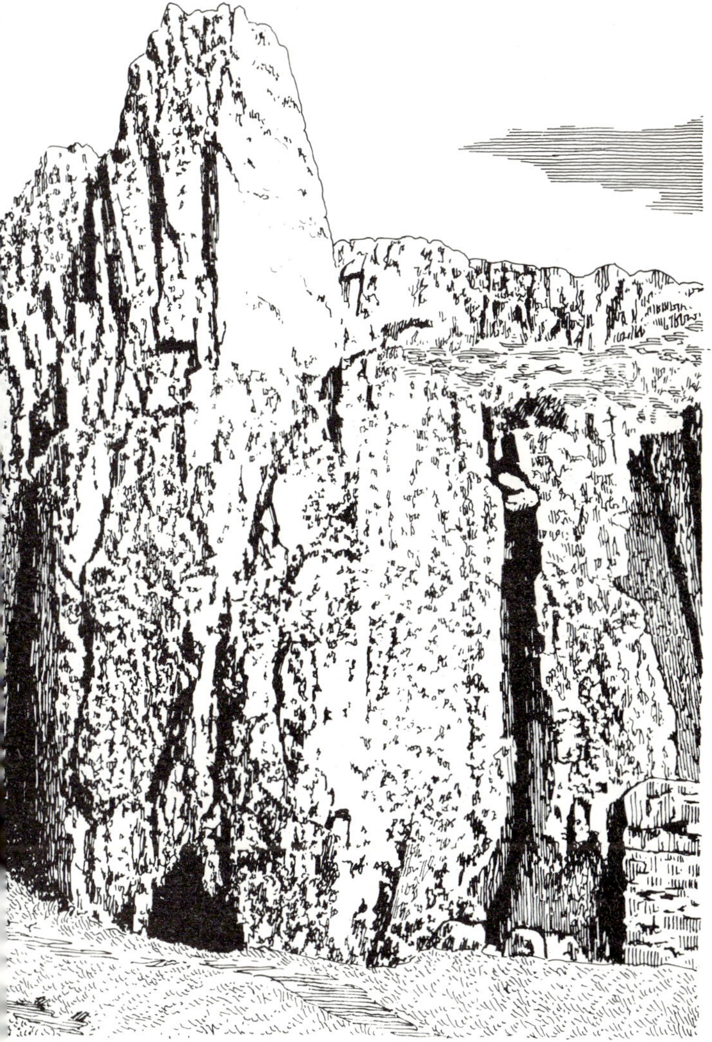

WALK 29   RAINSTER and HARBOROUGH ROCKS

from Middleton Top   9 miles

For the final two walks in this guide, we stray just outside the SE corner of the National Park to explore country which is not only scenically attractive, but holds a fascination for those interested in industrial archaeology. The two walks share a common start-point on the High Peak Trail at Middleton Top, where Derbyshire County Council's Countryside Service operates a combined picnic area, cycle-hire point and information centre. This penultimate walk ranges W with the Trail to discover the peculiar qualities of the intensely mined, quarried and pitted country above Carsington and Brassington. Both of these gorgeously homogeneous lead mining villages are visited before advancing to Rainster Rocks and another stretch of Trail-blazing, climbing to the bristling summit of Harborough Rocks for _the view._

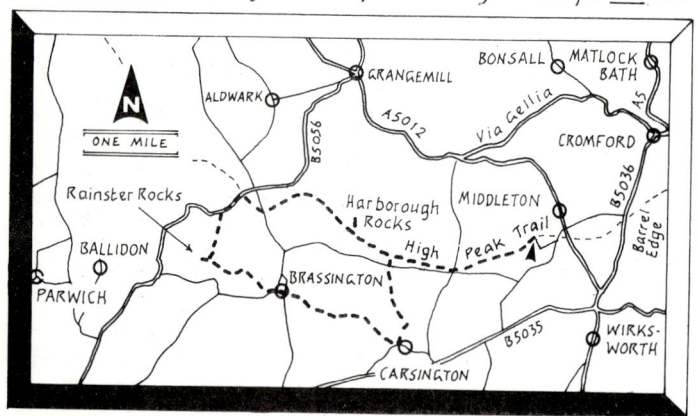

grid ref. 275 551

The walk can be limited rather neatly to a four mile circuit by starting beneath Harborough Rocks (by mile 7 on the map) and descending to Brassington via the truncated minor road, joining the main route at the Miner's Arms.

252

Daniel and Alison R. clambering on the topograph at Middleton Top

S Advance W along the level track (watchful of cyclists!). This first 1½ miles along the High Peak Trail to the top of the Hopton Incline may be duplicated on the return leg, but it surely no hardship to contemplate, for the walking is easy and enhanced by notable long-range views S. Hopton Tunnel is the first surprise of the walk, the craggy cutting culminating in a short rock arch tunnel carrying a farm lane. Beyond, the Trail crosses an embankment passing the at present derelict mineral processing works **1** and begins to rise up the 1 in 14½ (7%) Hopton Incline, which was the steepest in Britain where a conventional track locomotive was used. When first operated, wagons were drawn up the pitch by draught horses.

At the Hopton Works, where the Trail begins to drift away from the road, turn L, crossing the road to a stile/gate to enter Carsington Pastures. The strange pot-shaped building in the field below was formerly a windmill associated with Hopton Hall. In a region so seemingly comprehensively laced with walled enclosures this, large area devoid of division must seem odd on first acquaintance, but the reason is soon discovered. The overwhelming majority of field boundaries, despite their hoary grey, lichen-encrusted complexion, were built during the last two hundred years, a period which saw the lead mines upon Carsington Pastures and around Brassington at their most productive. Such a rich upland streaked with valuable mineral veins (scrins and flats) exploited in

———— *continued on page 254*

continued from page 253

an intensive frenzy, so there was no scope for agricultural use, lead spoil being notoriously poisonous for grazing livestock.

Walkers are warned that there are at least 230 mine shafts in this one area. Some, but by no means all, have been capped: some in fact are shielded by little more than a rash of nettles. Do not become an accident statistic because you choose to wander off the footpath!

The path keeps close order with the wall over the Old Knoll ridge ② and past the King's Chair: maybe this throne of stone has been modified at the humorous whim of miners (there being a similar seat near the summit of Harborough Rocks).

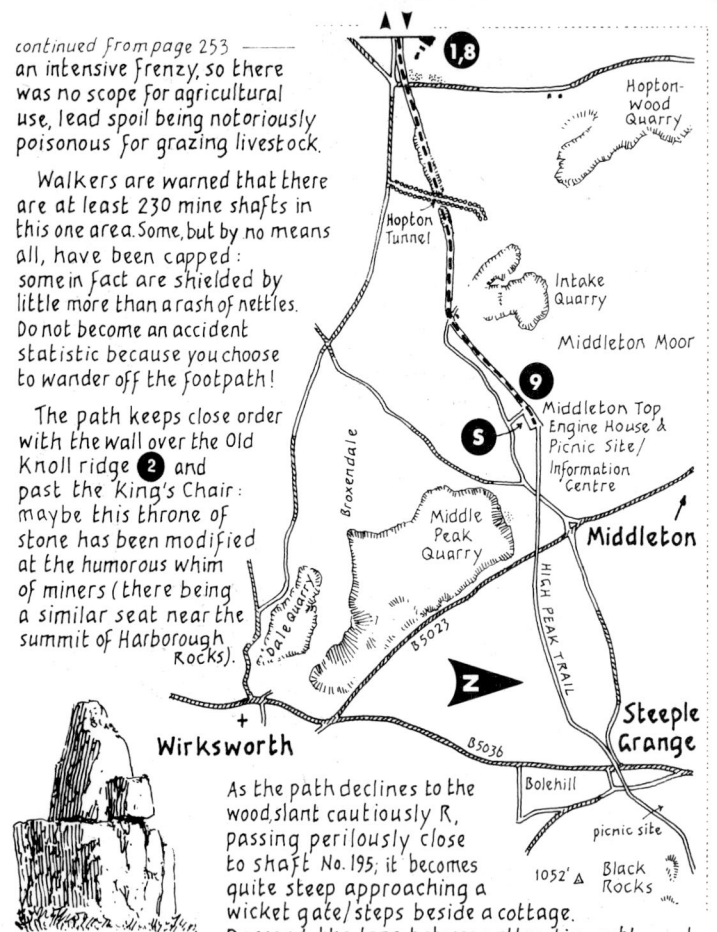

As the path declines to the wood, slant cautiously R, passing perilously close to shaft No. 195; it becomes quite steep approaching a wicket gate/steps beside a cottage.

Descend the lane between attractive cottages to the road junction in Carsington, which derives its name from 'Farmstead with cressbeds'. The recent history of Carsington has been broadcast nationally due to what can only be deemed the folly of Water Board engineers who failed to judge the hazards in the clay basin of Scow Brook, as they sank millions of pounds into the construction of a reservoir dam, only to see it slip-mercifully before the water had accumulated to threathen Ashbourne with an unwelcome deluge.

—— *continued on page 256*

254

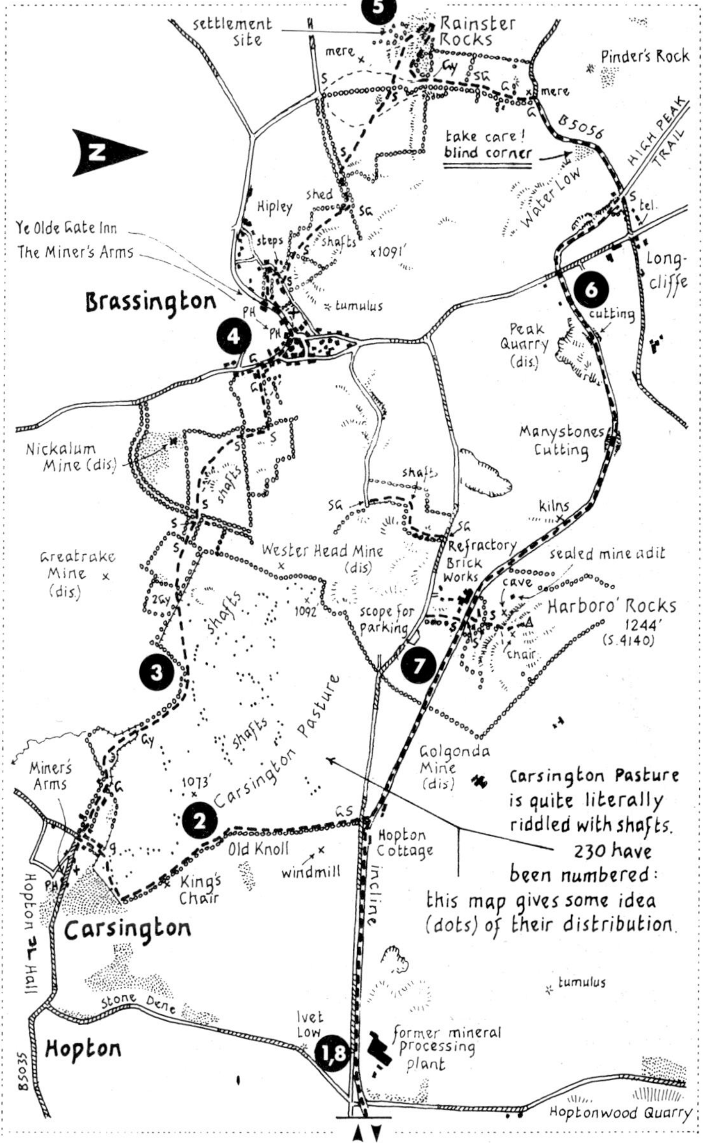

settlement site
Rainster Rocks
mere
Pinder's Rock
B5056
HIGH PEAK TRAIL
take care! blind corner
Water Low
Hipley
shed
shafts
1091'
Ye Olde Gate Inn
The Miner's Arms
steps
tumulus
Brassington
PH
tel.
Longcliffe
cutting
Peak Quarry (dis.)
Nickalum Mine (dis.)
Manystones Cutting
shafts
kilns
Greatrake Mine (dis.)
Wester Head Mine (dis.)
Refractory Brick Works
sealed mine adit
cave
Harboro' Rocks
1244' (S.4140)
1092'
scope for parking
chair
2Gy
shafts
Carsington Pasture
Miner's Arms
1073'
Golgonda Mine (dis.)
Carsington Pasture is quite literally riddled with shafts. 230 have been numbered: this map gives some idea (dots) of their distribution.
Hopton Cottage
Old Knoll
windmill
King's Chair
incline
Carsington
Hopton Hall
tumulus
Stone Dene
Ivet Low
former mineral processing plant
Hopton
B5035
Hoptonwood Quarry

continued from page 254

At the foot of the lane, turn R (W) along the farm lane which, at a stile/gate, becomes a track passing an old quarry to a further gateway. ❸
The track rises and, passing shaft No. 117, angles up the pasture, initially in a hollow way, going through two gateways in broken walls. Drop to a stile cross the small valley pasture, in a combe dotted with dolomitic limestone outcrops, to a stile. Go directly across the lane through the stile/gate onto a clear path cutting round the ridge with plenty of evidence of mine disturbance in the vicinity of the Nickalum Mine.

Brassington from the E.

The path slants down to a stile, following the wall to a stile L, then downhill to a gate into the farmyard. Go directly on to a gate onto the road. ❹ Turn R into Brassington, forking L by the Tudor House (1615).

Miner's Arms

Brassington appears to derive its name from 'farmsteam by the steep path', presumably the road running down from Longcliffe past the attractive village hall. The village rests snugly in a fold of the magnesian limestone hills, its steady growth inextricably linked to the fortunes of lead mining, hence the Miner's Arms which is passed on the way through to the church.

— *continued on facing page*

Tudor House

continued from facing page

St James' should not be passed by, its sturdy demeanour disguising a charming interior. The prominent Norman features, the tower, parts of the porch and S aisle were tastefully integrated during the necessary remodelling process of 1879-81. Notice particularly the 'Black Marble' (from Ashford-in-the-Water) columns between the nave and new N aisle.

Ye Olde Gate Inn (which vies with the Miner's Arms for walkers' custom) probably derives its name from proximity to the same 'steep path' (brant sty) or 'gate' held within the village name. Opposite the pub, the walk proceeds along the narrow passage between houses, climbing steps by 'Browtop' to reach the minor road. Go R to the stile/footpath sign short of the chapel. Cross the pasture to a stile (not the stile into the garden!), continuing to a stile/gate near a corrugated shed. Turn L down the lane, branching R at a stile taking a beeline down the pastures for Rainster Rocks. Keep just R of the intermediate dolomite outcrop, to reach a stile (·slightly obscured by a thornbush). You could go R here along the track, but there is every reason to make for the crest of Rainster (Rain's tor or thorn).

continued on page 259

Rainster Rocks

Young climbers delighting in the jug holds of Rainster Rocks

continued from page 257

Rainster Rocks, attained through the thorn scrub and boulders, is understandably popular with rock climbers, the S aspect coupled with the coarse character of the rock, deeply fissured and pock-marked with handy 'jugs,' making it the perfect challenge for developing technique and confidence for more serious limestone climbs elsewhere. The summit, easily reached through weaknesses to the L, is composed of huge irregular blocks of dolomite, and is a grand viewpoint.

5 Descend E, keeping within the scrub to join the track leading L through a gateway: proceeding via three more gates to join the B5056, where go R. In view W is the ivy-covered Pinder's Rock; the process leading to the survival of this isolated pinnacle is not fully understood, but, its name relates to a 'keeper of a pinfold,' which was an enclosure where stray farm livestock were held. The second corner demands respect as there is little verge to ameliorate the hazard for walkers. Pass under the old railway bridge, diverging R into the old Longcliffe station-yard and up onto the trackbed going L (SE). **6** The Trail leads via two interesting cuttings and the ruins of kilns (associated with a defunct paint factory) to the industrial complex beneath Harborough Rocks. Hoben's Brassington Works (refractory materials - bauxite process) nestles amid a sad scene of past and present mineral exploitation and processing, originally instigated by the railroad.

Diverge L between the ruinous farm buildings by three stiles to the jagged tiers of dolomite which offer exciting routes for all levels of rock-climbing ambition. The large cave (adopted by cattle as an impromptu cowshed!) has been excavated, revealing Romano-British pottery sherds. It is suggested that the name Harborough, which translates to 'army shelter,' may refer to the use of the cave as a refuge for militia. The summit commands a quite superb panorama, curiosity will draw walkers to examine the sculpted chair bearing initials and the date 1757. Regain the High Peak Trail, going L to **789** Middleton Top car park.

Hopton Tunnel

Bole Hill from Matlock Bath

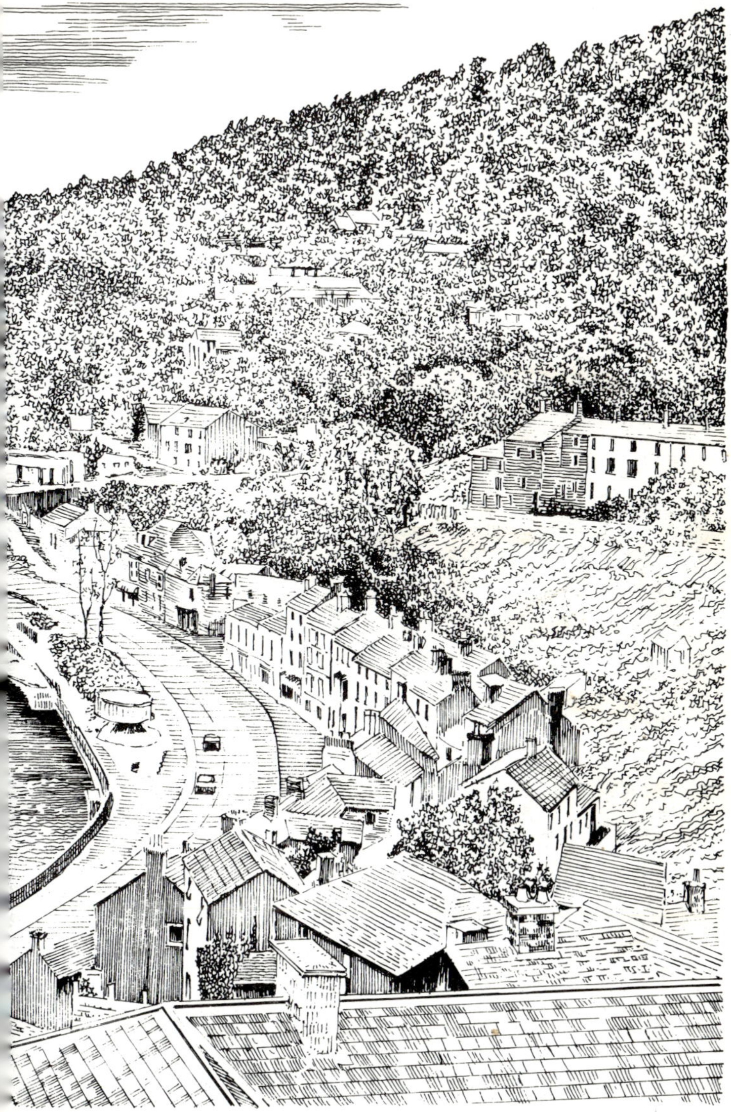

WALK 30   CROMFORD HEIGHTS
from Middleton Top   9¼ miles

By way of a finale, this walk manages to combine all the ingredients of the White Peak despite the fact that no portion of the route lies within the boundaries of the National Park. Whilst the harsh effects of mining and quarrying are not easy to dispel, there are numerous compensations to raise the anticipation for a good day's walking.

The High Peak Trail provides a splendid start via a severe incline to reach the Black Rocks of Cromford, where a spur route onto the outcrop revealing THE view of the day's undertaking may be taken. Approaching the Sheep Pastures Incline, the 'Little Switzerland' of the Derwent gorge may be admired from the promenade gallery of the Trail. The second long incline brings the route down to the Cromford Canal at Highpeak Junction. The level canal towpath is followed to Cromford Wharf; walkers may follow the road L past Richard Arkwright's famous factory complex or continue under Scarthin Rock to enter Cromford.

The full nine mile walk will not suit everybody's commitment, hence the short cut indicated curtailing the route along a delightful path up the valley from Cromford. Indeed, several plausible options

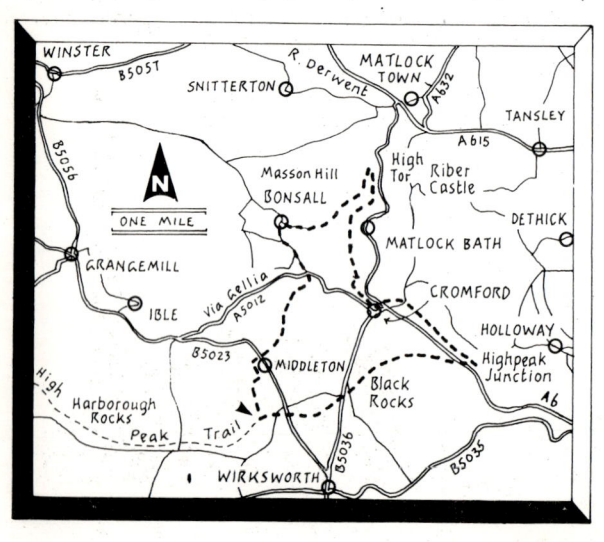

continued from facing page

exist using the Cromford Wharf car park as a valley base to explore Masson Hill, Bonsall or even High Tor (though there is an entry fee and access has a time limit).

The principal route enjoys Matlock Bath's wooded gorge without the need to dip deep into the pocket (the Heights of Abraham - an expensive luxury that can be avoided without trespass or blushes!). Bonsall (known as 'Bonser') is well worth a visit, though as a result it necessitates a plod down the oft busy road to the Via Gellia Mill.

The last stage of the journey evokes memories of the lattice work of grey-walled enclosures seen elsewhere upon the limestone plateau, a genuine White Peakscape.

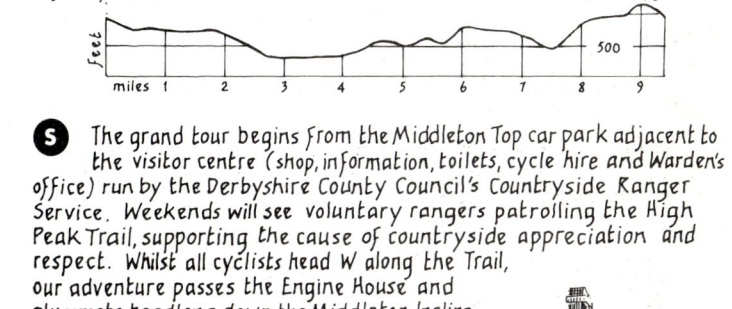

grid ref. 275 551

S The grand tour begins from the Middleton Top car park adjacent to the visitor centre (shop, information, toilets, cycle hire and Warden's office) run by the Derbyshire County Council's Countryside Ranger Service. Weekends will see voluntary rangers patrolling the High Peak Trail, supporting the cause of countryside appreciation and respect. Whilst all cyclists head W along the Trail, our adventure passes the Engine House and plummets headlong down the Middleton Incline, on course for the Highpeak Junction. The steam-powered beam winding engine hauled wagons up the 708 yard long, 1 in 8¼ gradient incline from 1830 until it ceased operation in 1963.

continued on page 264

Middleton Top Engine House

ALPORT HEIGHT

263

continued from page 263 ——

Restored by the Derbyshire Industrial Archaeological Society under the care of a Warden, the Engine House is opened to the public on Sundays, and the engine is 'steamed' (on compressed air) the first Saturday in each month from April - October. Perched tantalisingly close to the brink of the trackless incline rests a lone surviving wagon. When in service, wagons were attached to the winching cable by means of wrapped chains, a process performed by the 'hanger-on', and whilst the system proved mightily efficient the Middleton incline did become notorious, particularly in the early days, for broken-chain runaways (known as runs).

Descending over the 1980 bridge, part of the road improvement scheme demanded by lorries supplying the (ill-conceived?) Carsington dam project (with inviting direction signs luring custom to the Rising Sun). Now entering a cutting, pass under a bridge of lost purpose: when constructed it carried the original Wirksworth/Middleton road, now well and truly consumed by the Middle Peak Quarry. Cross the replacement B5023 before reaching the foot of the incline, where the original cable tension pulley remains in situ. With the Middle Peak branch line (difficult to distinguish) running back R, the Trail proceeds now with Coal Hills Quarry L (notice old water tanks) and the distinctive rock feature of Ravens Tor rising R, succeeded by the top of the old Midland Tramway Incline which led down into Wirksworth R. Next comes the former Steeplehouse Goods Stationyard L, though of more immediate interest for the teas provided at Station House R. The Killers Quarry branch line enters from the L as the Trail prepares to cross two roads, the first being the B5036, main Cromford/Wirksworth road. **❶**

Arriving within the Black Rock Picnic Area (two-tiered car park) above Dimons Dale (these mysterious 'demons' occur elsewhere in the White Peak e.g. Deep Dale near Ashford-in-the-Water), gird up your loins and accomplish the very worthwhile ascent R up the lead mine spoil to the crest of the Black Rocks. Although a footpath can be followed to the summit of Bole Hill, the prime viewpoint is unquestionably upon these massive whaleback gritstone buttresses. Within appreciative rock-climbing circles the proud, clean, pinnacled, arêtes and gullies are collectively known as the Black Rocks of Cromford. Looking N from this edge, admire the Matlock gorge with the Heights of Abraham L and High Tor R backed by Riber Castle, below which Willersley Castle, Masson Mill and Cromford stand out within the winding, wooded Derwent valley (see view opposite). With care it is possible to use the climbers' descent on the E end of the outcrop, thereby traversing L beneath the dark, almost forbidding crag back down to the Trail. Walkers seeking to shorten their journey are recommended to descend through the Dimons Dale woodland, as shown on the route map, and follow the Cromfordhill Road down to Cromford village.

—— *continued on page 267*

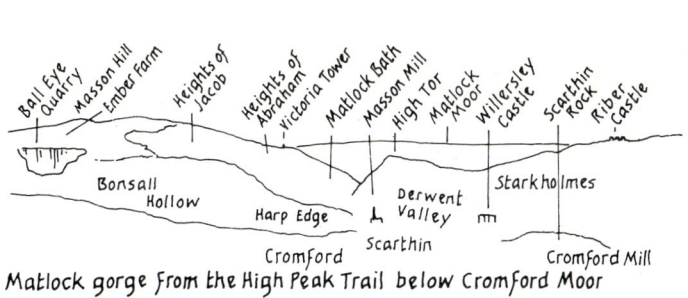

Matlock gorge from the High Peak Trail below Cromford Moor

(Labels, left to right: Ball Eye Quarry, Masson Hill, Ember Farm, Heights of Jacob, Heights of Abraham, Victoria Tower, Matlock Bath, Masson Mill, High Tor, Matlock Moor, Willersley Castle, Scarthin Rock, Riber Castle; Bonsall Hollow, Harp Edge, Cromford, Scarthin, Derwent Valley, Starkholmes, Cromford Mill)

W aspect of the Black Rocks of Cromford

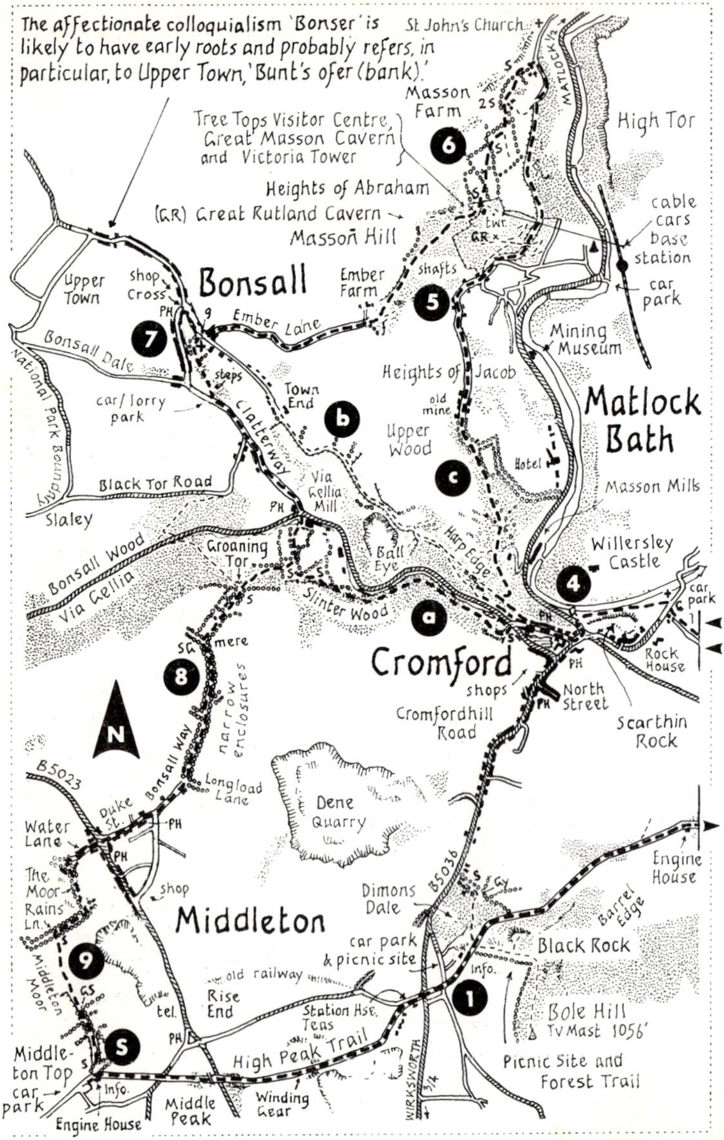
The affectionate colloquialism 'Bonser' is likely to have early roots and probably refers, in particular, to Upper Town, 'Bunt's ofer (bank)'.
St John's Church
MATLOCK 1/2
Masson Farm
High Tor
Tree Tops Visitor Centre, Great Masson Cavern and Victoria Tower
Heights of Abraham
(GR) Great Rutland Cavern
Masson Hill
twr.
GR
cable cars base station
car park
shafts
Bonsall
Upper Town
shop
Cross
PH
Ember Farm
Ember Lane
Bonsall Dale
National Park Boundary
steps
Mining Museum
Heights of Jacob
old mine
Matlock Bath
Town End
car/lorry park
Clatterway
Upper Wood
Hotel
Black Tor Road
Via Gellia Mill
Masson Mills
Slaley
Bonsall Wood
Via Gellia
Groaning Tor
Ball Eye
Harp Edge
Willersley Castle
Slinter Wood
car park
Cromford
mere
Rock House
shops
North Street
narrow enclosures
Cromfordhill Road
Scarthin Rock
N
Bonsall Way
B5023
Longload Lane
Dene Quarry
Duke St.
Water Lane
The Moor
Rains Ln.
shop
Middleton
Dimons Dale
B5036
Engine House
Barrel Edge
Black Rock
car park & picnic site
Info.
old railway
Middleton Moor
Rise End
tel.
Station Hse. Teas
Bole Hill
TV Mast 1056'
High Peak Trail
Middleton Top
car park
Picnic Site and Forest Trail
Info.
Middle Peak
Winding Gear
WIRKSWORTH 3/4
Engine House

continued from page 264 ————

Once more upon the Trail, continue E, revelling in the remarkable viewN, as from a gallery, upon the Matlock gorge (see view on page 265). Reaching the Sheep Pastures Incline Engine House (an empty shell), commence the final long descent of the old Cromford and Highpeak Railway (1291 yards at 1 in 8¼ gradient). The cinder track ensures a firm grip down the wooded bank ❷. Notice the old crane gear in the quarry just above the Intake Lane bridge, subsequent to which find the rock etchings immortalising 'W×B× Aug 13 1891' and 'WH1863'! Graffiti of this romantic type has a knack of appearing in handy outcrops of this amenable rock, the boiler-plates on top of Black Rocks being a prime site to discover such Victorian flights of fancy.

The view opens to the L where the incline is stabilised by a high retaining wall. Approaching the A6 underpass, a catch pit was installed in 1889 to pocket the occasional rogue wagons. The A6 bridge has an unusual skew elliptical arch, below which the incline concludes with a tiny portion of original track and the tension pulley in situ.

Resting in splendid isolation upon this track (1986) are two locomotives (the bulk of the railway lines were removed in 1967). The adjacent workshop (entry fee) and visitor information centre (entry free) are thoroughly well worth a few minutes of your precious time. With level going for the next mile or so to relish, cross the swing bridge, turn L and lengthen your stride along the Canal towpath.

———— *continued on page 268*

Originally the incline eased at this point to provide scope to transfer the wagons from one endless chain to another. A few dressed stones are all that remains of the intermediate Cromford Incline engine house, done away with in 1857.

267

continued from page 267

The Cromford Canal came into full operation in 1794, two years after the death of Richard Arkwright (a keen promoter of the project), initially using just the outflow from the cotton mill water power supply, supplemented in 1849 by the Leawood Pumphouse. Costing £80,000 to build, it ran the 14½ miles to Langley Mill, where it linked to the Erewash Canal. The canal was the first stage in the transportation explosion demanded by the burgeoning industrial age. Factory and quarry owners increasingly required to be able to shift both raw materials and their finished goods swiftly about the country. The railway age eventually brought about its demise, though for many years the Cromford & Highpeak Railway ensured a healthy working life for this canal. The principal commodities transported by the Cromford Canal were raw cotton, coal, lead; iron, limestone and gritstone. **❸** A small bridge (see above), linking to the Cromford meadows, is passed under: notice the grooves worn by tow ropes of the horse-drawn barges. Arriving at the Cromford Wharf, take a look around; though much has been removed to create the car park/picnic site amenity.

In its heyday, around 1830, the canal firm of Wheatcroft advertised a so called 'flying' service for passengers and goods using the canal system around central England. That such inflated terminology as 'flying', for such a slow (in present day terms) mode of transport was used, is proof of the abysmal state of the national road network at the time. From the broad winding pool (turning) the canal forks, the channel nearest the Rock House bank being for loading (notice the canopied warehouse beyond which is the counting office), whilst the near channel was for unloading. Joining the road two choices present themselves. Either go R, then L, to the church (as shown on the route map) advancing beneath the towering precipice of Scarthin Rock with the River Derwent and Willersley Castle prominent R - this track is not a public road but access is seldom withdrawn; however, on such occasion follow option two along Mill Road to the Derby road zebra crossing. The former must be the prime route given choice, despite the historical associations of the Mill. St Mary's church was begun in 1792, two years after the completion of Willersley Castle, but though both were the inspiration of Richard Arkwright, his untimely death meant that

continued on facing page

continued from facing page

he never lived in or worshipped at either. The church was completed in 1797 and Gothic embellished in 1857; it contains several Arkwright monuments. Willersley Castle is an imposing romanticised classical building, now owned by the Methodist church.

4 The Ab is reached at a gate precisely where it breaches Scarthin Nick. ¼ mile R are Masson Mills, the architecturally superb successor to Cromford Mill, built by Sir Richard Arkwright in 1783 and still in operation. Turn L to the zebra crossing, thereby entering Cromford village, created by Arkwright at the grey dawn of the factory system to house his cotton spinners.

Scarthin Rock

Cromford Mill's bastion image, when seen from Mill Road, was the result of discontent amongst the workforce, necessitating stronghold-like defences against possible revolt.   After experimenting with his horse-driven spinning frame in Nottingham, Richard Arkwright decided upon Cromford as a suitable location to develop his ambitious, innovative plans.   By harnessing Bonsall Brook and Cromford Sough (a lead mine drainage tunnel) on this site in 1771, he was able to accelerate production of cotton thread through a massive improvement in efficiency. This efficiency was won with the concerted involvement of a large labour force working long hours, the hardship being tempered by the security provided by this new working environment. The mill ran round the clock with whole families working the twelve-hour shifts.

The cast iron aqueduct, which replaced a wooden launder in 1821 supplying the head of water to the mill from the pond in the middle of Cromford, forms a bridge over Mill Road even today. Cromford Mill ceased cotton spinning in 1848, becoming a colour grinding works, the Masson Mills proving a better site powered from a convex weir in the River Derwent.   The place-name Cromford derives (as with Chrome Hill, WALKS 13/14) from 'curved', in this case a reference to the great loop of the river where a ford existed on the old road from Riber (where Cromford Bridge now stands). Incidentally, visitors to Cromford Bridge may glance upon the ruins of a C15[th] travellers' chapel and an C18[th] Fishing Pavilion (replica of Beresford Dale temple).

continued on page 270

continued from page 269

Entering Cromford Market Place, notice the grand façade of the Greyhound Inn, built in 1778 to offer comfortable lodgings for commercial guests to the factory complex. A brief detour up Cromfordhill Road enables visitors a chance to view North Street, the first 'Coronation Street', specifically built between 1771-6 for the mill workforce. The upper floor, originally one long room, contained knitting frames, permitting families to supplement their tiny incomes by making stockings, though the shift regime can have allowed precious little spare time.

The route continues from the Market Place up the narrow Scarthin Road, passing the Boat Inn, a name that harks back to canal times, after which the expanse of the mill pond fills the gulf L. One of a series of dams, this sheet of water plays host to a pair of graceless swans, who for some quirky reason can't stand ducks, chasing them off the moment they alight! The former corn mill, with waterwheel in situ, is refurbished as the Arkwright Museum, at the head of the pond.

Beyond Scarthin Books (a den which proves irresistible to the author and his like) a further important decision has to be made in terms of time and preference. Three rewarding options present themselves, viz:

ⓐ Save three miles by advancing up Bonsall Hollow to re-join the main route above the Via Gellia Mill. This navigationally easy route continues along Scarthin to its junction with the A5012. Go directly across onto a rising footpath, a few yards after the stile turn R, and adhere to the obvious path through the wooded glen. The path eventually rises sufficiently to enter the top of a rough bank pasture at a metal stile. Contour round to join the main route prior to re-entry into Slinter Wood on the ascent to Groaning Tor.

ⓑ The direct route to Bonsall. Scarthin was the old lead mining settlement expanded by Arkwright up from his mill site near Cromford Bridge. Leave the street R opposite the old Primitive Methodist chapel, ascending the cobbled footway, rising gradually along Harp Edge. Ignore the paths R: simply stick with the path till it merges with a broader path climbing up from the L. Pass the top access to Ball Eye Quarry (perhaps this name is a playful switch of Ible?), keeping beside the protecting fence to a larger track junction. Go L on the gated track with views into the richly wooded Griffe Grange valley (Via Gellia) L to enter Bonsall along Church Street.

Ball Eye Quarry

continued on facing page

Masson Mills

continued from facing page

C This, the principal route, embraces the wooded flanks of the anciently lead-mined Masson Hill, overlooking the Matlock gorge. Romanticised and exalted by writers as the 'Little Switzerland' of Derbyshire to enhance its spa appeal, and not without a modicum of justification.   Commence as per option **b** onto Harp Edge, though this time the tempting path over the ridge R is followed above the New Tribes Mission, with the famous Masson Mills, home of English Sewing Ltd, evident in the valley below. Notice traces of lead-mining, including an adit to the L of the path. Ignore the contouring path that

continued on page 272

continued from page 271

crosses a broken wall in the beechwood; instead, ascend to enter Upperwood Road by a footpath sign at the top of Wopping Lane (no fortress or new printing technology here!). Here you are above the Cumberland Cavern, once a show cave visited in 1832 by the then Princess Victoria.

Upperwood began life as a mining settlement on the old road between Matlock and Scarthin (the present course of the A6 only became feasible with the dynamiting of Scarthin Rock, creating the Nick, in 1815). Here are several, now inaccessible, mines. One, Jacob's Mine appears in the name Heights of Jacob, adopted in line with the Heights of Abraham, so christened in commemoration of the storming of Quebec by General Wolfe in 1759.

5 The sheltered combe developed in the C18th into an elegant spa resort, Matlock Bath blossoming upon the reputed health-giving properties of the thermal mineral springs. The Old Bath Hotel (later Royal) was built in 1698 upon the main springs. Through the next two centuries, notably the Regency period, hotels and smart houses of the well-to-do graced the steep banks of Masson Hill. The C19th saw the development of precariously perched homes in Gothic and Swiss styles, the latter in response to Lord Byron's allusion 'there are prospects in Derbyshire as noble as any in Greece or Switzerland.' Upperwood Road descends gently; just prior to the steepening, the Devonshire path leads L, passing the Devonshire Cavern to reach Ember Lane. The Pitchings of Upperwood Road lead down past the pedestrian entrance to the Heights of Abraham (entry fee). 50yds. after this, a fenced-off path (footpath sign 'Matlock') leads up steps L, crossing a wooden overflight isolating the right of way from the Masson Road footpath (entry fee) which climbs the commercially run Heights Gardens. Crossing the ridge, the trappings of commercialism, notably the cable cars emblazoned with Skol lager logos, can be cast to the back of one's mind, with glimpses through the trees of High Tor to attack the eye. Emerging at the entrance to Masson Farm (footpath sign 'Matlock Bath') with its B&B and camping notices, go R with the track to the entrance to Cliff House at the top of St John's Road. The chapel of St John is of visual note, being a fine example of Guy Dawber's work: built in 1897, it contains effects reflecting the current Arts and Crafts revival cultivated at the turn of the century.

A footpath sign here directs L up a potentially slippery path by a wall to 'Bonsall' with 'Great Masson Cavern' faintly discernible, painted on the wall. At the top of the rise, another sign directs L via a stile beneath the broken and tree-embowered Shining Cliff. Cross the field, passing round the back of Masson Farm. The name Masson appears to derive from 'Maessa's valley', probably a name associated with the Matlock gorge, later transferred to the flanking hill. Matlock, which consists

continued on facing page

continued from facing page

of five parts strung along the Derwent valley S of Darley Dale, probably gained its name from 'the meeting place (or enclosure) of the moot.' A moot was a Saxon court or administrative assembly. The well waymarked path proceeds by stiles and gateways ⑥ uphill to pass behind the Tree Tops Visitor Centre. The ascent provides splendid views back across the gorge to High Tor, possibly the most challenging limestone crag (in rock-climbing terms) in the district. From this angle, it is overtopped by Riber Castle, a late romantic folly built in the 1860s. Its grim, gritstone-castellated appearance (see below) may be an acquired taste; however, it has recently performed a useful function as a zoo.

Commanding a prominent crest, the Victoria Prospect Tower was built in 1844 to attract visitors to the Rutland and Great Masson show caves, a rôle it still performs, albeit at a price and subservient to the razzamatazz of the cable-car rides and café. There is a booth to the L of the public path dispensing authentic-looking paraffin lamps (exclusive to those who have paid their dues to the proprietors of the Heights emporium) for entry into the Great Masson Cavern, seen to the R. The deep cleft of Great Rake forms the approach, but despite the startling claims offered at the booth, the finest features of this very extensive labyrinthine mine are out of bounds.

Go L off the broad track, contouring through the upper woods. Evidence of lead mining continues: in fact, over 150 shafts pepper Masson Hill, so keep rigidly to the path and beware! The path emerges at a fence barrier/footpath sign by Ember Farm; from here simply follow Ember Lane (road) with no more ado down to Bonsall. At the foot of the hill, by Torber House, either go R to visit the focus of the village, the Cross, bearing the date 1671 on the shaft but with probably earlier origins, or

continued on page 274

Market Cross, Bonsall

continued from page 273

pass down through St James' churchyard. This recommended route does not, however, do real justice to the historically fascinating community of Bonsall (derived from 'Bunt's nook'). For centuries, a dual economy gave secure purpose here, lead mining and small-scale farming, hence the maze of fields across the plateau towards Winster. Arkwright's mills altered the lifestyle of this straggling settlement, subsequently new trades emerged to sustain what, even today, appears quite a remote village. The parish church hides its C13th features being engulfed by the total exterior re-building in the 1860s. Beneath the tower stands a knotted mountain ash: why was it contorted? The stepped path slips down from the churchyard, crossing the lorry park to join the Clatterway road: go L ❼. The name Clatterway derives from the sound of loose stones on wagon wheels; it leads down to the Via Gellia (A5012) road. Over the centuries, lead-smelters operated in this vicinity, hence the pub 'Pig of Lead' (formerly the Via Gellia Inn). Until the 1790s, there was not even a rude track down the Griffe Grange valley. At this time, Philip Gell of Hopton Hall constructed a drive to service his quarries and mill, this latter (now the Cromford Garnetters) being originally a corn mill. The late C18th saw a lead-smelting cupola developed here associated with the Ball Eye mine. In 1867 it became a cotton mill and in 1890 William Hollins and Co. took it over, conceiving the brand name Viyella from a corruption of Gell's Latinised affectation.

Cross the main road, following the footpath between the mill and pond which rises up the rough pastureland with the broken walls

continued on facing page

continued from facing page

to join route, ❼ entering Slinter Wood at a stile. Ascend quite steeply on a clear path to a stile above Groaning Tor. When lead smelting was at its zenith, most of the natural ashwood in this valley was consumed, hence the woodland floor ivy, characteristic of more open situations.

Follow Bonsall Way – simply oozing a long pedestrian history, this must be an old footway trod by burdened mules and men of old-rising to a stile/gate beside a mere, so typical of the limestone plateau. Go L within the lane ❽, notice the numerous shaft-top mounds littering the intense patchwork of walled strip fields. Advance beyond the junction with Longload Lane, the old pack road from the Derwent valley truncated forever by the Dene Quarry. Continue into Duke Street (named from the public house the 'Duke of Wellington'), thus reaching the main street in Middleton-by-Wirksworth.

Middleton (which means 'the middle farm' – between Bonsall and Wirksworth) has a long mining tradition. The proximity of the Cromford & Highpeak Railway, and its waxing and waning as a quarry centre over the last 150 years, have given the village a workaday air with few architecturally rewarding buildings to cause the walker to divert.

Journey's end is nigh. Cross the B5023 (nicknamed Nimblejack) into Water Lane, rising to turn L along the rough surface of The Moor, angling R round an old quarry into Rains Lane. A stile is sited in a short length of fence L; ❾ advance across the enclosed Middleton Moor, entering a lane at a stile/gate. Descend the lost fence corridor erected by a quarry firm for safety. This final stage affords   excellent views, notably S beyond the quarry-beleaguered Wirksworth (nonetheless well worth visiting on foot) to Alport Height. This hill appears to have figured long as a landmark on the ancient trading route that even the Saxons called 'Old Port Way'. For a more complete picture of precisely what is in view, consult the topograph in the car park.

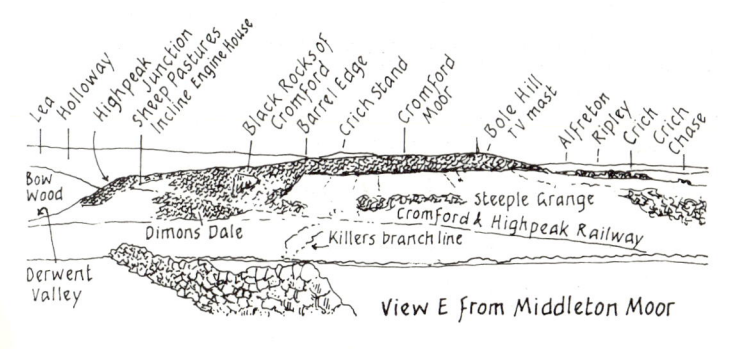

View E from Middleton Moor

275

POSTSCRIPT

Chatsworth Park in September 1987 saw in the first 'Festival of National Parks' the triumphant culmination of a two year campaign. Its aim was to heighten public awareness of the vital cultural and environmental importance of those areas of our precious country designated as National Parks. The momentum generated must not be allowed to wane, an irresistable political bandwagon must be developed to secure an enduring identity to the 'living' landscapes of wilder Britain.

The message Brian Redhead, President of the Council for National Parks, relayed to the fifteen thousand visitors on that sunny day must be our clarion call. We must ensure that succeeding generations have reason to applaud our custody of their inheritance.

We, who know, and dearly love, these ten (soon, eleven, with the Norfolk and Suffolk Broads designation) uniquely precious regions, should stand fast against their economic abuse. National Parks are no place for military training, extensive forestry, quarrying and mining, frivilous tourist gimmickry and grandiose road and building projects.

The pond and Dig Street, Hartington

Parrotts Restaurant, Chapel Street, Longnor

WALKERS' RESPONSIBILITIES

It is important to clarify and re-affirm that the name 'National Park' is only a title of convenience, clumsily borrowed from the great State-owned wildernesses of the U.S.A. Land ownership in the Peak Park, is in the main, as private as your own backyard. The National Trust has been bequeathed or purchased certain scenic or historically important estates and the PPJPB itself has purchased land to protect access and conserve specially sensitive country. These southern Pennine hills are therefore primarily enclosed farmland and walkers are obliged to respect rights-of-way and not roam assuming *de facto* access. Whilst the author has made every effort to confirm the status and advisability of the paths used in the book through consultation with the National Park, in practice walkers are responsible for their own actions. The Country Code guidelines are applicable (as ever) and walkers should be aware of their responsibilities which are:

1. Take all your litter home with you.

2. When picnicking use a liquid fuel stove, not a wood fire, and take care with matches and cigarettes. Forest and moorland fires are devastating in their effects on land and landscape.

3. Take pleasure in wildlife living and growing in its natural setting and do not carelessly destroy delicate habitats by picking plants or otherwise disturbing animals' environments.

4. Take care not to pollute water.

5. If you open a gate, then shut it securely.

6. Keep your dog under firm control on a lead. Dogs do not respect rights-of-way, but stray and pose a threat to farm livestock.

7. Avoid damage to walls or fences.

8. Avoid blocking gateways and access roads. Be mindful of hazards which your car may cause, and lock valuables out of sight in the boot. In other words, *park prettily, safely and thoughtfully.*

9. Take pleasure in the vital working elements of the countryside and leave only good report. The next group of townsfolk will receive a welcome consistent with *your* actions.

PRINTED BY MARTINS OF BERWICK

IF YOU LIKE ADVENTUROUS ACTIVITIES ON MOUNTAINS OR HILLS YOU WILL ENJOY READING:

CLIMBER
AND HILLWALKER

MOUNTAINEERING/HILLWALKING/TREKKING ROCK CLIMBING/SCRAMBLING IN BRITAIN AND ABROAD

AVAILABLE FROM NEWSAGENTS, OUTDOOR EQUIPMENT SHOPS, OR BY SUBSCRIPTION (6-12 MONTHS) FROM OUTRAM MAGAZINES, THE PLAZA TOWER, EAST KILBRIDE, GLASGOW G74 1LW

THE WALKERS' MAGAZINE

the great OUTDOORS

COMPULSIVE MONTHLY READING FOR ANYONE INTERESTED IN WALKING

AVAILABLE FROM NEWSAGENTS, OUTDOOR EQUIPMENT SHOPS, OR BY SUBSCRIPTION (6-12 MONTHS) FROM OUTRAM MAGAZINES, THE PLAZA TOWER, EAST KILBRIDE, GLASGOW G74 1LW